Discovering Lost Films of Georges Méliès in *fin-de-siècle* Flip Books (1896–1901)

Des fragments de films Méliès disparus ressuscités par des flip books (1896–1901)

Discovering Lost Films of Georges Méliès in *fin-de-siècle* Flip Books (1896–1901)

Des fragments de films Méliès disparus ressuscités par des flip books (1896–1901)

Thierry Lecointe, Pascal Fouché, Robert Byrne, Pamela Hutchinson

Research by / Recherche par Thierry Lecointe with the collaboration of / avec la collaboration de Pascal Fouché

Prefaces / Préfaces : André Gaudreault and / et Pascal Fouché
Introduction : Jacques Malthête

British Library Cataloguing in Publication Data

Discovering Lost Films of Georges Méliès in *fin-de-siècle* Flip Books (1896–1901)

Des fragments de films Méliès disparus ressuscités par des flip books (1896–1901)

A catalogue entry for this book is available from the British Library

ISBN: 9780 86196 750 6 (Paperback edition)

Published by
John Libbey Publishing Ltd, 205 Crescent Road, New Barnet, Herts EN4 8SB,
United Kingdom   e-mail: john.libbey@orange.fr; web site: www.johnlibbey.com

Distributed Worldwide by
Indiana University Press, Herman B Wells Library—350, 1320 E. 10th St.,
Bloomington, IN 47405, USA. www.iupress.indiana.edu

Contents / Sommaire

Remerciements / Thanks

Tout particulièrement à / Especially to :

Pascal Fouché, Onno Petersen et l'équipe du / and the staff of 24th San Francisco Silent Film Festival pour leur collaboration dans ce projet / for their collaboration in this project.

Jay Weissberg et l'équipe des / and the staff of 38èmes Gionate del cinema muto pour la programmation du corpus / for programming the corpus.

Jacques Malthête pour sa lecture attentive et les ultimes informations fournies sur le sujet / for his attentive reading and the ultimate information provided on the subject.

Pour leurs aides, collaborations ou soutiens / For their help, collaboration or support :

François Binétruy, Camille Blot-Wellens, Serge Bromberg, Bruno Carrière, Jean-Marc Combe, Roland Cosandey, Pascal Duclaud-Lacoste, Christian Fonnet, André Gaudreault, Laurent Guido, Frank Kessler, Eric Lange, Sabine Lenk, John Libbey, Laurent Mannoni, Carlo Montanaro, Jean-Claude Seguin, Jean-Pierre Sirois-Trahan et Frédéric Tabet.

Les institutions / The institutions : San Francisco Silent Film Festival, Le Giornate del Cinema Muto, Filmoteca Española, Cinemateca Portuguesa - Museu do Cinema et la Cinémathèque Française.

Marielle Lecointe pour ses relectures du texte français / for her proofreading of the French text.

Back from the Dead ...

André Gaudreault

To the memory of Madeleine Malthête-Méliès,
thanks to whom Méliès experienced a second birth

Unlike the Lumière brothers, whose reputation is based on the fact that these specialists of *motionless*[1] images had the gift of putting these images *into motion*, Thierry Lecointe on the other hand, has the gift of *immobilising* animated images, of stopping them. And he does this in order to let us have a better view of what they conceal and reveal. In fact, it was about twenty years ago now that he first offered us his composite panoramas of the amphitheatres in Nîmes or Béziers, where the bull fights or *corridas* took place that were captured by the Cinématographe Lumière.[2] These composite panoramas were made up of individual frames that he uses to fit time into a space that he "augments" by unfolding it, so that he can, as it were, extend it to produce spectacular panoramic views, such as this panorama of a *corrida* filmed in the Nîmes bull ring. This view was recreated using eleven different frames (see the illustration below) which, had it not been for his ingenuity, would only exist virtually, in a piecemeal fashion, in the series of Lumière views filmed in this location.

"Panorama of the bull fight or *corrida* filmed in the Nîmes amphitheatre on 24th September 1899 by two technicians from the Lumière company" (Thierry Lecointe, *Le Cinématographe-Lumière dans les arènes*, Montpellier: UBTF, 2007, p. 107).

What Lecointe wanted to achieve by doing this was to detect the *clues* which would establish a precise chronology of the different shoots "from the position of the shadows of the bull ring architecture in the *plaza*".[3] The shadow of the buildings as a clue to establish the chronology… A trick worthy of the talent of a true sleuth, which Lecointe will make use of once again, in this book, when dealing with the folioscope *Arrivée d'un train*. I'll come back to this.

For Lecointe the sleuth has more than one gift, as the readers will discover when they consult (or rather devour) the present book. Like all good detectives, he succeeds in getting his sources to talk, amongst others the "paper characters" that feature on the images (once again individual frames) of Léon Beaulieu's "pocket cinematograph", and which are "paper" characters quite simply because the "films" involved are not set *on film* but *on paper* since they are destined to be viewed by flicking through.

"Films on paper"… the expression can only evoke to all specialists of early cinema, the famous paper prints from the Library of Congress, whose images were "re-animated" in the 1950s, thanks to that former detective (surprise, surprise …) Kemp Niver.[4]

There is no need for me to go here into the many other talents of Lecointe – who brilliantly carries out the "investigation" that he presents in the present work, based on "documents" which, as he writes here, are "at the crossroads between celluloid, paper print and books" – since Méliès's great-grandson, Jacques Malthête, takes charge of this in the Introduction, he who, just like his mother, Madeleine Malthête-Méliès, granddaughter of the Magician of Montreuil, has done so much to give Méliès back his place in history.

What Lecointe manages to achieve here (just like Niver who succeeded in bringing inert images back to life) is a kind of miracle that consists of resurrecting, before our very eyes, as if they were brought "back from the dead" – to mention a literary piece the reading of which gives one the shivers, or even a spell of dizziness (not to say "vertigo", as well as sweats, *cold* ones of course[5]) –, views which in fact had not been *viewed* for a long time, a very long time even, and the existence of which (of part of them at least) we actually had no suspicion. What is more, the work of investigator Lecointe makes it possible to reveal, to uncover, a rather peculiar artistic and commercial activity of the Magician of Montreuil. Yes, Lecointe the investigator is a real sleuth, but unlike Hitchcock's Scottie, he does not have vertigo… It is he in fact, and the frantic spiral of his questionings, that give us vertigo. We are, unfortunately, not used to reading works in which the author constantly revises his hypotheses – as Lecointe does here – as we advance in the reading of the results with which he presents us, and then does not hesitate to abandon those invalidated by the results of his research – which is why he deserves our total respect.

How many "among the dead" will turn in their graves when the present work comes out, I cannot say, but there will be many of them. Because Thierry Lecointe announces to us here a fabulous discovery: he has indeed *rescued from oblivion* Méliès's oldest "films"! No less! Not that he himself discovered the flip books concerned (we have Pascal Fouché to thank for that). That is not Lecointe's feat. The real *tour de force* performed by Lecointe is to have managed to transform these dumb witnesses into voluble informants, going as far as to "undo them so as to extract potential information"[6] and by using a thousand and one tricks, to make them finally spit out the truth and give him… Georges. Amongst these tricks are certain operations that we had forgotten all about since primary or secondary school: geometric triangulation, smallest common multiple, but also the calculation of the focal distance, location and measurement of the shadows used to determine the date and time of the shooting of the images, to name but a few.[7] Like a demiurge given to transubstantiation, Lecointe shows us the recipe to be followed in order to gradually transform a mass of individual frames into invaluable incunabula, that can now take their place in the filmography of the Magician of Montreuil. Before Lecointe, we generally did not know that Méliès had produced flip books, and now we know.

Lecointe is never short of resources to satisfy his curiosity and his need to get to the bottom of his intuitions. What is more – rather like Méliès – he is a fan of a certain kind of transformism: he, too, nimbly performs substitutions, metamorphoses, apparitions and disappearances. Thus, in 2013, he gets hold of exhibit No. 1, a flip book known by the title *Arrivée d'un train gare de Vincennes* [Arrival of a Train at the Station of Vincennes] and which he thinks MIGHT be the reproduction for the folioscope, by God-knows-Who (since everyone knows that Méliès WOULD NEVER HAVE produced folioscopes) of a cinematographic film that MIGHT itself be by Méliès.

After the kind of sleight-of-hand that is his speciality, he shakes up these uncertainties. And the *Arrivée d'un train gare de Vincennes* suddenly transforms itself (nothing in my hands, nothing up my sleeves!) into… *Arrivée d'un train (gare de Joinville)* [Arrival of a Train (Joinville Station)]. With one wave of his magic wand, the Station of Vincennes disappears and it is the Station at Joinville that appears in its place. As in every good film by Méliès, one element replaces another… and we can now confirm that this view IS by Méliès and that IT IS, definitely, a reproduction BY Méliès for the folioscope of one of his views, BY a Méliès whom we now know DID produce folioscopes… And yet, people would insist in every tribune or article that the images in this flip book were too poor, that no one would ever be able to prove that the images were by Méliès. Curators, archivists and even a great-great-granddaughter of Méliès considered the task impossible.[8] But Lecointe, like Méliès, was clearly ready to "achieve the impossible".[9]

The references to Hitchcock which I have made here up to now may seem gratuitous, but is it not *troubling* to think that Lecointe believes he recognizes Méliès making "a furtive appearance à la Hitchcock", on the platform at the Joinville-le-Pont train station, during the first seconds of the folioscope entitled *Arrivée d'un train* [Arrival of a Train]? To paraphrase the Lecointe terminology, I would add that I too have a high level of confidence that this pseudo-Mr. Anybody who does not behave at all like somebody "waiting for his train or a passenger" is well and truly Méliès himself, whom we see on the virtual "screen" of this "little book that can be flicked through very fast"[10] that is the folioscope showing the platform of the station at Joinville.

I know that, from now on, whenever I see a folioscope in a flea market, the following sequence will immediately come into my mind: Lecointe/Proust/madeleine/Méliès. A single one of these four words begins with a small letter, but it could also have begun with a capital… Indeed there is, and we all know, a Madeleine in the home of our favourite *manufacturer of animated photographs*, but there is also one with the *manufacturer of anguished suspense stories*, one of whose works I have already mentioned.

In *Vertigo*, the sight of Judy acts on Scottie just like the taste of madeleines on Proust: seeing Judy brings back the memory of his own Madeleine (although she is a false Madeleine since in fact her name is Judy Barton and she once personified – another substitution – Madeleine Elster, whom her husband has murdered and who seems to have come back from the dead … in the form of Judy).

Jacques (and the other people close to Madeleine) will forgive me if I say that, were she still here with us, "our own" Madeleine, we the Méliès *aficionados*, might have been able to recognise Georges from his slightest movements, having been brought up by him, and could have guaranteed Lecointe that it was indeed her grandfather who was pretending to be the Mr. Anybody on the platform of the station at Joinville…

And this would have allowed Lecointe, who classifies his *Arrivée d'un train* amongst the "probable Méliès – high level of confidence", to be able to move it into a "confirmed Méliès" category. And to lift the veil on a Méliès, that incorrigible "transformist", someone who substitutes everything for its opposite, and vice versa, and who does not need to come back from the dead to continue to play some almighty tricks on us. These are found regularly and there is a long list of effects that have revealed[11] things, as the years go past during the decades which separate us from the death of Georges, amongst which the most recent one, as far as I know, concerns a film which has not survived (if indeed it ever existed) dated 1896. In fact, being the incorrigible transformist that he is, endlessly trying to make us take sows' ears for silk purses, Méliès has been trying to make us believe for aeons that it was on the Place de l'Opéra, in Paris, that he was hit by a sudden flash of inspiration:[12]

> Do you want to know how the idea of using trick effects in kinematography first came to me? Very simply, upon my word. One day, when I was photographing as usual in the Place de l'Opéra, the camera I used in the early days [. . .] jammed and produced an unexpected result. It took a minute to disengage the film and to start the camera up again. In the meantime, the passersby, horse trolleys, and other vehicles had, of course, changed positions. When I projected the strip of film [. . .] I suddenly saw a Madeleine-Bastille horse trolley change into a hearse and men become women. The substitution or stop-camera trick had been discovered.

In fact, this may well not have been the case, as I announced in 2018.[13] Because in fact certain clues allow Jacques Malthête and I to believe that it was more likely to have been in the Place Saint-Augustin that Méliès went through his famous camera jam episode, that is if this event ever really took place.[14] In the series of words pronounced by Méliès, the "Place Saint-Augustin" disappears and it is the "Place de l'Opéra" which appears, thus substituting the most famous of the two squares (the most glamorous as well), for a Parisian square that also had the privilege of appearing in the Méliès catalogue and, wait for it, not just anywhere in this catalogue…, since it "appears" just before (at No. 69) the first Méliès trick film: *Escamotage d'une dame chez Robert-Houdin* (*The Vanishing Lady* at No. 70)… And the one might perhaps explain the other…

One last word on Lecointe's work about folioscopes: this book is not a flip book – the "little book that is flicked through very fast" – although you might find it *flippant*[15] and read it from beginning to end "like a novel", like a … captivating page-turner.

Finally I would add a simple remark: for his work as a detective of paper prints, in 1955, Kemp Niver received an Honorary Oscar, an award given to him in 1955 for having developed a process that made it possible to resuscitate the films stored on paper at the Library of Congress.[16] Perhaps France should give back to Caesar what is Caesar's[17] and honour Madeleine (posthumously) as well as, by the same stroke, Jacques and Thierry, who have striven so hard to bring Georges back from the dead …

Notes

1. Cf. their production in the 1880s of millions of photographic slides of the "Étiquette bleue" brand.

2. Three examples of these paranoramas can be found in his article "Les tournages multi-caméras chez Lumière" [Multi-Camera Filming in the Lumière films], in François Albera, Marta Braun and André Gaudreault (eds.), *Stop Motion, Fragmentation of Time: Exploring the Roots of Modern Visual Culture*, Lausanne: Payot Lausanne, 2002, pp. 271–296.

3. *Ibid.*, p. 282.

4. According to Paul Spehr and Erik Barnouw, who respectively wrote the Foreword and Introduction to the work by Kemp Niver, published in 1985; see Paul Spehr, "Foreword", and Erik Barnouw "Introduction", in Kemp R. Niver, *Early Motion Pictures: The Paper Print Collection in the Library of Congress*, Washington: Library of Congress, 1985, pp. vii and xv.

5. I am referring here, of course, to the book by Pierre Boileau and Pierre Ayraud, aka Thomas Narcejac (Boileau-Narcejac, *D'entre les morts*, Paris: Denoël, 1954), of which the Hitchcock film *Vertigo*, of 1958, is the adaptation. Translator's note: The book's title literally means "back from the dead"; the French title of its filmic adaptation is *Sueurs froides*, which means "cold sweats".

6. Thus he takes to pieces, page by page, a spoilt and incomplete copy of a folioscope of *Arrivée d'un train* that belongs to him, so as to to "confirm that the flip book is made up at the printer's of eleven strips of eleven frames placed one after the other, perfectly aligned from left to right".

7. Dear readers, did you know that the shadow thrown by an architectural element can give two dates, just two, in a single calendar year for the day when it could have been filmed? Did you know that the direction and length of a shadow can even allow you to calculate the approximate time that a shot was filmed?

8. "[…] film preservationists, archivists, and even a Méliès' descendant think it's *an almost impossible task*" (Maane Khatchatourian, "George Melies Flip Book Sets off Crowdsourcing", *Variety*, 24 July 2013, https://variety.com/2013/film/global/george-melies-flip-book-sets-off-crowdsourcing-1200564564).

9. "[…] needless to say, you must absolutely *achieve the impossible* [.,.]" (Georges Méliès, in André Gaudreault, *Film and Attraction: From Kinematography to Cinema*, translated by Timothy Barnard, with a critical edition of Georges Méliès's *Kinematographic Views (1907)* established by Jacques Malthête, Champaign: University of Illinois Press, 2011 [2008], p. 141; emphasis in the original).

10. *Dixit* Méliès's second wife, Jehanne d'Alcy, quoted here by Jacques Malthête in the Introduction.

11. We know that Méliès was in favour of magicians' secrecy and that, in his view, a true professional of magic had to be discreet in relation to this. So he was careful never to "revea[l] the secret of the trick" (Georges Méliès, in André Gaudreault, *op. cit.*, p. 149).

12. *Ibid.*, pp. 147–148.

13. In a conference paper about the camera jam episode in the Place de l'Opéra called "Que n'a-t-on pas dit sur le fameux épisode du blocage de l'appareil sur la place de l'Opéra (point d'interrogation et point d'exclamation)" [What has not been said about the famous episode of the jammed camera in the Place de l'Opéra (question mark and exclamation point)], presented in Paris, in March 2018, during the symposium *Truquer, créer, innover. Les effets spéciaux français* [Tricking, Creating, Innovating. French Special Effects] of which the proceedings will be published in 2021.

14. A discovery made with the complicity of Stéphane Tralongo, whom I wish to thank.

15. In the sense of "which surprises, or even stupefies" (https://dicocitations.lemonde.fr/dico-mot-definition/62704/flippant.php).

16. "Long months of effort finally established the feasibility of the project. New negatives – then projection prints – *could* be made from the paper rolls. The old films could, in short, be brought back from the dead. [...] For his mutiple role in the restoration miracle, Niver received an Oscar" (Erik Barnouw, "Introduction", in Kemp R. Niver, *Early Motion Pictures, op. cit.*, p. xv–xvi); note here the use of the expression "back from the dead", which recalls the title of the book by Boileau-Narcejac and that of the present piece.

17. Translator's note: The author refers here to the French equivalent of the Oscar, the Cesar award. See: https://en.wikipedia.org/wiki/C%C3%A9sar_Awards.

The Flip Book, a Curious Object, Half Book, Half Cinema

Pascal Fouché

t is very probable that our forebears had been flipping through successions of drawings for a long time to watch them come to life, but it was not until 1868 that the first patent industrialising the flip book was filed by an English printer, John Barnes Linnett. Others followed in different countries but the principle varied little and the flip books that are published today are still very close to what they were in the 19th Century: a small format booklet held in one hand which is flipped through by the other to give a series of images produced in a sequence the illusion of movement.

The illustrations for the first of them were hand drawn, but photography and cinema were soon to supply them with images. The discoveries made by Etienne-Jules Marey and Eadweard Muybridge around chronophotography, together with the birth of cinema, became inexhaustible sources for the production of new flip books.

Extracts from the films of cinema pioneers were made into flip books from the 19th Century onwards, particularly by the American, Thomas Edison, and the German, Max Skladanowsky, who self-edited them, or by the Frenchman, Léon Gaumont, whose copyright has been found on some of them. The flip book is silent, like these early films, and so is a perfect reflection of them. Later on, it was more common to feature certain cult scenes when the flip book became a by-product or promotional object to accompany the launch of a film. This is why there are flip books for almost all the films produced by Disney.

But the cinema is only one of the numerous areas covered by flip books. Often thought of as a toy, it would also be designed for children and would frequently have a quite simple drawing with a format which made it easier to flip through it. For adults, it soon became a publicity gimmick to promote different brands or products, and a training manual for many different sports so as to show the ideal swing or the best way of hitting a home run … The most mythical figures of sport all had at least one flip book celebrating their exploits.

Current affairs and anniversaries of outstanding events also often served as a pretext for producing flip books and eroticism also provided inspiration for the manufacturers, particularly when they showed a body being gradually unveiled.

In addition, since the end of the 19th Century, books of all kinds also had drawings or photos on the edge of pages which could be flipped through as a complement to illustrate the subject matter or as an additional feature to attract readers.

From the 50s, it was the turn of artists to adopt flip books, vying with each other to create the most imaginative techniques, formats or covers for their books. And finally, a hundred years after the invention of cinema, the Internet has opened up new possibilities by allowing all and sundry to design his or her flip book using drawings or photos that only have to be printed to assemble one's very own flip book.

All in all, it is a very varied universe because the flip book is both timeless and universal.

They can be found everywhere with different names (*flick* or *flicker* book in the UK, *Daumenkino* in Germany, *para para* book in Japan, etc.) where, since they generally have very little written text, they can be understood by everyone. The inhabitants of Quebec and sometimes the French have adopted the term 'folioscope' which was originally the name of a brand invented by a French toy manufacturer at the end of the 19th Century. This term has the disadvantage of bearing no etymological relation to the object it describes.

Children much appreciate the workshops where they learn to make their own flip books and this is an excellent way of introducing them to the mysteries of animation and cinema. Sometimes informative, always fun, the flip book is designed to surprise; it has to tell a story in a few seconds and, depending on how quickly it is flicked through, it can also reveal details that may not have been seen at first glance.

The flip book is a fragile object, the kind that is qualified as 'ephemera', because the more it has been flicked through, the more it may have been damaged, which is why it is hard to find some of the oldest ones in good condition; and this is also the sign that they have been much used. This is the case of many of those dating from the end of the 19th Century and in particular, with the extracts of films which, for the main part, have not been identified and may be the only trace today of films which have been lost.

This first attempt to identify some of them, led jointly by Thierry Lecointe and Robert Byrne, could well open up the way to some priceless discoveries.

Introduction

Jacques Malthête

At the turn of the last century, a trader in knick-knacks, Léon Beaulieu (1857–1901) had some little booklets of photos on sale which, when you flicked through them, made the trains and figures which they featured move as if in a picture house. This was in Paris, between about 1896 and 1901. Many of these *folioscopes* – the French term – (Beaulieu had christened them pocket cinematograph, while Pascal Fouché preferred the term *flip book*) are today to be found in private collections, including Pascal Fouché's own, and he is here the author of a biography on Beaulieu. The present study, mainly under the brilliant direction of Thierry Lecointe, tells the story of 27 Beaulieu flip books that belong to this collection, to which have been added some examples from the same manufacturer coming from collections belonging to François Binétruy, Carlo Montanaro and Thierry Lecointe.

When examining such a corpus, apart from a few flip books whose images are attributed to Pathé, Edison,

© Robert Byrne – Collection Pascal Fouché.

Skladanowsky and Gaumont, Lecointe believes he has identified about 20 films by Georges Méliès, after a long and meticulous process of research, a tight and systematic analysis, not to say a scientific one, which has led to some very solidly-argued hypotheses. For example, by classifying the flip books in several categories, based on the number of pages – with a maximum of 121 – and according to the direction in which they are flipped over, from front to back or the other way round – Lecointe has managed to figure out some of the essential characteristics of Beaulieu's production.

Having said this, as we all know, providing proof is not always easy when you are trying to attribute, in this case to Méliès for example, what at first might seem a partial reproduction of one of his films.

Lecointe is a very talented clue-spotter: a postcard allows him to discover a station where the train featured in an animated flip book stops, while the direction and length of a shadow shows him the approximate time and season of a shot in the open air, and an element of the decor or a costume featured in a flip book are rediscovered in one of the Méliès films that has been saved or in an advertisement promoting one of the films which has been lost … .

Unfortunately, the bad quality of the photograms reproduced by photo-engraving (lack of pixels and thus definition and re-inking of some of the contours) makes the identification of the actors somewhat risky. Thanks to a process of re-animation of the photograms – photographed by Onno Petersen and re-animated by Robert Byrne – the effect of the lack of definition is reduced and it may thus be possible to recognize the body movements if not the face of a well-known actor or actress, such as Georges Méliès, Jehanne d'Alcy or Élise De Vère.

About twenty flip books have thus been considered to be extracts from so far unknown films by Méliès. Of course, the enormous interest aroused by this discovery can be imagined. The arguments supporting the premise are numerous but, for my part, particularly concerning these characters, I believe I can really only recognize Méliès in a single flip book, *Pose chez l'artiste. Vénus. (A Pose at the Artist's. Venus)*. In *Nuit Agitée (Agitated Night)*, it is also apparently him (wearing a false white beard) who is acting, wearing a similar costume to the one in the corresponding film which has been saved, *Une Nuit Terrible (A Terrible Night)*. Thanks to her size and body language, Jehanne d'Alcy is almost certainly present in *Le Coucher de la mariée (The Bride's Bedtime)* and quite probably in *La Puce (The Flea)* and *Le Bain (The Bath Tub)*. Apart from this, we discover a bed here, an element of the decor there or, somewhere else again, a piece of clothing, coming from one of the Méliès films that has been saved, or which is seen on one of the promotional photos that has been kept in an archival collection.

Now the question arises as to the material status of the film source. As far as the twenty odd flip books supposedly coming from a Méliès film are concerned, it so happens that none of them corresponds exactly to a film that has been saved. Basing himself on a number of considerations, Lecointe proposes the hypothesis that they come from an early version of films of which they strangely constitute the only trace.

The example of the flip book *Nuit agitée (Agitated Night)* is one of the rare duplicates that perfectly illustrates Lecointe's theory because its twin brother, the Méliès film *Une nuit terrible (A Terrible Night)* has been saved. The scenarios are indeed identical, but nevertheless they have notable differences. First of all, their length: *A Terrible Night* measures 20 m, that is one minute at 16 frames per second, while the flip book is made up of only 121 photograms, which corresponds to a length of film of 2m 30, that is 10 seconds according to the speed of the recovered folioscope (12 frames per second). It's already quite remarkable to be able to manage to include the essential part of an action that takes 60 seconds in the film in such a short space of time. As if Méliès had shot this version with a flip book in mind, having managed to squeeze the main part of the action, the gag, into a dozen seconds. This special tape may also have measured 20 metres, perhaps even a little less, out of which the extract designed for the flip book has been removed.

The other notable difference (without mentioning the camera being closer to the ground in the film, the headboard being on the left in the film and on the right in the flip book, the bedside table and the chair in the film being transformed into stools in the flip book, with the chamber pot standing on the right hand stool while it is on the left in the film), apart from these there is the black background as featured in the Marey and Edison pictures. This particular characteristic is, for Lecointe, an argument in favour of the flip book version being earlier. One can in fact understand the use of a black background to bring out the characters when the lighting is rather poor and the film not very sensitive, but why then should Méliès have re-shot the same film that same year (1896), and perhaps even at a few days interval, without using the black background? Whatever the reason, if we judge from the films of his that have been saved, he would only use it in his films with multiple exposures. Moreover, in the films from flip books with black backgrounds which are attributed to him, there is paradoxically, no multiple exposure, nor, in fact, are there any special effects. Was this a deliberate choice on his part, if it is true that the corpus studied here is representative of the entire production of the Méliès flip books?

It is surprising that no known text written by Méliès, nor any of the interviews of his that have been transcribed, mention this singular activity. We only possess one account, by his second wife, Jehanne d'Alcy, who declared during a session of the Commission for Historical Research of the French Cinémathèque (17 June 1944):

> M. Langlois. – He [Méliès] did everything Lumière did, according to the catalogue, and he began to shoot all his scenes very fast.
>
> [...].
>
> Mme Méliès. – He did *Le Bain de la Parisienne* (*The Parisian's Bath Tub*) and the little book you flick through very fast.

It will be obvious that these folioscopes, arising as they do from the very early days of cinema, have not yet revealed all their secrets. A full and passionate dossier now awaits the reader, with its fascinating discoveries, its questions, its attractive hypotheses and its daring conclusions.

1

Léon Beaulieu's Pocket Cinematograph (1896–1901): Discovering Lost Films of Georges Méliès in *fin-de-siècle* Flip Books

Thierry Lecointe, Pascal Fouché,
Robert Byrne, Pamela Hutchinson

Based on research by Thierry Lecointe
with the collaboration of Pascal Fouché

Chapter One

M. Méliès and His Movies, M. Beaulieu and His *Bimbelots*

Georges Méliès was a man who knew more than most about vanishing tricks. A Paris-born conjuror-turned-filmmaker, he is celebrated by cinephiles for the spectacular visions he created in the cinema's earliest days, extravaganzas such as *Voyage dans la lune* (1902) and *Voyage a travers l'impossible* (1904). More specifically, he is remembered for the simple special effect achieved by pausing the camera mid-filming, and removing an object, person or fantastical creature from the frame before turning again. People, objects, and circumstances appeared, transformed, and vanished as if by magic. Méliès produced hundreds of films, some of them lavish, many of them brilliant, beginning in the spring of 1896. Audiences around the world enjoyed his movies, and his peers tried to imitate them.

By the time the Great War began, though, it looked like Méliès himself was about to vanish. As the war ended, he had lost his reputation, his status in the industry, his money, his studio, his theatre and most of his films, selling what remained of his stock in the early 1920s.

A few years later though, Méliès's luck turned around. It had to. In December 1925 Méliès married his long-time companion Jehanne D'Alcy, who had appeared alongside him in many of his films, but they were no longer in the film business. D'Alcy rented a toy kiosk in the Gare du Montparnasse, from which they made a small living. This was when a journalist named G.-Michel Coissac sought out the once-great filmmaker to give him his due: interviews, a public screening of his available work and even the *Légion d'honneur* soon followed. Whatever else Méliès had lost, his reputation was returned to him. He died in 1938, at the age of 76, and while he never made another film, he had been rehabilitated from obscurity and his place in film history was assured. Now, interest in his beautiful, distinctive work is growing, and historians and archivists continue to uncover a precious few of his missing films. The story in these pages concerns one of the most unconventional approaches for doing just that.

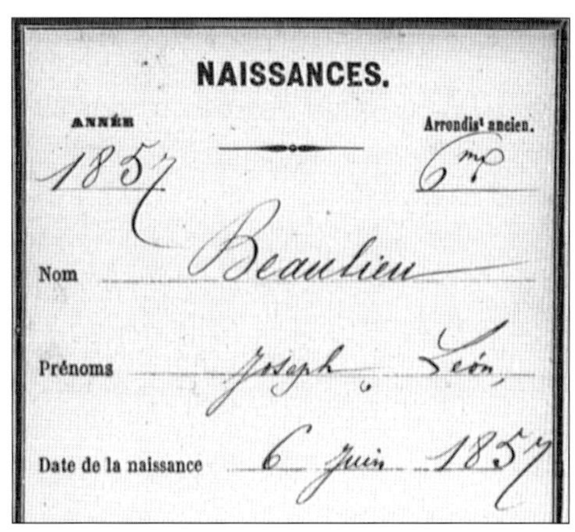

Léon Beaulieu's birth certificate © Private collection.

The Petit Biograph Parisien © Pascal Fouché.

Fellow Parisian Léon Beaulieu may have had less to lose than Méliès, but he did his best. His life was much shorter and remains far more obscure. He was born in the sixth arrondissement of Paris on 6 June 1857 and he died a few miles away on the other side of the river in 1901. In the 43-and-a-half years in between those two dates he led a hectic and apparently turbulent life: he never married but he moved frequently, and he saw military action, as well as the inside of a jail cell more than once. He died in his house at 257 rue Saint-Denis, on 22 February 1901, but he left future generations some artefacts of distinctive charm – marvellous miniatures that provide clues to the lost work of that other, far more celebrated man, who was living and working in Paris at the same time.

On his death certificate, Beaulieu's occupation was registered as *bimbelotier*. That's a word that has almost vanished from the French language. It means that he sold *bimbelots*: little trinkets, knick-knacks or playthings for children. Among those *bimbelots* were his flip books, which captured a few seconds of film in an analogue, portable, pocket-sized format. Each of the miniature books is comprised of approximately a hundred pages of card bound with tape, to be animated by a thumb flicking the pages from back to front (and sometimes vice versa), or in Beaulieu's own invention, the Petit Biograph Parisien, an enamelled metal device he patented in 1898[1] as an "*Effeuilloir mécanique pour cinématographe de poche*": a mechanism for turning the leaves of a pocket cinematograph.

Pascal Fouché, a historian and collector who specialises in flip books, has looked into the life of Beaulieu, and his research brings the memory of the man to life, even though many of the details remain sketchy. Beaulieu's parents were named Louis Beaulieu and Marie Coudert, but they had both died by the time Léon was 20. That's when, on 12 September 1878, Beaulieu joined the 2nd Military Infantry Section of the French army, giving his residence as Aubervilliers (just outside Paris), and his current occupation as *fumiste*, a word that can mean a "humbug" but here refers to a heating engineer. He had brown hair, grey eyes and stood 5ft 1in tall. He could read and write but was only educated to primary school level – he never earned his high-school diploma.

Before being discharged from active service in 1884, Beaulieu spent six months on a campaign in Algeria (6 November 1883 – 18 May 1884), but prior to that he had served two years of a three-year sentence in prison for insulting and threatening a superior.

After joining the reserves in 1885, Beaulieu continued to have trouble following the rules: first he was sentenced to two months in prison for assault, then to two years and a fine of 50 francs for fraud in 1886, and then again to two months in prison in 1888 for another violent incident. He returned to the military in 1888 and 1889, before finally leaving in 1896 due to his asthma and obesity. During this period, the military records show Beaulieu as living both in Aubervilliers and also at two separate addresses in Paris: 25 rue de Montmorency in 1893 and 23 rue de Bretagne in 1895. There was just one more conviction on Beaulieu's record in his short life. On 29 January 1901, less than a month before he died, Beaulieu was sentenced to pay a fine of 100 francs for indecency.

At some point between leaving the military for good, and that final indecency charge, Beaulieu became a *bimbelotier*. After he died, his estate included goods or *bimbeloterie* that were sold at auction for 220 francs – which is more than his furniture raised. We know that he made his pocket cinematographs at five different residences in Paris and Aubervilliers[2] because the addresses are printed on the flip books themselves and 37, rue du VertBois in Paris appeared on his patent for the Petit Biograph Parisien.

Various addresses printed on Beaulieu's flip books
© Robert Byrne – Collection Pascal Fouché.

Beaulieu was listed under the heading 'Cinematograph' in *L'Annuaire du Commerce et de l'Industrie 1898* but as far as we know, he had no direct contact with the people who made the original films.

Unless … One of the addresses printed on Beaulieu's booklets is 144 rue Oberkampf, Paris, and it was here, from the end of 1896 to the middle of 1897 that he probably produced his first flip books. Across the street, at numbers 141 and 143, a man called Alban Lapipe had premises for manufacturing tools, but on 26 March 1896, he had filed his own patent for a *"Machine à perforer les matières flexibles avec amenage automatique"* in other words, a device for punching holes in flexible film, and Georges Méliès is known to have been one of his early customers. If Beaulieu and Méliès ever met, it could have been here, on the rue Oberkampf in 1896 or 1897.

Nearly fifty years later, when Méliès's widow Jehanne d'Alcy recalled her husband's early films in 1944, she mentioned *"le petit livre qu'on feuilletait très vite"*, or the little book that one leafs through very quickly.[3] Did they collaborate on these pocket cinematographs? Perhaps, or perhaps not. But it is now time to skip even further ahead, to the 21st century, and the lucky discovery of one of Beaulieu's bimbelots in a second-hand bookshop in Germany.

Endnotes

1. See pictures 27-1/-2/93/-4 and 28 for patent.
2. See Appendix 2 for summary of Léon Beaulieu's addresses.
3. A conversation with Henri Langlois reported by Jacques Malthête to Thierry Lecointe, Commission de recherches historiques de la Cinémathèque française, meeting on 17 June 1944.

Chapter Two

The "One Percent Chance"

Bernhard Richter discovered one of Léon Beaulieu's flip books in 2013, when he and his daughter Sara were looking for a raffle prize in a shop in Germany. Richter is the co-founder of a computer animation company, and he was hunting for a piece of historical cinematic ephemera that would be a tempting prize at a computer graphics conference. However, when he saw the flip book, he guessed he had found something far more important. Leafing through the flip book revealed a soft, pale view of a train coming to a halt behind the camera, next to a canopied train platform where men with hats and canes were milling around.

Richter believed that the images in the flip book could come from a lost film: Georges Méliès's 1896 *Arrivée d'un train (gare de Vincennes)*. "We haven't found anything 100 percent conclusive tying the book to Méliès", his daughter told *Variety* journalist Maane Khatchatourian, but they had identified the double-decker train as the kind of model running in suburban stations in Paris and they knew that Beaulieu, whose name appeared on the flip book, was producing flip books at this time.

To add to this circumstantial evidence, the Richters decided to crowdsource their research. As *Variety*[1] reported, they produced a rough animation of the flip book's images and uploaded it to YouTube[2], asking for more information. However, the experts that Khatchatourian quoted in the article doubted that the trail would stay hot. There was too little detail in the image, no signs, no landmarks. Serge Bromberg rated the chances of learning more at "one percent" for all these reasons, and Jan-Christopher Horak pointed out that the film was actually very similar to the Lumiere brothers' famous *L'Arrivée d'un train en gare de La Ciotat* (1895), filmed several hundred miles away on the south coast of France. "The camera angle, the camera looking down the platform, the train coming in and riding past the camera – that's identical to the Lumière film", he said.

Khatchatourian had also contacted Domitor, the international society for the study of early cinema, before publishing her article, and for the next two to three months, its scholars took an intense interest in the problem of identifying the film from the folioscope. Although they mostly agreed that it was a near-impossible task, some Domitor members, including Méliès's great-grandson Pascal Duclaud-Lacoste, Mélies expert Jean-Pierre Sirois-Trahan, a professor at Laval University in Quebec City, and independent researcher Thierry Lecointe stayed with the hunt.

As soon as Lecointe saw Richter's images he was convinced that they contained enough clues for him to locate the station, and he hypothesised that this booklet could belong to a bigger set of flip books. If he could find more of Léon Beaulieu's work, he reasoned, he would be able to identify additional films – perhaps by Méliès or his peers. An online search swiftly led Lecointe, Sirois-Trahan and Duclaud-Lacoste to Pascal Fouché, who had several Beaulieu flip books in his collection, and who was able to research the biography of their maker.

For a while the trail appeared to grow cold, but in late 2017, Lecointe and Fouché had a meeting in Paris with Robert Byrne of the San Francisco Silent Film Festival and the Pocket Cinematograph project was off to a new start. Which meant the chance of identifying the film in the flip book had become significantly higher than one percent.

Endnotes

1. *Variety*, "George Melies Flip Book Sets off Crowdsourcing", 24 July 2013, https://variety.com/2013/film/news/george-melies-flip-book-sets-off-crowdsourcing-1200564564/

2. "Early Film by Georges Méliès survived as flip book?" https://www.youtube.com/watch?v=UTqQeCJLHdE

Chapter Three

Which Train? Which Station? Which Film?

Arrivée du train / Arrival of the train (handwritten title, 121 frame-images)

© Onno Petersen – Collection Pascal Fouché.

Trains, a potent symbol of the progress of the industrial revolution, were popular both with postcard manufacturers and early filmmakers in the 1890s. The Lumière brothers were far from the only filmmakers to aim their cameras at trains arriving and leaving stations. Pathé, Gaumont, and many others made this kind of film. Georges Méliès is known to have shot at least two train-arrival films, listed in the Méliès catalogue:[1] No. 8, *Arrivée d'un train (gare de Vincennes)* and No. 35 *Arrivée d'un train (gare de Joinville)*. Both are thought to be lost.

Within his extensive collection, Pascal Fouché, it turned out, had more than two dozen Beaulieu flip books, including a more complete version of the one Bernhard Richter found in the German bookshop – Fouché's copy comprised 121 images rather than 109 in the example bought by the Richters. Lecointe analysed this copy frame by frame to extract all the information it contained. On these pages, he was able to see more detail of the train, including the text that was written on it: EST and the number 634 or 654. It turned out that the train was owned by the Eastern Railway, and the locomotive could be further identified as a 031T (T for tender) series 8 pulling Bidel double-decker passenger carriages – a model that used by this company on the "Vincennes line" between Paris-Bastille and Verneuil-l'Étang.

Trains on this line stopped at 23 stations, but Lecointe focused his search on just six of them, ones that were known to have been filmed at this time, and that were close to Paris. In addition to the locomotive and the railcars, there were also clues from the natural world: the short length of the shadows and the leaves on the trees suggested the film was shot in high summer, around noon. After searching through images of the stations on his list online, Lecointe was able to eliminate those in urban areas since the geographical settings didn't match but photographic analysis of the Joinville-le-Pont station, in a south-eastern suburb of Paris revealed great promise. When Duclaud-Lacoste located a postcard featuring a "bird's-eye view" of the station, the discovery allowed Lecointe to pinpoint the precise locations in the film, and determine with 100% certainty that this particular flip book train arrived in Joinville-le-Pont station from Paris, in summer, a little before noon.

By positively identifying the station pictured in the flip book as Joinville-le-Pont, Lecointe eliminated the possibility that the flip book was derived from Méliès' *Arrivée d'un train (gare de Vincennes)* but simultaneously raised the possibility that the book derived from another Méliès lost film: Arrivée d'un train (gare de Joinville). Perhaps the only fly in the ointment being that Georges Méliès was one of two filmmakers known to have recorded a train arriving at that same station, the other being Auguste Baron. However, Baron's film, unlike the one filmed by Méliès, has survived and a comparison of the two elements confirms that the flip book does not derive from Baron's work. Lecointe's conclusion, with 99.9% certainty, is that the flip book derives from Arrivée d'un train (gare de Joinville), which would have been shot by Georges Méliès in the second half of July 1896. It is an astonishing fragment of film history we never expected to see, not quite the film itself but a physical copy of a copy, and an animation of a few of its frames.

There was more to discover from this flip book, however. With the help of Robert Byrne's smooth animation of the images in the flip book, and using the movement of the human figures on the platform and the decelerating train as a guide, the researchers deduced that an appropriate frame rate for animating this flip book would be about five/six images a second, whereas the original film was shot at 10/12 frames a second. There are short breaks in continuity, perhaps because there are frames missing in the flip book that were present in the original film. The team could also see that the outlines of one figure's trousers and the edge of the platform roof appear to have been emphasised, with bold lines etched into the printing plate itself, suggesting that the image needed to be touched up. This flip book was made, one may presume, from either a well-worn print or a shoddy printing plate – or both (see Section 2, images 1 to 26).

Endnote

1. *Liste complète des films cinématographiques de G. Méliès, fabricant, 13, passage de l'Opéra, Paris,* [ca 1898], (No. 1 to 166).

Chapter Four

One Down, 26 to Go

The identification of one lost Méliès film was exciting in itself, but it was the start of a project, not the end. And it was a very promising start. Analogous to the way that the flip books are leafed from back to front, might it be possible to identify more films, including lost ones, from Beaulieu's paper-and-card reproductions? Fouché had 26 more Beaulieu flip books in his collection (one of these is only tentatively attributed to Beaulieu), and it seemed, after searching in other archives online, that this may well be all that survives of his work. What stories could these tiny books tell?

First, Robert Byrne and photographer Onno Petersen created digital, animated versions of the flip books. Petersen devised an innovative mount that allowed each page to be photographed without risk to the pages or their fragile binding. In the final tally, some 2,642 photograms were photographed and can now be played like miniature movies, or frozen, and analysed frame by frame.[1] Byrne animated the images, turning them back into moving pictures, working with Lecointe to approximate a likely frame rate for each in the process. In 2019 the animated flip books had their world premiere at the San Francisco Silent Film Festival and were subsequently shown at Le Giornate del Cinema Muto in Pordenone – returning these lost images to the big screen.

The Corpus of Léon Beaulieu – © Onno Petersen – Collection Pascal Fouché.

Anatomy of a Flip Book

How to proceed with the Beaulieu investigations? At first glance, some of the flipbooks were more mysterious than others, and they weren't all the same shape and size – the page-counts ranged from 64 to 121. By disassembling one of the books, Lecointe deduced how they were manufactured. The pages of a book were printed on a single sheet pressed from a single printing plate consisting of a matrix of images (see Section 2, image 32). The halftone images (similar to newspaper photography printing) engraved on the printing plate produced a sheet that was then cut apart and assembled into the small finished books. The dimensions of the matrix on the sheet correspond to the number of pages in the flip book. A matrix of 11 x 11 images produced a book of 121 pages, a matrix of 7 x 12 yielded 84 flip book pages, a printing plate of 9x10 images resulted in a 90-page flip book, and so on.

Names and Identification

To begin the analysis, the research team needed to assign names to the flip books, which were produced without printed titles. They are not numbered either, and while some have handwritten titles on the covers others do not, so in those cases the research team used titles informally given to the books by Fouché. Several of flip books, in fact, have multiple titles – one could be written on the cover by an unknown person at an unknown time, as well as a title assigned by the researchers, and of course (if identified) the title of the film that is represented in the book. Lecointe's next task was to sort the booklets into groups with matching specifications, page counts, paper thickness, address, size etc. With the booklets named and categorised, the plan was to try to attribute each flip book to a filmic source, with either low, medium or high confidence, otherwise "unknown" or "confirmed". For example, that first flip book of the lost Joinville station film was attributed to Méliès with high confidence.

Of all the possible strategies for attributing the films, the first preference was matching the flip book photograms against existing film prints. Failing that, in the case of missing films, the aim was to match actors, props and even décor to identify the original filmmaker, studio and even the specific film. Along the way, the team hoped to learn more about the flip books and their construction, as well as the cinema of the 1890s. Might they be able to unearth lost films, remakes or films that were never catalogued? Very possibly. Anything can happen when you read back to front, using your thumbs.

Endnote

1.   Animation of all 27 Beaulieu flip books can be found online at: https://silentfilm.org/preservation/flipbooks.

Chapter Five

Freezing the Flip Books

Two Backwards Booklets: Kisses and the Can-Can

Les Deux baisers / The Two Kisses (handwritten title, 75 frame-images)

© Onno Petersen – Collection Pascal Fouché.

Four of the flip books are very easy to attribute, and this one is a doddle. This flip book is taken from the famous, in fact notorious, film *The May Irwin Kiss*, shot in April 1896 by the Edison company in New Jersey. Two actors, May Irwin and John Rice, are seen in close-up enjoying a smooch, a few moments from a scene from the stage musical *The Widow Jones*. The film was advertised salaciously in the Edison catalogue as follows: "They get ready to kiss, begin to kiss, and kiss and kiss and kiss in a way that brings down the house every time". There may be little doubt as to why two of these embraces were reproduced and distributed in flip book form.

This flip book scrolls smoothly at the speed of 12 frames a second, which proves that it was actually taken from every other frame of an Edison film shot for a Vitascope at 24fps, and not a flip book-style device in a Kinetoscope. There are two versions of this 75-page flip book in Fouché's collection: one bearing an address in Rue Volta, which scrolls from front to back, and another that scrolls from back to front, Beaulieu-style, and has an address associated with Beaulieu in Aubervilliers. In both variations, the printed numbering on each page is the same, thereby confirming that the same printing plate was used and the only difference is the order of the bound pages. This version is also much smaller in size than the other Beaulieu flip books.

La Danse du Cancan / The Cancan (handwritten title, 84 frame-images)

© Onno Petersen – Collection Pascal Fouché.

The appeal of the film source in this next flip book may be similarly self-evident. The origin of this folioscope is the Gaumont Studio's *Moulin Rouge: quadrille* (1896) and it features four dancers in their distinctive lace skirts high-kicking in a square formation.

This booklet also scrolls from front to back, running naturally at speed of around 16 frames a second and it is one of only three examples in this collection to have 84 pages. There are a few continuity breaks that show it is made up of different sequences put together.

This flip book bears no specific mention of Beaulieu, there is no page bearing his name or address, but it comes from a lot that contains more of his work and its first page has been torn off, as is often the case with Beaulieu's flip books (we'll come back to this). Again, there is another version similar to this one by Beaulieu, using the same Gaumont images, in Fouché's collection. This second version is complete and bears two stamps: one for the printer "Imp. Prissette, Paris" and another for "Clichés, L. Gaumont et Cie, Paris".

What could be the link between Beaulieu and the Prissette press? If Beaulieu did not own his own printing press, was *Prissette* his press of choice?[1] Could Prissette have used Beaulieu's photo plates after his death to sell flip books under their own brand? These questions remain unresolved. There are seven Prissette flip books in Fouché's collection, all of which bear the words "Clichés, L. Gaumont et Cie, Paris". Aside from *Moulin Rouge: quadrille*, the two others read from back to front as with most Beaulieu booklets.

Scrolling from the front to the back is the more the natural method for operating a flip book. These two booklets, taken from Edison and Gaumont sources were either not designed by Beaulieu for use in his Petit Biograph Parisien, which runs booklets back to front, or were produced before it was developed in March 1898. That said, all the back-to-front flip books are spread across all five of Beaulieu's known business addresses. Probably Beaulieu conceived the "Petit Biograph Parisien" early in his flip book career, and so these two front-to-back booklets are the exception that proves the rule. It's also possible that they were not Beaulieu's original work, and instead he opportunistically exploited some pre-existing booklets under his own brand.

Guaranteed Gaumont: Fighting Before Bedtime

Duel de Femmes / Women's Duel (handwritten title, 84 frame-images)

© Onno Petersen –
Collections Pascal Fouché et Thierry Lecointe.

There are two more flip books in Pascal Fouché's collection comprised of 84 pages and bearing the name "Clichés, L. Gaumont et Cie, Paris", with the Prissette brand printed on the back cover. They clearly correspond to two Gaumont films, No. 24 *Duel de femmes*, a fight scene featuring two women, and No. 142 *Une Nuit agitée*, in which a man is rudely disturbed from his slumbers.

Unlike *La Danse du Cancan*, these two flip books scroll from back to front as do most Beaulieu booklets. In this case because they are designed to be used in the Petit Biograph Parisien. This detail is specific to Beaulieu in Paris-Nord in the very late 1890s, which suggests a relationship between Prissette (printer-manufacturer) and Beaulieu (manufacturer).

As with *La Danse du Cancan*, pre-cinema expert and collector François Binétruy has an unbranded version of the *Duel de femmes* flip book in his archive. The first page, where the address should appear, is torn but the page where you would expect to see the copyright details is not. Could it be that this flip book was made in two versions: one with the Gaumont copyright intact, attributable to Prissette, the other without, from Beaulieu?

For further confirmation, *Duel de femmes* can be identified by comparison with three frames on a Gaumont poster showing the same scene. All of which adds up to the conclusion that flip book is attributed to Gaumont.

Le Coucher or *La Puce* / *Bedtime* or *The Flea* (handwritten titles, 84 frame-images)

© Onno Petersen – Collections Pascal Fouché, François Binétruy et Thierry Lecointe.

Le Coucher or *La Puce* can also be easily traced back to a Gaumont source, the 1897 film *Une Nuit agitée*, directed by Alice Guy. Its action matches two consecutive photograms in a Gaumont catalogue from January 1900, allowing us to attribute this to Gaumont with high confidence.

As with *Duel de femmes*, we have logged two copies of this flip book, one complete and one with a torn cover. Again, it may be that there exist both Prissette and Beaulieu versions. Whether a link between Beaulieu and Prissette can be proven or not, it is clear that only booklets made from Gaumont films are 84 pages long. Paradoxically, the choice of the number of photograms seems to be the choice of the film producer, not the booklet manufacturer.

Méliès Mysteries: Bed, Bath and Beyond

Nuit agitée / Restless Night (handwritten title, 121 frame-images)

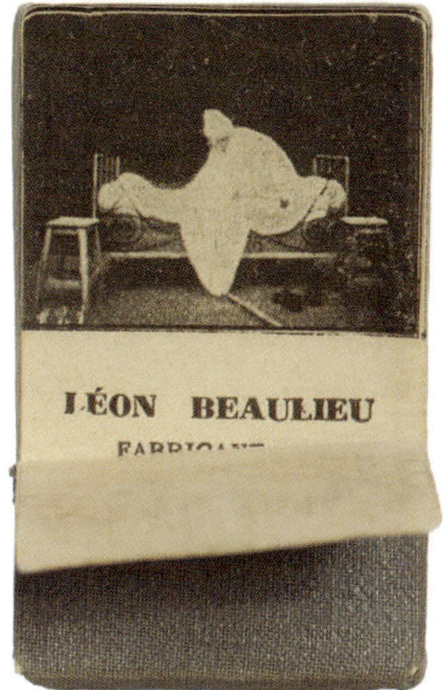 

© Onno Petersen – Collection Pascal Fouché.

Those were the easy ones. None of the other booklets in the Beaulieu collection can be so simply traced back to a pre-existing, extant film source, so this is where the real detective work begins. The sleuthing starts with *Nuit agitée*, a comic skit in which a sleeping man has his slumber disturbed by a giant bug, panics and then swats at it with first a broom and then a chamber pot – the scatological implications of which are happily left for the audience to imagine.

These images must be from the Méliès studio (see Section 2, image 29). The bed with iron scrolls, the stools alongside it, the costume and even the fake beard are familiar from his films (see Section 2, images 33 to 41). In fact, the distressed sleeper is most likely the director himself – a view shared by both the Beaulieu research team and Méliès scholar Jacques Malthête. It also runs smoothly at a speed of 12 frames a second, as in several early Méliès films.

The film this scene most closely resembles is *Une Nuit terrible* (1896), but the action is not an exact match. Closer analysis, using the size of the bed as a guide, reveals that this film was shot with the camera closer to the bed than in that film (2.75m rather than 5.38m). Jacques Malthête has made many studies of the evolution of Méliès's studio, and if you look at his films across this period, you find the camera moving further and further away from the field of action. This suggests that the scene captured in this flip book was filmed by Méliès before he made *Une Nuit terrible*. *Nuit agitée*, or rather the film it was made from, is the earlier film of this bedbug skit and *Une Nuit terrible* is a remake. *Nuit agitée* is therefore confirmed as a previously unseen film by Méliès, transferred to flip book form.

Le Bain / *The Bath* (handwritten title, 80 frame-images)

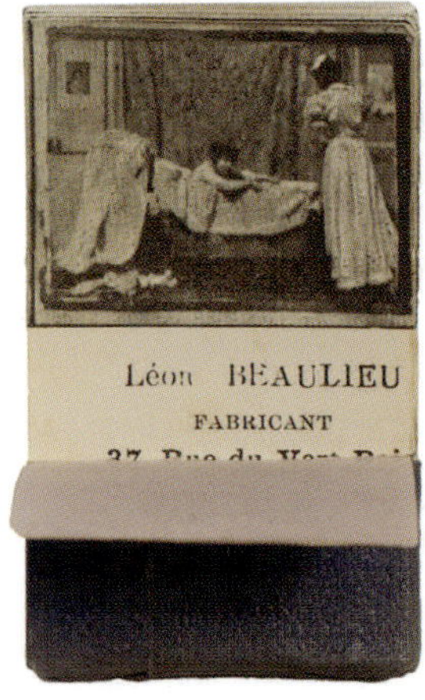

© Onno Petersen – Collection Pascal Fouché.

From bedtime to bathtime, and this slightly risqué scene of a woman disrobing, with her maid's assistance, prior to a soak in the tub. After watching this scene several times to study the details in the background, Lecointe realised that the action in the foreground itself was familiar from four different Méliès films, and the director's wife Jehanne d'Alcy was most likely playing the lead role. D'Alcy wears a gown in this scene that is identical to the one she wears in a Méliès film called *Après le bal (le tub)* from 1897. Georges Sadoul features an image from this film in his book *Histoire générale du cinéma – II*[2] with the title *Le Bain de la Parisienne*, but it is not a match to any of the pages in the flip book – the shadows are different, for one thing. Again, this appears to be an earlier version of a film that we know – in this case a missing film that we know only from a picture in a history book (see Section 2, images 30 and 31).

It is a scenario with a very obvious appeal. And this may be the only flip book for which we can speculate a collaboration between Méliès and Beaulieu. In 1944, when d'Alcy mentioned "*le petit livre qu'on feuilletait très vite*", she mentioned it in the same sentence as this film: "Il a fait *Le Bain de la Parisienne* et le petit livre qu'on feuilletait très vite. J'ai fait *Le Tub* aussi". In English: "He made *Le Bain de la Parisienne* and the little book that one leafed through very quickly. I acted in *Le Tub* also" (see Section 2, images 42 and 43). It appears that Méliès contributed to the creation of flip books, even if he never discussed it.

The scrolling rate of this film looks natural at eight frames a second, but it was made using every other image from a filmstrip, so the original film would be expected to play at 16fps.

Le Coucher de la mariée / The Bride's Bedtime, aka *Le Déshabillé de la mariée / The Bride Undressed* or *La Toilette de la mariée / The Bride Undresses* (handwritten title) and *L'Amant surpris / The Surprised Lover* (handwritten title, 90 frame-images)

Le Coucher de la mariée © Onno Petersen – Collection Pascal Fouché.

L'Amant surpris © Onno Petersen – Collection Pascal Fouché.

There are more Beaulieu flip books in the same voyeuristic or licentious vein as *Le Bain* and two of them use the same boudoir setting. The first of these is called *Le Coucher de la mariée* or *The Bride's Bedtime*, though there are also versions called *Le Déshabillé de la mariée* or *La Toilette de la mariée*. The second is called *L'Amant surpris*, or *The Surprised Lover*.

The bride preparing for bed is very probably Jehanne d'Alcy once more. Again, she is undressing with the assistance of her maid, but this time in preparation for bed, and just in the final moments, a man in evening dress rushes into her room. Also again, this film is a near-miss match for a Méliès film pictured in the Sadoul book: *Le Coucher de la mariée* (1899). So, it is possible that as before the source for this flip book is an earlier version of a known film.

L'Amant surpris nudges the theme of *Le Coucher de la mariée* a little further into x-certificate territory, with not just more sex but also some violence. A man and woman are rapidly unpeeling their clothes, in a bedroom, in front of the familiar bed with iron scrolls. He attempts to embrace her, but she pushes him away and demands payment by pointing at her open palm. He puts his hands in his trouser pockets, but when his hands come out empty, she starts shooing him out of the room, at which point another man leaps into the frame and aggressively pursues the departing lover (or customer?) – who might at this point be described as more embarrassed than surprised.

L'Amant surpris, *Le Coucher de la mariée* and *Le Bain* – © Onno Petersen – Collection Pascal Fouché.

L'École des gendres, [*The School for Sons-in-law*], Méliès film No. 102 – © Cinémathèque Française.

The same boudoir appears in three different flip books and Méliès film No. 102 (see Section 2, images 44 to 47).

The presence of a woman who looks very much like d'Alcy (although Malthête questions this) and the familiar setting suggest this is a Méliès film, but it does not correspond to any known title in his filmography. This suggests the existence of certain "off-catalogue" scenes as part of a "*grivoise*"[3] or bawdy slate that Méliès alluded to briefly in 1907. When listing the subjects of films, he mentioned scenes such as "risqué subjects and model poses"[4]. Although Méliès was writing about films more generally, his account is possibly coloured by his own memories and examples from his own cinematic career.

Both of these flip books are confirmed as originating from Méliès film sources, and both scroll nicely at a rate of eight frames a second, with the flip book using every other image from a strip of celluloid.

Petites Performances

Prestidigitation / Conjuring Trick (handwritten title, 121 frame-images)

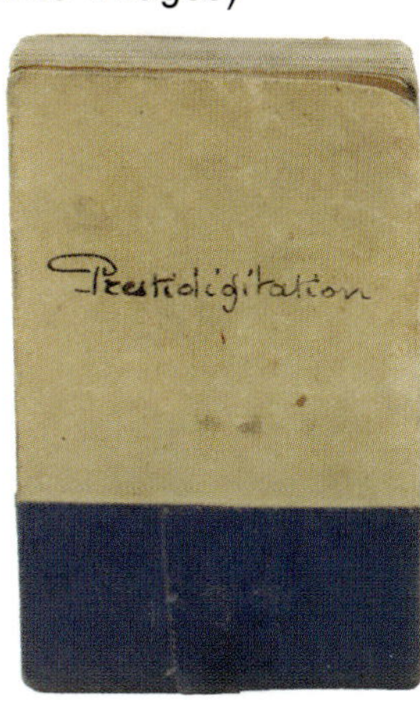

© Onno Petersen – Collections Pascal Fouché et François Binétruy.

A picture is emerging now that suggests all the flip books containing either 80, 90 or 121 pages come from Méliès films. There are seven more 121-page flip books in the set, all scenes of performers doing their acts: dancing, conjuring or in several cases, fighting. This first booklet shows us a magician, a celebrated conjurer called David Devant, pulling a rabbit out of an apparently empty opera hat. He performs the trick with flair, first looking into the hat to make sure it is empty, then casting a spell over it with a flourish and finally removing the rabbit and holding it aloft bearing a delighted smile.

Devant was an English magician, born in Holloway, north London in 1868 who was considered to be one of the greatest magicians of his time. He became the first president of The Magic Circle.

He also had a rock-solid connection to early cinema, beginning in 1896 when he staged an early British film screening. Méliès used one of Devant's stage acts in his *The Spiritualist Photographer* (1903), and Devant himself appeared in three films made by Paul and one by Méliès.

This appears to be a short section from that Méliès film, *David Devant*, which was probably shot in mid-1897 at the latest, given its catalogue number, 101. In the catalogue, which was published in late 1898, early 1899, the full film is described as follows: "Conjuror pulling cards, live rabbits, a carafe full of wine, glasses and a pot of flowers from a top hat, which he transforms into a cage containing a dove and makes disappear".[5] The few seconds of the flip book's running time only contain the white-rabbit sequence, but this scene can be attributed to Méliès with high confidence. The flip book scrolls well at a rate of 12 images a second, and therefore the original film probably does also. The booklet is printed with the address in Rue Oberkampf, which supports the idea that that Beaulieu was still living there at the end of the first half of 1897.

La Danse / *The Dance* (handwritten title, 121 frame-images)

© Onno Petersen – Collections Pascal Fouché et François Binétruy.

Another British performer, and another blank, dark backdrop. The flip book shows a single figure, a young woman in a white tutu, dancing charmingly but somewhat eccentrically. There were many, many similar films produced in the early period of cabaret and music hall dancers performing for the camera, which meant almost endless opportunities for comparison: Caroline Otéro, Liane de Pougy, Emilienne d'Alençon, Yvette Guilbert, Louise Willy, Carlotta Zambelli and Régina Badet to start with. None of these dancers were a match to the distinctive character cavorting in this flip book, however – most of them were too old for one thing.

Could this perhaps be a fragment from another missing Méliès film? One possible candidate was No. 45 *Miss de Vère (Gigue Anglaise)* / *Miss de Vere (English Jig)*, evidently a film made of British music hall star Elise de Vère performing an English jig. She would have been 17 at the time the film was made (1896), which corresponds to the youthful figure in the flip book, and she was known for her beauty – there are several postcard images of her with her dark hair piled on top of her head in the fashionable *fin-de-siècle* style. She was the daughter of Charles de Vère, a magician who ran a magic shop in Paris in the 1890s, and was good friends with Méliès. Young Elise began her French career in January 1897 at the Théâtre-Concert-Parisiana, and was very successful, although some critics, such as Valerian Tranel, were unimpressed by her wriggling movements and cat-calls, saying she danced "like the Irish in the suburbs of London".

Although the dancer is wearing a tutu in this flip book, the choreography is far from classical ballet, but according to dance scholar Laurent Guido, there is nothing to confirm that this is a bona fide English jig, either:

> "obviously, one can imagine, by projecting the information that we have on Miss de Vère, that this is a young girl who puts on a tutu and makes some choreographic gestures vaguely related to the spirit of the jig – the fact that she almost loses her balance at the end of some movements testifies to either a certain carelessness or a lack of professionalism."[6]

Guido also pointed out that Méliès may have described these few steps as a jig purely

Postcard of Elise de Vère – Collection of Thierry Lecointe.

because he knew that was her speciality, so it was wise to make reference to it, as he did with the other dancers, music hall artists and gymnasts he filmed.

The tutu may be more important than the dance. Of the several actresses mentioned above, none were photographed in this kind of costume. Most pictures of De Vère are from around 1900, but when the Lecointe discovered an image of her from a few years beforehand, she was wearing a tutu (see Section 2, images 54 to 56). It's not possible to be entirely sure, but this flip book likely represents a portion of Méliès' *Miss de Vère* (*Gigue Anglaise*) from 1896: another lost film, glimpsed through a Beaulieu booklet. So that's another high-confidence attribution to Méliès, for this flip book that plays smoothly at 12 frames a second.

Lutte de cuisiniers / Cooks' Fight (handwritten title, 121 frame-images)

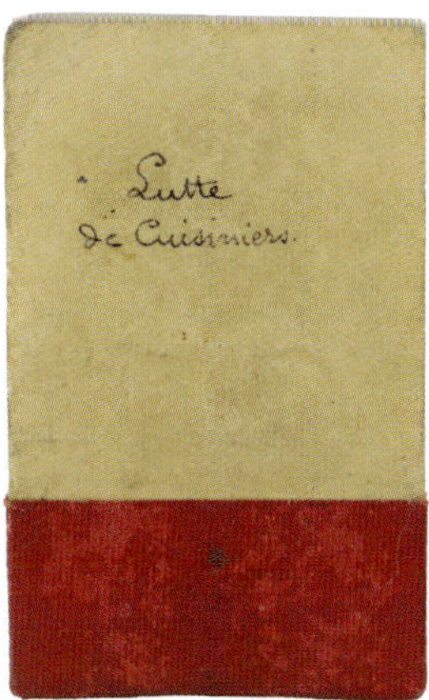

© Onno Petersen – Collections Pascal Fouché et François Binétruy.

In this rough-housing skit the gag-violence rapidly escalates as two cooks brawl in a kitchen. One soon gains the upper hand, pushing his opponent into a barrel and attacking him with a knife, a pan and a pot of water. The scene ends just as his victim wriggles free and prepares to fight back; the two square off again like boxers at the start of a bout.

The backdrop is dark and empty as in many early Méliès films, and the barrel may be similar to one he used elsewhere, but it is not possible to match this flip book with a specific film. However, enough of the specifications are the same (including the likely scrolling speed of 12 frames a second, the size and number of pages) as other Méliès-sourced flip books. This flip book is therefore classified as probably taken from a Méliès source, with medium confidence.

Four duels: *Le Duel*, *Le Bâton*, *Boxe*, *Escrime* or *Duel au sabre* (handwritten titles, 121 frame-images)

Le Duel © Onno Petersen – Collection Pascal Fouché.

Le Bâton © Onno Petersen – Collection Pascal Fouché.

Boxe © Onno Petersen – Collections Pascal Fouché et François Binétruy.

Escrime or *Duel au sabre* © Onno Petersen – Collections Pascal Fouché et François Binétruy.

These four combative booklets should be considered together, because they appear to be a series. Each scene is a duel, whether with sabres, swords, sticks or fists, against a black background. As they are all also 121-page flip books, scrolling happily at 12 frames a second, it's reasonable to assume a single supplier for all of them. It seems unlikely that many different filmmakers have used a technique that provides the same number of images.

Although Méliès is best remembered as the innovator who made trick movies and fantasy films, in his early days, he also made the same kinds of films as his peers and many of them were quite bare-bones productions. Most of his early films from 1896 and 1897 have disappeared, but those that remain show a certain distinct style in the making. As he later recalled, "I first projected Kinetoscope films, fencers, boxers, Loïe Fuller. My characters appeared in white on a black background".[7] The fencers and boxers in question are likely those found in the Méliès filmography, numbered 136 and 148: *Match de boxe, professeurs de l'école de Joinville* and *Assaut d'escrime, école de Joinville*. The catalogue numbers don't quite tally with Méliès's memories – they suggest shooting dates of late 1897 and 1898. The Loïe Fuller film, *Danse Serpentine*, is numbered 44 and therefore dates from the beginning of Méliès's filmmaking career (he started making films in spring 1896).

Therefore, we can conclude that films 136 and 148 are remakes and the duel scenes captured in these booklets are the originals – which likely date right back to the beginning of Méliès's filmmaking career, probably shot around the same time as the film of the train arriving in Joinville station. Given the similarities between these four scenes, the stick fight and the sabre duel could confirm the existence of an "off-catalogue" slate from the Méliès studio[8] – in the same way that we know the Lumière brothers filmed many scenes that were not included in the official catalogue.

The flip books scroll well at 12 frames a second and do not appear to be missing any images, so they correspond to the 10–12fps rates used by Méliès at the start of his career. Sadly, there are no details in the images here that can strengthen our classification – we can only say we have medium confidence that these booklets are made from Méliès films.

The Nineties

La Méprise / *The Mistake* (handwritten title, 90 frame-images)

© Onno Petersen –
Collection Pascal Fouché.

The Beaulieu collection contains eight booklets with 90 photograms apiece, two of which are identified as Méliès movies – *Le Coucher de la mariée* and *L'Amant surpris*. The remaining six all have handwritten titles: *La Nourrice, La Puce, Le Coup du père François, Pose chez l'artiste. Vénus* and *La Méprise*. The title of the last booklet in that list translates as *The Mistake*, and it's a simple comic sketch hinging on a mistaken identity. A figure in long black skirts and carrying an umbrella approaches the window of a boutique, with their back to the camera. Along comes a likely chap in a straw boater using a cane and puts his hand on the black-clad figure – who then turns haughtily around, revealing himself to be, not an elegant lady in a dress, but clergyman in his robes.

The scenario suggests a match with lost Méliès film 36, *Salut malencontreux (scène comique)* or *The Unlucky Greeting*, but it's not that simple (we will talk about it again later when we get to *La Nourrice*). The backdrop appears to be unique to the film, and although the bald man in the boater looks a little like Méliès, Jacques Malthête does not recognise a resemblance. There are several similarities between this flip book and one discussed below called *Le Voyeur*, though, including that boater and the cane, as well as the staging and the saucy subject matter. The source for this booklet can be stated as Méliès with medium confidence.

This flip book scrolls smoothly at eight frames a second, with every other image being used from a 16fps film.

Pose chez l'artiste. Vénus / Posing for an Artist as Venus (handwritten title, 90 frame-images)

© Onno Petersen – Collection Pascal Fouché.

A cheekily funny, and surprisingly complex, comic scenario set in an artist's studio. A model poses as Venus for a painter, who appears to be played by Méliès. The artist, overcome with lust, gurns at the camera-audience and leaps on to the model's dais to embrace her, with wildly wandering hands. Insulted, the model knocks him flat on his back, and briefly recovers her classical pose, before deciding to enjoy the moment and take the time to laugh at the painter, who is squirming with distress on the studio floor. He picks himself up and they appear to call it a truce – the session will resume, and continue as long as the artist keeps his professional distance.

It may also be taken from an off-catalogue Méliès movie. There is not an extant film print that duplicates this scenario, but there is a corresponding photograph, reproduced in *Georges Méliès mage*[9] that nearly-but-not-quite matches the booklet scene. Even interpreting the evidence of this picture takes a good deal of detective work. The positions of the painter and the model, general framing and perspective, position of the easel and set dressing is similar but not identical. Méliès's costume leaps out, though. Not just the artist's smock but his beautiful plaid trousers are identical. And unmistakable. Méliès also wore a very similar trouser in film No. 112 *Entre Calais et Douvres* and then again No. 312/313 *Le Déshabillage impossible* (see Section 2, images 59 to 63).

Returning to the flip book, that dais turns out to be the most devilish of details. The small coffee table on which the model stands can be seen in seven other Méliès films from No. 78/80 *Le Manoir du diable* (1897) to No. 371/372 *Le Chapeau à surprises* (1901) (see Section 2, imagess 64 and 65).

A second version of the same scenario: [*Le Modèle irascible*], © Lobster Films.

Pages 1, 10, 15 and 20 of the flip book – © Onno Petersen – Collection Pascal Fouché.

This flip book is therefore confirmed as being taken from a Méliès film. The comparison of the photograph and the booklet is another reminder that once Méliès not only made remakes but also off-catalogue films, although there are two titles in his filmography that may be related to the film excerpted in the flip book (No. 130/131 *Le Modèle irascible* and No. 166 *Rêve d'artiste)*. The address printed on this booklet (rue Vert-Bois) points to the conclusion that this booklet uses images from an earlier version of *Le Modèle irascible*. The most likely frame rate for this booklet is eight frames a second, based on using every other image from a source film that was photographed at 16 frames a second.

La Nourrice / The Nanny (handwritten title, 90 frame-images)

© Onno Petersen – Collection Pascal Fouché.

This boisterous slice of slapstick combines a balancing trick and a visual joke, and is populated by easily recognisable comic types including the nanny of the title. On a simple bench, the only piece of scenery here, a flamboyantly uniformed soldier and a nanny cosy up together, playing with the baby in her charge. At the other end, an older gentleman settles down to read his newspaper. The soldier looks down at his lap – the baby has wet him – and he and the nanny both leap to their feet, toppling the bench and throwing the gentleman to the floor, much to their amusement. The clarity of the images is probably the lowest in the set, so it is not possible to identify the actors, but it is clear they are wearing theatrical makeup, as was common in early Méliès films.

Jacques Malthête suggests the flip book could have been sourced from Méliès film No. 36, *Salut malencontreux*, alternatively titled *A Soldier's Unlucky Salutation* in the American Méliès catalogue. One of the first French catalogues includes three images that feature a soldier and nurse similar to the figures in our flip book. It can therefore be attributed to Méliès with high confidence, also by comparing its technical specifications to others in the collection.

This film is certainly one of the oldest in the set and the optimal speed for this flip book has been estimated by Robert Byrne as a quite slow 10 frames a second, which will be the same as the film it is sourced from.

Photogram 45 from flip book *La Nourrice*
© Onno Petersen – Collection Pascal Fouché.

Three surviving photograms of *Salut malencontreux*,
© Cinémathèque Française.

La Puce / The Flea (handwritten title, 90 frame-images)

© Onno Petersen – Collection Pascal Fouché.

Another case of a bug disturbing a good night's rest, but this time it is a flea (*puce*) and the interrupted sleeper is a woman. Instead of attacking the flea with a broom, the unfortunate lady loses the culprit somewhere in her nightgown: cue lots of wriggling, skirt-lifting and thigh-scratching. In other words, this is another cheeky excuse for a flash of flesh laced with humour. The title of the flip book brings to mind a Pathé film (No. 783: *La Puce* (1897–99)) but the leading lady appears to be Jehanne D'Alcy – and page 35 offers a good look at her face.

The black background is familiar, well as familiar as it can be, and although the bed is very distinctive, it doesn't match the two other beds found in existing Méliès films. However, the patterned quilt on top of the bed can be seen in two: No. 82 *Le Cauchemar* from late 1896 and No. 122/123 *L'Auberge ensorcellée* from 1897 (see Section 2, images 66 to 68).

Despite the scant evidence, the source for this booklet can be classified as Méliès with high confidence. This is because of that decorative counterpane, and the fact that the flip book's manufacture matches that of others that are certified as Méliès-adapted. The flip book plays well at 10 frames a second as the source film would have done.

Le Coup du père François / The Father François Attack (handwritten title, 90 frame-images)

© Onno Petersen – Collection Pascal Fouché.

The name of this booklet is a phrase that has almost disappeared from the French language – so it is fairly safe to assume it is a contemporary title. A "*Coup du père François*" is a term that originated in the second half of the 19th century and refers to a specific kind of assault. The victim, walking alone at night, is approached by a first assailant who engages him in conversation as a diversion while the second assailant sneaks up behind him and strangles him violently with a cord. While the victim struggles with the rope around his neck, the first assailant empties his pockets. In a true *Coup du père François* the victim should be lifted off the ground by the force of the strangulation. French linguistics expert Gaston Esnault has suggested that the name came from a celebrated French wrestler called Charles Arpin who was also nicknamed "the terrible Savoyard" and "Father François". He died in 1883, but during his time in the ring, strangulation moves were legal in French wrestling.

In the scenario, which neatly illustrates this gruesome phenomenon, the decoy is a woman, who closely resembles the actress playing the maids in *Le Coucher de la mariée* and *Le Bain*. The victim has a look of Méliès himself, with a familiar boater, but minus the traditional bald cap. These details and that fact that the booklet has similar specifications to three certified Méliès flip books combine to give *Le Coup du père François* a classification of Méliès with high confidence. This flip book plays best at eight frames a second, probably taken from a film shot at 16fps.

The Odd Squad

There are three more flip books with unique numbers of photograms – 64, 88, 96 and 98. Some of them are far easier to identify then others.

Déguisement / Disguise (handwritten title, 88 frame-images)

© Onno Petersen – Collection Pascal Fouché.

This diverting flip book shows a master of theatrical disguise transforming himself into different characters solely by manipulating a soft cloth cap. It's not a great leap to guess that this is a section of the lost Méliès film No. 42, *Dix chapeaux en 60 secondes* (1896). Sadly, there are no visible details to corroborate this supposition further.

Examining the construction of the booklet, however, reveals that despite the shorter length, it has been made in much the same way as the 121-page booklets that have been attributed to Méliès. It has been built out of eight lines of 11 photograms. Therefore, this flip book, which looks natural playing at 12 frames a second, is attributed to Méliès with medium confidence.

Le Voyeur / The Voyeur (handwritten title, 80 frame-images)

© Onno Petersen – Collection Pascal Fouché.

Proof, if it were needed, that the cinema was exploring the illicit thrills of voyeurism long before Hitchcock came on the scene. In this scenario we see a woman partially hidden by a wall, hitch up her skirts to sit down behind it, and another smiling fellow in a straw boater nods at the camera before kneeling down to observe her through a crack in the brickwork. In a moment, she's up and off and the Peeping Tom likewise leaves the frame. The wall itself can been seen in three other Méliès films, No. 180 *Luttes extravgantes*, No. 183 *L'Illusionniste fin de siècle* and No. 309/310 *Nouvelles luttes extravagantes*, only here the lower half has been repainted, to show potted plants, suggesting the action takes place in a garden (see Section 2, images 48 to 51). The straw boater is also familiar, as are both the risqué subject and the leading man's comic gestures. The cane looks like the one used in *La Méprise* too … However, despite the research team's instincts, it's not possible to positively identify the leading man as Méliès. There certainly is a lot in common between this scenario and *La Méprise*.

All in all, there is just enough evidence to mark this flip book as "Méliès certified". It plays smoothly at eight frames a second using every other frame of a 16fps original.

"Partie de cartes à trois" / *Card Game for Three* (96 frame-images)

© Onno Petersen –
Collection Pascal Fouché.

During the animation process, Robert Byrne discovered that while this flip book is made up of 96 pages, they represent 48 frames, repeated, instead of 96 unique images. The purpose of doubling up images seems to be to make a short flip book seem the same size as the others. Neither the unusual format nor the scenario (three men play cards around a table, and move to start a scuffle) suggest a link to Méliès, even though his first film was called *Partie des cartes*. The surviving version of that film is probably a remake of his first film (from a hypothesis of Lecointe), shot on 10 June 1896. This is not a match to the surviving version and neither is it a match to the lost version, as according to the memory of his granddaughter, Madeleine Malthête-Méliès, that scene contained four adult male actors, one more than here. There is also a reproduction labelled as frame of the first film in the book *Georges Méliès* by Maurice Bessy and Lo Duca, clearly showing the four men at the table. According to Jacques Malthête, both the attribution of the photograph to Méliès and the identification of the characters is uncertain.

Each of the 48 images in this booklet has a clearly marked black frame, as has also been noticed in flip books made from Gaumont titles. This led the Beaulieu research team to look at Gaumont film No. 72, *Partie de cartes*. Again, there was no direct match, although there were a couple of clear similarities: the rather tight framing and the number of characters.

Skladanowsky flip book / 48 pages – © Private collection.

However, further research led Lecointe to discover a flip book using the same images for sale on an online auction site. This flip book was completely unlike the Beaulieu books in form but it was presented as a copy of a booklet by the German inventor and filmmaker Max Skladanowsky. We can share that conclusion and attribute this book to Skladanowsky, even though the images do not match those in another of his card-party flip books, *Eine Parthie Klabrias* / *A Game of Klaberjass* (however, same table and actors).

Lutte / *Wrestling* (handwritten title, 98 frame-images)

© Onno Petersen – Collections Pascal Fouché et François Binétruy.

Lecointe was able to analyse three different versions of this flip book, which nevertheless has many singular qualities. One copy in Fouché's collection bears the address of the Prissette printer on the top page and flips from back to front for use in the Beaulieu's patented device. When we consider the second copy in Fouché's collection and the one owned by François Binétruy the link to Beaulieu seems more doubtful. These copies have no identifying marks and the first page is torn as with most Beaulieu flip books. However, all three copies have a paper binder over a staple, elements, which associates them more closely with Prissette. It is possible that flip books were sold by both Prissette and Beaulieu.

There are probably only two films that correspond to this flip book and they are both from 1896: *Wrestlers (three),* directed by George William De Bedts, and *Wrestlers,* from Pathé. The De Bedts film is often advertised in the regional press as *Wrestlers Folies-Bergères,* and sometimes in colour – useful to distinguish the three figures in combat. As there are only two figures in this flip book it seems more likely that the images originated with Pathé.

It is also curious that both wrestlers seem to be suspended in mid-air, against a black background – there is no difference in shading to suggest a flat ground. This kind of treatment is not seen in any of the other flip books, which reinforces the idea of a different provenance for these images. This flip book is therefore classified as probably from a Pathé source, but with low confidence.

"*Train en marche*" / *Train in Motion* (64 frame-images)

© Onno Petersen –
Collection Pascal Fouché.

This is another intriguingly constructed flip book, consisting of 64 pages, but just 32 repeated images. It's not put together in the same way as the Gaumont card-party flip book, however, and it has handwritten numbers in the corner of each page, as seen on a few Méliès-attributed booklets (one certified, one high confidence and four medium confidence). That said, its construction is also similar to the Gaumont booklets. It plays best at eight frames a second, using every other frame from the original film.

It seems bizarre that this booklet only has 32 images. It's a scene of a train in motion through open countryside and this short length doesn't give the opportunity even to see the whole train. Perhaps Beaulieu was making do with the material he had and no more was available to him.

It might seem impossible to identify such a brief snippet of film, reproduced with such comparatively reduced clarity, but there are clues to be found, even in these 32 images. Not many, though, and it proved impossible to match the train or carriages to any used on the French railways. So Thierry Lecointe contacted two rail experts, Jean-Marc Combe (former director of the French Railway Museum in Mulhouse) and Christian Fonnet (former librarian at La Vie du Rail), who were most helpful. They agreed that the train shown was undoubtedly a 120 (1110) 3-cylinder Teutonic class compound model used on the London North Western Railway in England, serving stations from London to Liverpool, via Birmingham, Crewe, Chester and Manchester.

Although Méliès went to England to buy equipment, he never filmed there (see Section 2, images 71 to 73). There is an off-catalogue R.W. Paul film called *Royal Train*, but that doesn't match the action here. However, there are 38 consecutive titles in the Gaumont filmography that mention locations in England and Dublin – which is easily reached from the port at Liverpool. Gaumont film No. 55 is called *Train à corridor* and it appears in the catalogue between *Queen Victoria's Jubilee Views* from 22 June 1897 (Nos 7 to 23) and *The Duke and Duchess of York's Visit to Dublin* from 18 August 1897 (No. 62). It was probably filmed by British camera operators using a 60mm Gaumont machine who sent their film back to the company's headquarters for processing.

This flip book, which was previously classified "unknown" can now be attributed to Gaumont, with medium confidence.

A Serpentine Mystery
Loïe Fuller (handwritten title, 90 frame-images)

© Onno Petersen – Collections Pascal Fouché et Thierry Lecointe.

These booklets pose a puzzle. In the collection there are five identical flip books featuring a performance of the serpentine dance made famous by Loïe Fuller – a familiar, yet always beautiful scene popular in early cinema– and they are all individually hand-coloured. They all contain 90 pages, are 42mm wide and scroll back to front, looking natural at 10 frames a second. The kind of numbering found on these flip books is seen on other Beaulieu booklets, but also one by Prissette. Only one of the booklets carries a manufacturer's name and address: "Prissette, Imprimeur

Fabricant. Passage Kuszner, 17, Paris". The other four have torn front pages. All the mutilated flip books in the collection are attributable to Beaulieu, while all the Prissette booklets are intact. Many of the Beaulieu booklets in Fouché's collection have the covers torn away, and all of those in Lecointe's collection. One hypothesis is that the mutilations took place after the posthumous sale of Beaulieu's stock so they could be claimed by the new owner.

The good news is that this particular serpentine dance does appear to correspond with a lost Méliès film. Early film scholar Jean-Claude Seguin has identified a serpentine dance painted with "four colours" among other Méliès films projected in Lisbon in August 1896.[10] In these three flip books, "Fuller" turns and twists both her body and her billowing white skirts in shades of blue, green, yellow and red.

The *Loïe Fuller* flip books can therefore be attributed to Méliès with high confidence, as a match to film No. 44 *Danse serpentine*, even if the manufacturer is uncertain. The evidence of a Spanish version of this flip book that it could be a match to a Gaumont film, No. 12 *Danse serpentine*, but this is less likely.

There a more perplexing mystery: the dancer's identity. Many serpentine dance films incorrectly claim to be Fuller, and the resemblance here is not convincing, and according to opinion of Fuller scholars Zeva Oelbaum and Sabine Krayenbühl, the dancer is clearly not Loïe Fuller.

While the Méliès film does not identify the dancer, contemporary press articles imply it is Fuller. It could perhaps be American dancer Crissie Sheridan, for example, but the likeness is not any more convincing. If you compare these images to Méliès' No. 188 *La danse du feu* (1899), the dancers appear to be very alike, although the definition does not allow for a confident match. Who is the dancer in this booklet? Was the book sold using Fuller's name or did some latter-day wishful-thinking owner write the name? Perhaps we'll never know.

Endnotes

1. Although the lengths of flip books vary (between 52 and 70 mm), the width of Prissette flip books, 42mm, is common to most Beaulieu booklets.

2. *Histoire générale du cinéma – II, Les pionniers du cinéma 1897-1909,* Éditions Denoël, Paris, 1973.

3. This could support Sadoul's assertions about a repertoire of saucy films, in Sadoul, 1973, *op. cit.* pp. 107 and 115.

4. In Georges Méliès, "Les vues cinématographiques. Causerie par Geo. Méliès", reproduced in André Gaudreault, *Cinéma et attraction. Pour une nouvelle histoire du cinématographe*, CNRS, Paris, 2008, p. 201.

5. In "Liste complète des films cinématographiques de G. Méliès, fabricant, 13, passage de l'Opéra, Paris", quoted in Jacques Malthête, *Méliès, images et illusions*, Exporégie, Paris, 1996, p. 216.

6. Letter from Laurent Guido 12 November, 2013.

7. Georges Méliès, *Noir et Blanc*, 10 July 1929, quoted in Jacques Deslandes, *Le boulevard du cinéma à l'époque de Georges Méliès*, Éditions du Cerf, Bourges, 1963, p. 27.

8. For non-catalogued films already inventoried see Malthête, 1996, p. 243.

9. In Maurice Bessy and Lo Duca, *Georges Méliès, mage*, Jean-Jacques Pauvert, Paris, 1961, p. 147, *Le peintre et son modèle*. The silver print (11.5 x 16 cm), representing his wife in the role of the model and himself in the role of the painter, entitled "*Le Modèle narcissique*", 1896 , was auctioned on 17 March, 2018 by Galerie de Chartres, 7, rue Colin d'Harleville, 28000 Chartres.

10. In the Lisbon newspaper *A Vanguarda*, 22 August, 1896.

Chapter Six

Lessons from the Flip books

Just as discrete images combine to form a smooth motion, out of the analysis of each flip book, patterns emerge. First, all the booklets attributed to Méliès films consist of 121, 90, 80 or 88 pages, and it seems most probable that higher pagecounts correspond with earlier films. This is substantiated by looking at the backdrops: the older films are shot on plain dark backgrounds (apart from the film shot at Joinville station), with increasing use of décor and scenery as Méliès progressed in his filmmaking. As corroboration, the three flip books printed with the address on Rue Oberkampf all contain 121 photograms – and this is where the researchers believe Beaulieu began to produce his booklets.

All this research confirms a general evolution, for flip books taken from Méliès films, towards using fewer and fewer images. Could this be a scheme to reduce manufacturing costs?

A hypothesis also emerges that all the 121-page flip books, and those with 90 images from one of the last three commercial addresses, are re-editions, as well as those with 90 and 80 images using painted scenery. The nine flip books, originally taken from Méliès or other films, would be *La Danse* (rue Oberkampf), *Prestidigitateur* (Oberkampf), *Arrivée d'un train* (Oberkampf), *Le Coup du père François* (rue Volta), *Le Voyeur* (Volta), *Les Deux baisers* (Volta), *Le Coucher de la mariée* (rue du Vert-Bois), *Pose chez l'artiste. Vénus* (du Vert-Bois) and *Le Bain* (du Vert-Bois).

The scenes captured in these flip books provide further evidence that Méliès's style evolved very swiftly from simple sketches to more elaborate scenarios the beginning of 1897. None of the painted sets in the Méliès scenes contain his Star Film branding, which can be seen in his films from 1897 on. Undoubtedly, Beaulieu produced his flip books between late 1896 and early 1898, but probably not beyond that.

Léon Beaulieu therefore seems have concentrated on producing filmic flip books, as his primary business, only during this fairly short period. This coincides with his listing in commercial directories under the specific heading "cinematograph" and the filing of his patent for the Petit Biograph Parisien. After the middle of 1898, it appears that he returned to selling *bimbelots* – flip books were just part of his stock. His return to Aubervilliers and the address in rue de la Courneuve marked a change, and possibly a decline in his business. After 1898, while he no longer produced new flip books but continued to reissue his old ones.

Finally, what was the relationship between Prissette and Beaulieu? One can surmise that Prissette may have had access to the same suppliers as Beaulieu: Gaumont for flip books with 84 pages and Méliès for those with 90 pages.[1] The five Prissette flipbooks with photographic images are 42mm wide, same as the Beaulieu flip books. The cutting of the photo strips seems to have been done the same way, with the same tools. There is likely a link between these two manufacturers, but it is tricky to say exactly what it is. The Beaulieu project's research leads towards the conclusion that Beaulieu himself had only a minimal role in the process of making flip books: at most it seems he was only physically involved in binding and, of course, selling them.

Endnote

1. For the last flip book, *Lutteurs*, we know only two films corresponding to this title. One from the filmography of George William De Bedts, *Lutteurs (à trois)* and the other Pathé *Lutteurs*, both 1896. The De Bedts was sometimes known as *Wrestlers at Folies-Bergères*, announced a few times "in colour". The colour could actually be justified by the number of wrestlers (three). Knowing that there are only two in the flip book suggests a Pathé source, which would explain the flip book's unique 98-page format. It seems unlikely, however.

Chapter Seven

Torn Pages

At this point it is still not clear why so many of Beaulieu's flip books have their first pages torn off, but it may have something to do with what happened to them after he died. The most obvious suggestion is that someone wanted to remove the branding in order to sell them under their own marque. No other explanation seems as likely. This would further suggest that less than 37% of the collection was sold in Beaulieu's lifetime, under his own brand – and this proportion may well fall as more research is completed.

As part of his research, Pascal Fouché noticed that the subjects of some of Beaulieu's flip books were also used by a toy company in the early 20th century. This company manufactured a well-known optical device called the Cinématographe-Jouet. Researcher Éric Lange[1] found an article from *La Nature*, on 13 December 1902, which tells us that this device dates from that year and was invented by a man named M. Mathieu.

A comparison of a strip for the
Cinématographe-Jouet Mathieu and a Beaulieu
flip book © Pascal Fouché.

Cinématographe simplifié. — Ce petit jouet est des mieux réussis de l'année. Le mécanisme est d'une simplicité re-

Cinématographe simple.

marquable ; c'est ce qui en fait tout le charme et le rend bon marché. L'appareil se compose d'une bande de papier noire parcheminée mesurant 0ᵐ,30 de longueur sur laquelle on a collé les unes à côté des autres, à une distance de 2ᵐᵐ, des photogravures d'une scène quelconque prises au cinématographe et représentant une cinquantaine de positions successives. On a réuni ensuite les deux extrémités de la bande afin d'en former un anneau ; dans cette bande on y dépose une simple et grosse bille ordinaire, puis on suspend la bande sur une manivelle qui traverse un petit carré de bois de 2 millimètres d'épaisseur correspondant aux intervalles laissés entre les images, puis on descend la bande dans une grande boîte rectangulaire en introduisant les deux extrémités de la manivelle dans les deux petites fentes réservées à cet effet. Sur la face supérieure de la boîte est fixée une petite patte en métal qui vient heurter chaque image à son passage. Il suffit de tourner la manivelle de gauche à droite pour voir s'animer toutes ces figures qui passent successivement. On y voit un duel, une danseuse, des chiens savants, des clowns, un train en marche, etc., etc. La bille emprisonnée et entraînée par cette petite manivelle donne la tension nécessaire à la bande, suivant le mouvement rotatif. Ce petit cinématographe est un jouet ingénieux, amusant et vraiment curieux. Le cinématographe se trouve chez M. Mathieu, 29, rue de Valois, à Paris.

Le Nature, 13 December 1902 – © Private collection.

The Mathieu strips consist of only 48 images and among Cinématographe-Jouet's dozen cassette strips are five Beaulieu subjects: *Nuit agitée, La Danse, Le Duel, Boxeurs* and *Lutte de cuisiniers*[2] (the *La Nature* article also mentions *Train en marche*). However, a detailed examination reveals no perfect match between the Beaulieu and Mathieu frames. The Mathieu images are not photographic reproductions, but pictures drawn from Beaulieu photograms, and of markedly lower resolution. In Mathieu's version of *Nuit agitée* for example, the bed has been redesigned and there is only one stool (which has been slightly been modified) holding the chamber pot. The character himself has been outlined in ink.

It continues. The images on the other strips are drawings strongly inspired by the original photograms in the Beaulieu booklets. The chronology of the Cinématographe-Jouet seems to support the idea of Beaulieu's booklets being appropriated after his death. Note also that Mathieu operated his flip books with a device just as Beaulieu did, scrolling back to front.[3]

Endnotes

1. His website is dedicated to early cinema technology http://cinematographes.free.fr/

2. The Mathieu collection is also composed of two strips made from photographs whose origin is unidentified and five others composed of drawings.

3. Back-to-front scrolling used by Watilliaux, Beaulieu and Mathieu (flip books of French origin, contemporary with the beginnings of the cinematograph) is related to the use of mechanical scrolling devices. When the pages are scrolled by thumb, the pages in Western countries use a left-to-right motion, like handwriting, scrolling from the front as shown in a photograph where Max Skladanowsky is flipping through a flip book of its manufacture made from its cinematographic views [ca 1896]. This seems to confirm that the Prissette flip books, which scroll from back to front could be ersatz Beaulieu flip books.

Conclusions and Data

We started with a word that has more or less vanished from the language, *bimbelot*, and continued via one that has not yet made its way into French, crowdsourcing. The global hunt for information about the Beaulieu flip books began with a chance discovery of French artefact in a German bookshop by two people who live in Bolivia. Via a magazine article published in Los Angeles, and the involvement of an international research organisation, Domitor, the project has spread to San Francisco and back to France. The animation and digitisation of the flip books means they can be studied by scholars anywhere in the world and screened at cinemas and festivals around the globe. It's an adventure that began with the new media of the late 19th century, and has been facilitated by the new media of the late 20th.

These trinkets have revealed much about early cinema: about the recurrence of remakes, about the proliferation of off-catalogue films and even the suggestion of a separate, risqué slate of film production. Animating the flip books confirms the proposed slow shooting speeds of very early cinema: from 12fps or even 10fps rising to 16fps.

Most romantically, this crowdsourcing has made it possible to reverse a vanishing trick. The Beaulieu booklets reveal fragments of films that were unknown, or only known to have disappeared. With these tiny possibly pirated copies, Léon Beaulieu unwittingly preserved some of the legacy of Georges Méliès, which disappeared along with his negatives a century ago.

Here is the ledger. The project has uncovered 25 fragments of films from earliest days of cinema, in a non-film repertoire of 27 trinkets, that is to say flip books. At the meeting point of film, paper and book, these flip books, which have been collected by Pascal Fouché, captured by Onno Petersen's photography, researched and analysed by Thierry Lecointe, and magnified by Robert Byrne's animation, reveal even more of Méliès' work – even his very oldest films that few people ever imagined seeing again. There is no doubt that these tiny flip books have yet more secrets to reveal.

Beaulieu Flip Books

121 images

- *Nuit agitée*, (12fps – 12fps), confirmed Méliès, possible early version of *Une Nuit terrible, No. 26*. Photos exist but no known copy of the film survives;
- *Arrivée du train*, (5fps – 10fps), probably Méliès – high confidence, *Arrivée d'un train (gare de Joinville), No. 35*. No known copy of the film survives;
- *La Danse*, (12fps – 12fps), probably Méliès – high confidence, *Miss de Vère (gigue anglaise), No. 45*. No known copy of the film survives;
- *Prestidigitation*, (12fps – 12fps), probably Méliès – high confidence, *David Devant, No. 101*. No known copy of the film survives;
- *Boxe*, (12fps – 12fps), probably Méliès – medium confidence, possibly first version of *Match de boxe, professeurs de l'école de Joinville, No. 136*. No known copy of the film survives;
- *Le Duel*, (12fps – 12fps), probably Méliès – medium confidence, possibly first version of *Assaut d'escrime, école de Joinville, No. 148*. No known copy of the film survives;
- *Le Bâton*, (12fps – 12fps), probably Méliès – medium confidence, no associated title. No known copy of the film survives;
- *Duel au sabre*, (12fps – 12fps), probably Méliès – medium confidence, no associated title. No known copy of the film survives;
- *Lutte de cuisiniers*, (12fps – 12fps), probably Méliès – medium confidence, no associated title. No known copy of the film survives;

110 images

- *Arrivée du train*, (5fps – 10fps), probably Méliès – high confidence, *Arrivée d'un train (gare de Joinville), No. 35* – variant of the 121-photogram version (without images 111 to 121);

90 images

- *Le Coucher* (or *Le Déshabillé* or *La Toilette*) *de la mariée*, (8fps – 16fps), confirmed Méliès, possibly first version of *Le Coucher de la mariée, No. 177/178*. No known copy of the film survives;
- *L'Amant surpris*, (8fps – 16fps), confirmed Méliès, no associated title. No known copy of the film survives;
- *Pose chez l'artiste. Vénus*, (8fps – 16fps), confirmed Méliès, possibly first version of *Le Modèle irascible, No. 130/131*. A fragment of this film is known to exist but has not been restored;
- *La Puce*, (10fps – 10fps), confirmed Méliès, no associated title. No known copy of the film survives;
- *La Méprise*, (8fps – 16fps), probably Méliès – high confidence. No known copy of the film survives;
- *Le Coup du père François*, (8fps – 16fps), probably Méliès – high confidence, no associated title. No known copy of the film survives;
- *La Nourrice*, (10fps – 10fps), probably Méliès – high confidence, could correspond to a first version of *Salut malencontreux, No. 36*. No known copy of the film survives;

80 images

- *Le Bain*, (8fps – 16fps), confirmed Méliès, possibly first version of *Après le bal (le tub), No. 128*. No known copy of the film survives;
- *Le Voyeur*, (8fps – 16fps), confirmed Méliès, no associated title;

96 images

- (48 x 2): *Partie de cartes à trois*, (12fps – 12fps), confirmed Skladanowsky. No known copy of the film survives;

75 images

- *Les Deux baisers*, (12fps – 24fps), confirmed Edison, *May Irwin Kiss, No. 155*.

Prissette/Beaulieu Flip Books

98 images

- *Lutte*, (12fps – 12fps), probably Pathé – low confidence, *Lutteurs*, no catalogue number. No known copy of the film survives;

90 images

- *Loïe Fuller*, (10fps – 10fps), probably Méliès – high confidence or Gaumont – low confidence Méliès/ *Danse serpentine, No. 44* or Gaumont *Danse serpentine: Loïe Fuller, No. 12.* No known copy of the film survives.

88 images

- *Déguisement*, (12fps – 12fps), probably Méliès – medium confidence, *Dix chapeaux en 60 secondes, No. 42.* No known copy of the film survives;

84 images

- *La Danse du Cancan*, (16fps – 16fps), confirmed Gaumont, *Moulin rouge: quadrille, No. 3.* No known copy of the film survives;
- *Duel de femmes*, (16fps – 16fps), confirmed Gaumont, *Duel de dames, No. 24.* No known copy of the film survives;
- *Le Coucher*, (8fps – 16fps), confirmed Gaumont *Nuit Agitée, No. 142.* No known copy of the film survives;

64 images

- (32 x 2): *Train en marche*, (8fps – 16fps), Probably Gaumont – medium confidence, *Train à corridor, No. 55, série L.* No known copy of the film survives.

Appendices

APPENDIX ONE: A CHRONOLOGICAL RECONSTRUCTION

This is a suggested chronology for the films used to make the flip books – not a chronology for the flip books themselves. After each title the following information is recorded: the number of frames per second relating to recording speed of the film; the number of photograms in the flip book; the associated film; the shooting date and the date of the first known screening.

Fragments attributed to Méliès

- *Boxe:* (12fps), 121 images, possibly first version of *Match de boxe, professeurs de l'école de Joinville, No. 136;*
- *Le Duel:* (12fps), 121 images, possibly first version of *Assaut d'escrime, école de Joinville, No. 148;*
- *Le Bâton:* (12fps), 121 images;
- *Duel au sabre:* (12fps), 121 images;
- *Lutte de cuisiniers:* (12fps), 121 images;
- *La Puce:* (10fps), 90 images;
- *Nuit agitée:* (12fps), 121 images, possibly first version of *Une Nuit terrible, No. 26;*
- *Arrivée du train:* (10fps), 121 images, *Arrivée d'un train (gare de Joinville), No. 35,* film March 1897 (date of first known screening August 1896)*;*
- *La Nourrice:* (10fps), 90 images, possibly first version of *Salut malencontreux, No. 36;*
- *Déguisement:* (12fps), 88 images, *Dix chapeaux en 60 secondes, No. 42;*
- *Loïe Fuller:* (10fps), 90 images, *Danse serpentine, No. 44,* flip book published July 1897 (date of first known screening August 1896);
- *La Danse:* (12fps), 121 images, *Miss de Vère (gigue anglaise), No. 45,* flip book published between October 1896 and March 1897*;*
- *Prestidigitation:* (12fps), 121 images, *David Devant, No 101,* flip book published between October 1896 and March 1897*;*
- *Le Coup du père François:* (16fps), 90 images, flip book published between April and September 1897;
- *Le Voyeur:* (16fps), 80 images, flip book published between April and September 1897;
- *La Méprise:* (16fps), 90 images;
- *Le Bain:* (16fps), 80 images, possibly first version of *Après le bal (le tub), No. 128,* flip book published between October 1897 and May 1898;
- *Le Coucher de la mariée:* (16fps), 90 images, possibly first version of *Le Coucher de la mariée, No. 177/178,* flip book published October 1897 and May 1898;
- *L'Amant surpris:* (16fps), 90 images, flip book published October 1897 and May 1898;
- *Pose chez l'artiste. Vénus:* (16fps), 90 images, possibly first version of *Le Modèle irascible, No. 130/131,* flip book published October 1897 and May 1898.

Fragment attributed to Edison

- *Les Deux baisers*, (24fps), 75 images, *May Irwin Kiss, No. 155*, known filming date April 1896.

Fragment attributed to Skladanowsky

- *Partie de cartes à trois*, (12fps), 2 x 48 images.

Fragments attributed to Gaumont

- *La Danse du Cancan*, (16fps), 84 images, *Moulin rouge: quadrille, No. 3*, date of first known screening December 1896;
- *Duel de femmes*, (16fps), 84 images, *Duel de dames, No. 24*, date of first known screening July 1896;
- *Le Coucher*, (16fps), 84 images, *Nuit Agitée, No. 142*, catalogue date August 1897;
- *Train en marche*, (16fps), 2 x 32 images, *Train à corridor, No. 55, série L*, filming date probably July 1897, catalogue date November 1897.

Fragment attributed to Pathé

- *Lutte*, (12fps), 98 images, *Lutteurs*, no catalogue number, filming date presumed spring 1896.

APPENDIX TWO: LÉON BEAULIEU'S ADDRESSES

Keeping track of Beaulieu's movements is not straightforward, but here is a tally of the addresses where he is known to have done business, the time he spent there, and the number of flip books bearing that address.

Late 1896 to mid-1897
144, rue Oberkampf, Paris, four flip books;

September 1897 to February 1898
46, rue Volta, Paris, three flip books;

End of February 1898 to October 1898
37, rue du Vert-Bois, Paris, nine flip books;

End of 1898 to mid-1900
1, rue de la Courneuve, Aubervilliers, twenty flip books;

Mid-1900 to his death in February 22, 1901
257, rue Saint-Denis, Paris, thirteen flip books.

2

Proof in Pictures /
Des preuves en images

Illustrations 1-2-3 : type 031T série 8.
On notera les positions aléatoires des inscriptions (numéro, EST et SERIE 8)
Note the random positions of the inscriptions (number, EST and SERIE 8)
© Collection Thierry Lecointe.

Illustrations 4-5-6 : wagons dit « Bidel » à double étage utilisés par la Cie de l'Est sur la ligne de Vincennes. En haut [4] le gare de départ Paris-Bastille.
Double-decker "Bidel" wagons used by "Cie de l'Est" on the Vincennes line. Above [4] the Paris-Bastille departure station. 4-5 © dans Didier Leroy, *La ligne de Vincennes*, La Vie du Rail, Paris, 2006 / 6 © Collection Thierry Lecointe.

Illustrations 7-8-9 : arrivée de la 031T n° 683 avec ses wagons « Bidel » en gare de Paris-Bel-Air en direction de Paris-Bastille.
Film Joly-Normandin.
Arrival of the 031T N° 683 with its "Bidel" wagons at Paris-Bel-Air station travelling to Paris-Bastille. Joly-Normandin's movie. © Col. Cinemateca Portuguesa-Museu do Cinema.

Illustrations 10-11-12 : film d'Auguste Baron *Arrivée d'un train* [en gare de Joinville-le-Pont] (ca 1897–1901).
Auguste Baron's film, *Arrivée d'un train (Arrival of a Train)* [at Joinville-le-Pont station].
© Collection Filmoteca Española.

Illustrations 13-14-15 : les gares de Saint-Mandé, Vincennes et Nogent-sur-Marne ne correspondent pas à celle du flip book. Les 031T n° 664 et 678 arrivent en gare. The stations of Saint-Mandé, Vincennes and Nogent-sur-Marne do not correspond to those of the flip book. 31T N° 664 and N° 678 arrive at the station.
© Collection Thierry Lecointe.

Illustrations 16-17-18 : la gare de Joinville-le-Pont (au fond en provenance de Paris-Bastille). Joinville-le-Pont station (in the background, train arriving from Paris-Bastille).
© Collection Thierry Lecointe.

Illustration 19 : La gare de Joinville-le-Pont (sens inverse).
Joinville-le-Pont station (from the opposite direction).
© Collection Thierry Lecointe.

Illustration 20 : La gare de Joinville-le-Pont, arrivée d'une 031T n° 658 en provenance de Paris-Bastille.
Joinville-le-Pont station, the arrival of a 031T N° 658 from Paris-Bastille.
© Collection Thierry Lecointe.

Illustration 21 : la gare de Joinville-le-Pont, train en provenance de Paris-Bastille.
Joinville-le-Pont station, train arriving from Paris-Bastille.
© Collection Thierry Lecointe.

Illustrations 22 et 23 : la gare de Joinville-le-Pont (détail).
1 : l'appentis visible sur les photogrammes du flip book / 2 : position de la caméra.
Joinville-le-Pont station (detail).
The annexe (roof) visible on the photograms of the flip book / 2: Position of the camera.
© Collection Thierry Lecointe.

Illustrations 24-25 : la gare de Joinville-le-Pont (depuis le village). Joinville-le-Pont train station (view from the village).
© Collection Thierry Lecointe.

Illustration 26 : le chef de gare avec son pantalon blanc à Verneuil-L'Etang, à droite les wagons « Bidel ».
The station master with his white trousers at Verneuil-L'Etang, on the right the "Bidel" wagons.
© Collection Thierry Lecointe.

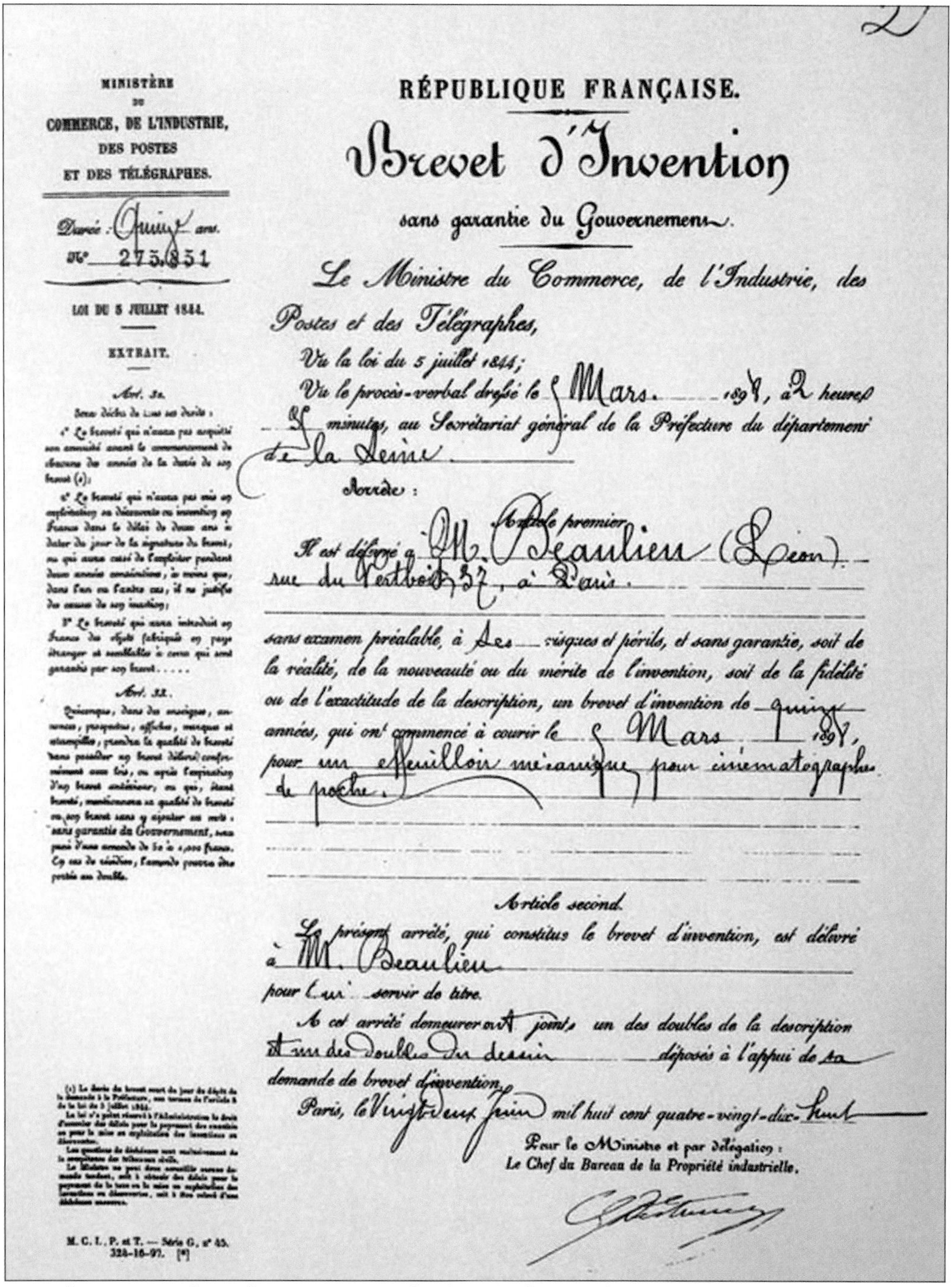

MINISTÈRE DU COMMERCE, DE L'INDUSTRIE, DES POSTES ET DES TÉLÉGRAPHES.

Durée : Quinze ans.

N° 275.851

LOI DU 5 JUILLET 1844.

EXTRAIT.

Art. 32.

Sera déchu de tous ses droits :

1° Le breveté qui n'aura pas acquitté son annuité avant le commencement de chacune des années de la durée de son brevet (1);

2° Le breveté qui n'aura pas mis en exploitation sa découverte ou invention en France dans le délai de deux ans à dater du jour de la signature du brevet, ou qui aura cessé de l'exploiter pendant deux années consécutives, à moins que, dans l'un ou l'autre cas, il ne justifie des causes de son inaction;

3° Le breveté qui aura introduit en France des objets fabriqués en pays étranger et semblables à ceux qui sont garantis par son brevet.....

Art. 33.

Quiconque, dans des enseignes, annonces, prospectus, affiches, marques ou estampilles, prendra la qualité de breveté sans posséder un brevet délivré conformément aux lois, ou après l'expiration d'un brevet antérieur, ou qui, étant breveté, mentionnera sa qualité de breveté ou son brevet sans y ajouter ces mots : sans garantie du Gouvernement, sera puni d'une amende de 50 à 1,000 francs. En cas de récidive, l'amende pourra être portée au double.

M. C. I. P. et T. — Série G, n° 45. 324-10-97. [*]

RÉPUBLIQUE FRANÇAISE.

Brevet d'Invention

sans garantie du Gouvernement.

Le Ministre du Commerce, de l'Industrie, des Postes et des Télégraphes,

Vu la loi du 5 juillet 1844;

Vu le procès-verbal dressé le 5 Mars *189*8, *à* 2 *heures* 5 *minutes, au Secrétariat général de la Préfecture du département de* la Seine.

Arrête :

Article premier.

Il est délivré à M. Beaulieu (Léon) rue du Vertbois, 37, à Paris.

sans examen préalable, à ses *risques et périls, et sans garantie, soit de la réalité, de la nouveauté ou du mérite de l'invention, soit de la fidélité ou de l'exactitude de la description, un brevet d'invention de* quinze *années, qui ont commencé à courir le* 5 Mars 1898, *pour* un effeuilloir mécanique pour cinématographe de poche.

Article second.

Le présent arrêté, qui constitue le brevet d'invention, est délivré à M. Beaulieu *pour* lui *servir de titre.*

A cet arrêté demeureront joints un des doubles de la description et un des doubles du dessin *déposés à l'appui de* sa *demande de brevet d'invention.*

Paris, le Vingt-deux Juin *mil huit cent quatre-vingt-dix-* huit

Pour le Ministre et par délégation :
Le Chef du Bureau de la Propriété industrielle.

Illustration 27-1 : brevet d'invention Léon Beaulieu (page 1). The patent for Léon Beaulieu's invention (page 1).
© Collection Pascal Fouché.

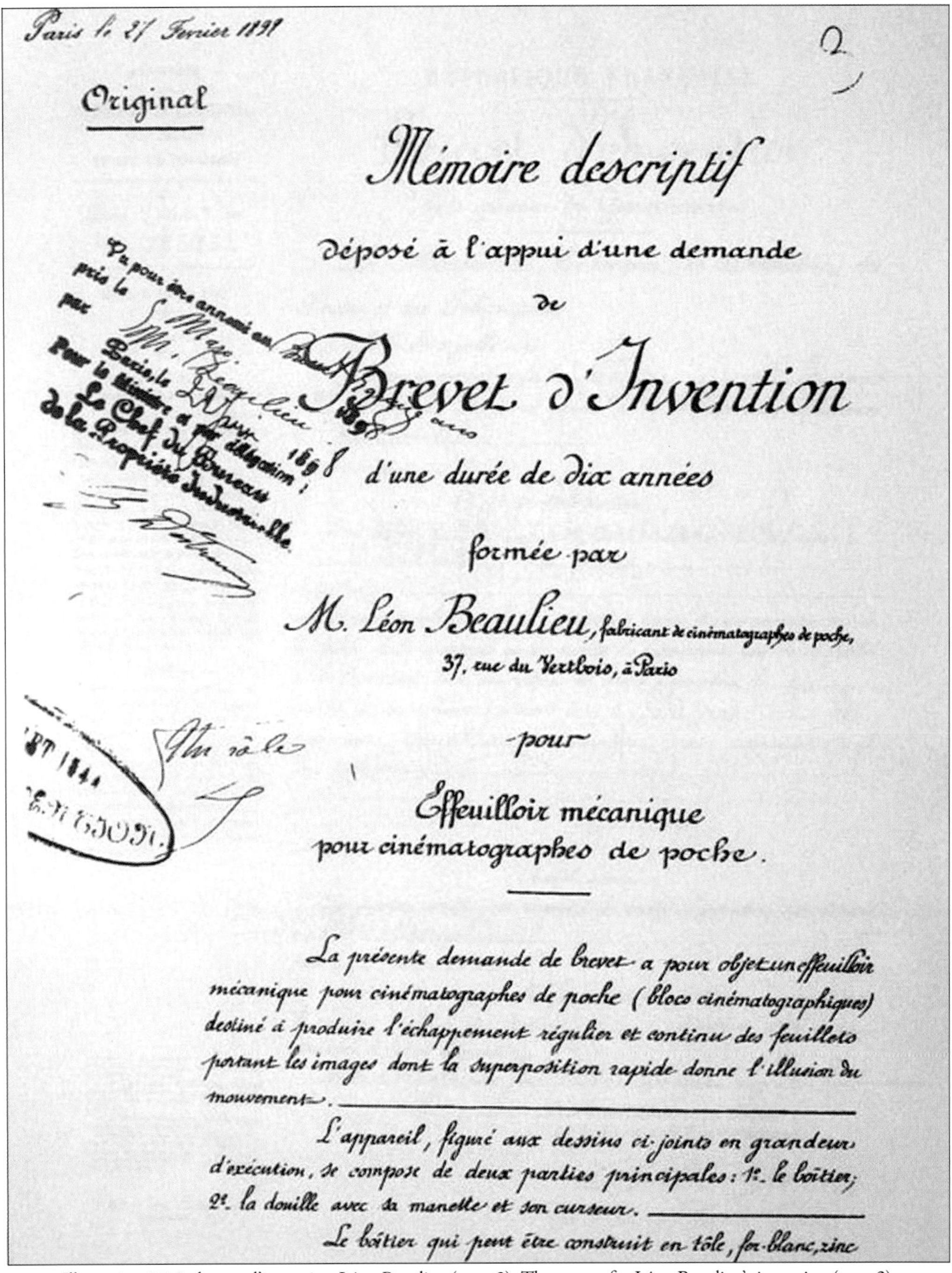

Illustration 27-2 : brevet d'invention Léon Beaulieu (page 2). The patent for Léon Beaulieu's invention (page 2). © Collection Pascal Fouché.

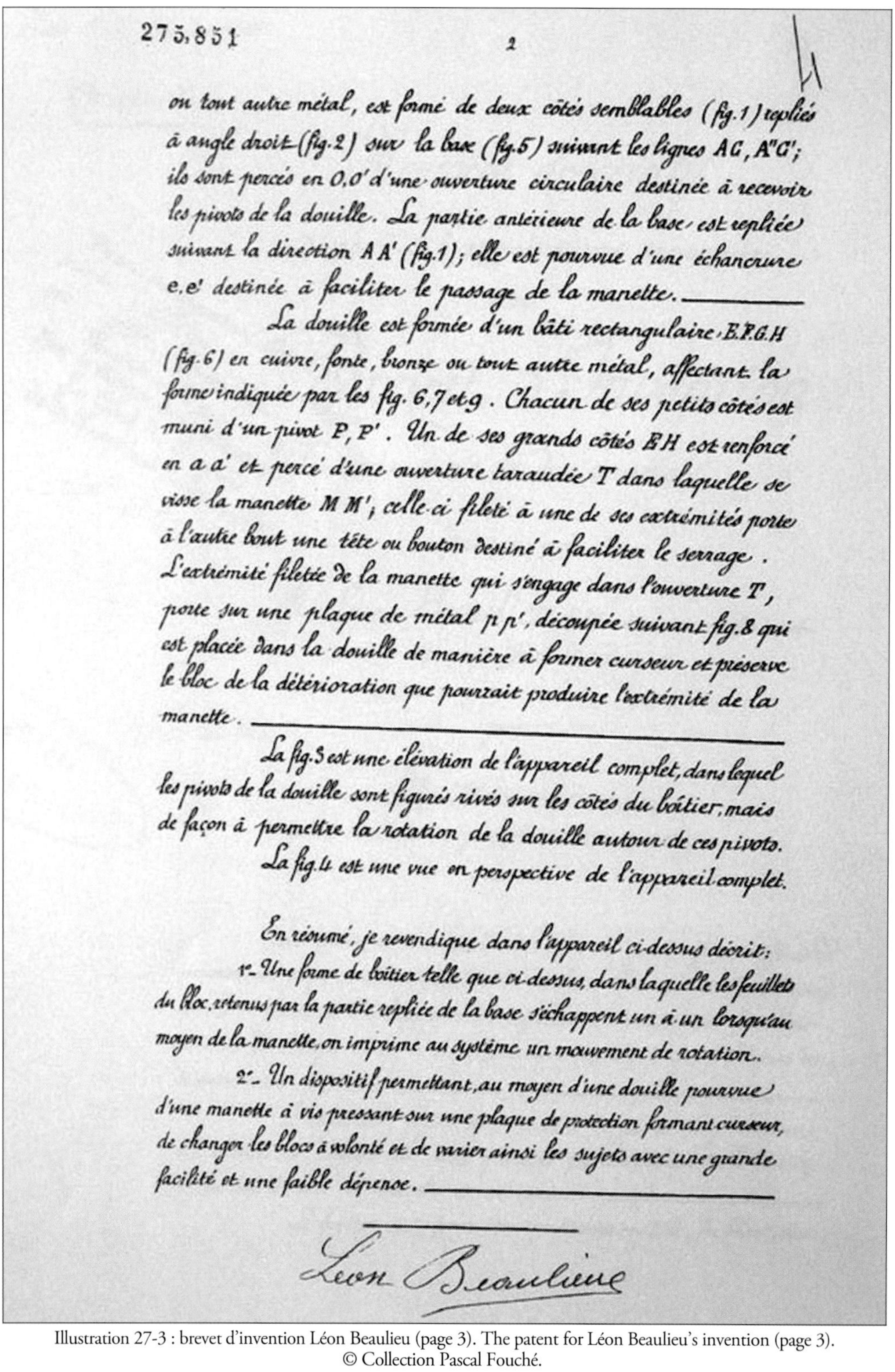

273,851   2

on tout autre métal, est formé de deux côtés semblables (fig. 1) repliés à angle droit (fig. 2) sur la base (fig. 5) suivant les lignes AG, A'G'; ils sont percés en O, O' d'une ouverture circulaire destinée à recevoir les pivots de la douille. La partie antérieure de la base est repliée suivant la direction AA' (fig. 1); elle est pourvue d'une échancrure e, e' destinée à faciliter le passage de la manette. ________

La douille est formée d'un bâti rectangulaire E, F, G, H (fig. 6) en cuivre, fonte, bronze ou tout autre métal, affectant la forme indiquée par les fig. 6, 7 et 9. Chacun de ses petits côtés est muni d'un pivot P, P'. Un de ses grands côtés EH est renforcé en a, a' et percé d'une ouverture taraudée T dans laquelle se visse la manette MM'; celle-ci filetée à une de ses extrémités porte à l'autre bout une tête ou bouton destiné à faciliter le serrage. L'extrémité filetée de la manette qui s'engage dans l'ouverture T, porte sur une plaque de métal p, p', découpée suivant fig. 8 qui est placée dans la douille de manière à former curseur et préserve le bloc de la détérioration que pourrait produire l'extrémité de la manette. ________

La fig. 3 est une élévation de l'appareil complet, dans lequel les pivots de la douille sont figurés rivés sur les côtés du boîtier, mais de façon à permettre la rotation de la douille autour de ces pivots.

La fig. 4 est une vue en perspective de l'appareil complet.

En résumé, je revendique dans l'appareil ci-dessus décrit:

1°– Une forme de boîtier telle que ci-dessus, dans laquelle les feuillets du bloc, retenus par la partie repliée de la base s'échappent un à un lorsqu'au moyen de la manette, on imprime au système un mouvement de rotation.

2°– Un dispositif permettant, au moyen d'une douille pourvue d'une manette à vis pressant sur une plaque de protection formant curseur, de changer les blocs à volonté et de varier ainsi les sujets avec une grande facilité et une faible dépense. ________

Léon Beaulieu

Illustration 27-3 : brevet d'invention Léon Beaulieu (page 3). The patent for Léon Beaulieu's invention (page 3).
© Collection Pascal Fouché.

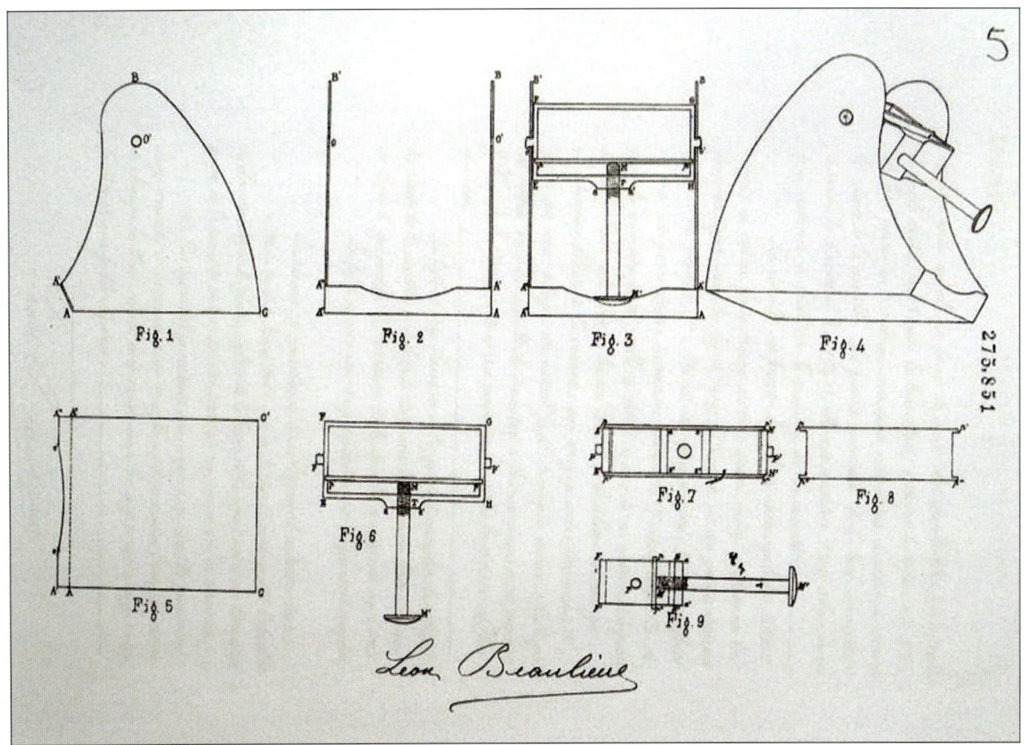

Illustration 27-4 : brevet d'invention Léon Beaulieu (page 4). The patent for Léon Beaulieu's invention (page 4).
© Collection Pascal Fouché.

Illustration 28 : « effeuilloir mécanique pour cinématographes de poche ». Mechanical flip through machine for Pocket Cinematograph.
© Collection Pascal Fouché.

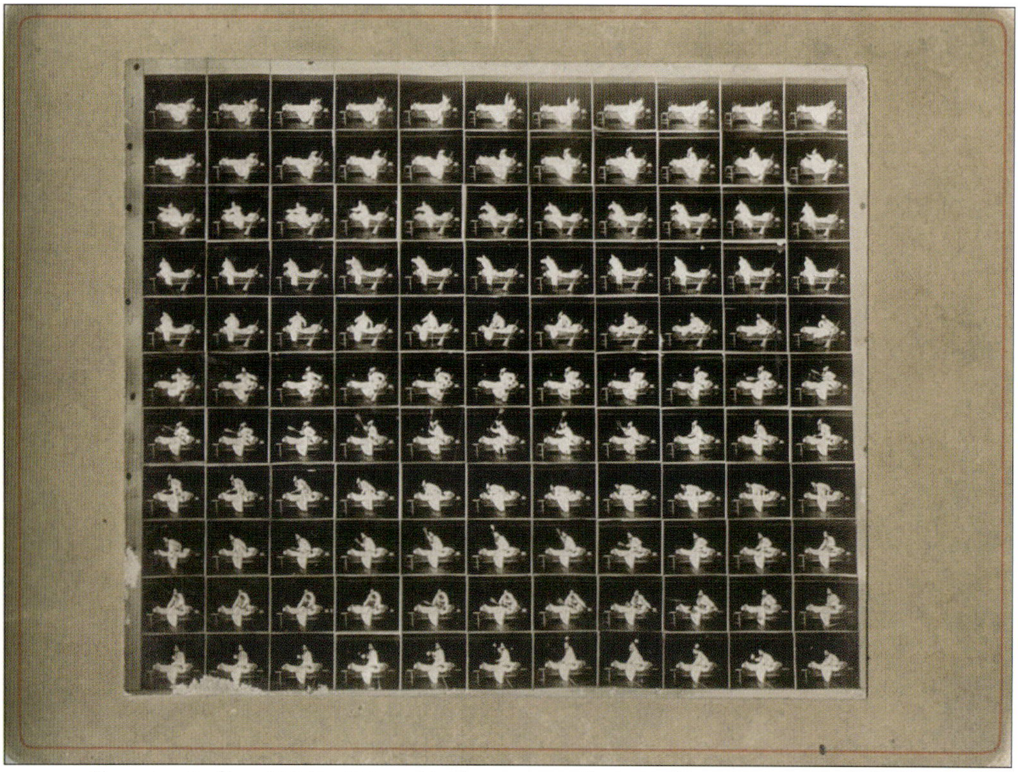

Illustration 29 : film n ° 26 *Une Nuit terrible* (photogrammes d'une première version ? ceux du flip book).
Film N° 26 *A Terrible Night* (frames of a first version? featured in the flip book).
© Cinémathèque Française.

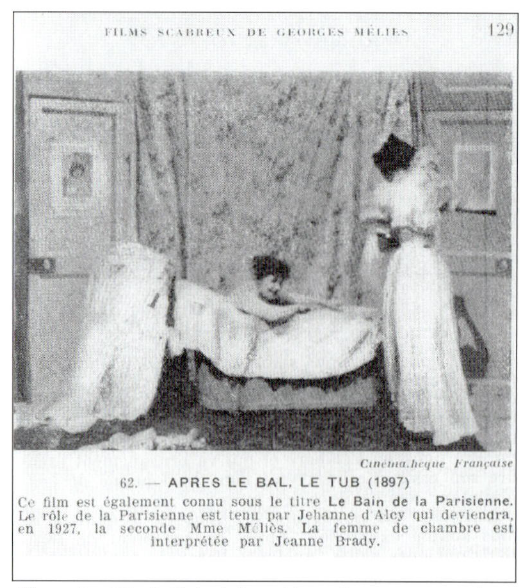

Illustration 30 : *Le Bain de la parisienne*, image correspondant
à la scène du flip book (photographie disparue du fond de la
Cinémathèque Française). Image corresponding to the flip
book scene (the photograph hes disappeared from the
Cinémathèque Française archive).
© Cinémathèque Française.

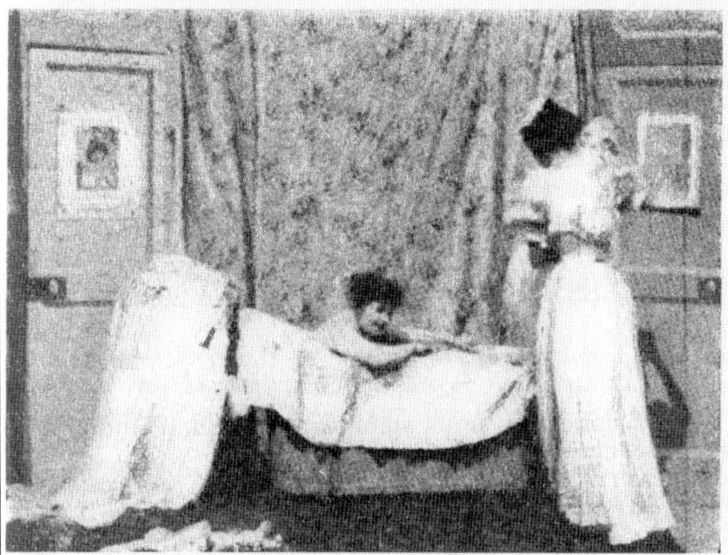

62. — APRES LE BAL, LE TUB (1897)

Ce film est également connu sous le titre **Le Bain de la Parisienne**. Le rôle de la Parisienne est tenu par Jehanne d'Alcy qui deviendra, en 1927, la seconde Mme Méliès. La femme de chambre est interprétée par Jeanne Brady.

63. — LE COUCHER DE LA MARIEE (vers 1900)

Ce film, qui ne figure pas au catalogue américain de la Star Film, est interprété par l'actrice Bairal, qui joue le rôle de Cendrillon dans le film réalisé en 1899. Le rôle du vieux beau est tenu par Georges Méliès.

Illustration 31 : reproduites dans / reproduced in Georges Sadoul, *Histoire générale du cinéma – II, Les pionniers du cinéma 1897-1909*, Paris, Éditions Denoël, 1947. © Cinémathèque Française.

Arrivée du train – **Version à 110 photogrammes / frames**

Bande 1 (photogrammes 1 à 11) / strip 1 (frames 1 to 11).

Bande 2 (photogrammes 12 à 22) / strip 2 (frames 12 to 22).

Bande 3 (photogrammes 23 à 33) / strip 3 (frames 23 to 33).

Bande 4 (photogrammes 34 à 44) / strip 4 (frames 34 to 44).

Bande 5 (photogrammes 45 à 55) / strip 5 (frames 45 to 55).

Bande 6 (photogrammes 67 à 77) – erreur de numérotation [de l'imprimeur]. Stripe 6 (frames 67 to 77) - numbering error [by the printer].

Bande 7 inexistante (photogrammes 78 à 88) – erreur de numérotation [de l'imprimeur] et [oubliée au montage par Beaulieu ?].
Strip 7 nonexistent (frames 78 to 88) - numbering error [by the printer] and [forgotten during editing by Beaulieu?].

Bande 8 (photogrammes 56 à 66) – erreur de numérotation [de l'imprimeur].
Strip 8 (frames 56 to 66) - numbering error [by the printer].

Bande 9 (photogrammes 89 à 99) / Strip 9 (frames 89 to 99).

Bande 10 (photogrammes 100 à 110) / Strip 10 (frames 100 to 110).

Illustration 32 : flip book *Arrivée du train* (le démontage met en évidence le processus de fabrication). Flip book *Arrivée du train* (disassembly highlights the manufacturing process).
© Collection Thierry Lecointe.

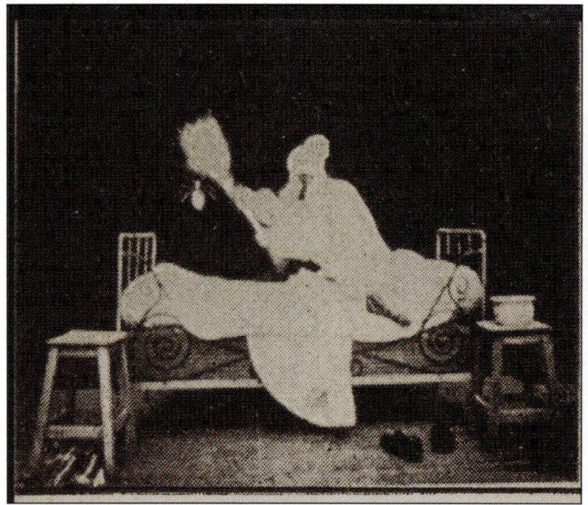

Illustration 33-34 : flip book et film n° 95 *L'Hallucination de l'alchimiste* (1897) / les deux tabourets à chaque extrémité du cadre.
Flip book and film No. 95 *An Hallucinated Alchemist* (1897) / the two stools at each end of the frame.
© Onno Petersen – Collection Pascal Fouché / © Collection Lobster films.

Illustration 35 : film n° 26 *Une Nuit terrible* (1896) / probable remake du flip book avec le même lit en fer.
Film No. 26 *A Terrible Night* (1896) / Probable remake of the flip book with the same iron bed.
© Collection Lobster films.

Illustration 36 et 37 : le lit en fer à l'écran dans les films n° 211 *Affaire Dreyfus, entrevue de Dreyfus et de sa femme à Rennes* (1899) et n° 325-326 *La Maison tranquille* (1900) / photographie de plateau : le lit en fer à l'étage.
Iron bed on the screen in movies No. 211 *Dreyfus Affair, Dreyfus in Prison of Rennes* (1899) and No. 325-326 *What is Home without the Boarder* (1900) / On set photography: the iron bed is upstairs.
© Collection Lobster films / © Cinémathèque Française.

Illustrations 38-39 : film n° 26 *Une Nuit terrible* (1896), version primitive (flip book) et son probable remake. Le lit se présente sous une perspective différente conséquence de l'éloignement de la caméra.
Film No. 26 *A Terrible Night* (1896), an early version (flip book) and its probable remake. The bed is viewed from a different angle because of its distance from the camera.
© Onno Peterson – Collection Pascal Fouché / © Collection Lobster films.

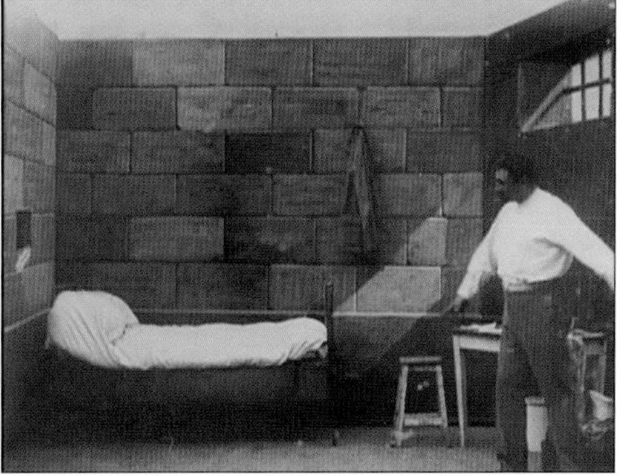

Illustrations 40-41 : films n° 122-123 *L'Auberge ensorcelée* (1897) et n° 209 *Suicide du colonel Henry* (1899). Le lit se présente sous une perspective différente conséquence de l'éloignement de la caméra. Il est retourné dans le n° 209.
Films No. 122-123 *The Bewitched Inn* (1897) and No. 209 *Suicide by Colonel Henry* (1899). The bed is seen from a different angle because of its distance from the camera. The bed is on the opposite side in No. 209 (note the stool again).
© Collection Lobster films.

Illustrations 42-43 : flip book *Le Bain* et film n° 128 *Après le bal, le tub* (1897), la transparence de la robe de nuit laisse entrevoir la forme de la combinaison.
Flip book *Le Bain (The Tub)* and Film No. 128 *After the ball* (1897), the transparency of the night dress suggests the shape of the underwear.
© Onno Petersen – Collection Pascal Fouché / © Collection Lobster films.

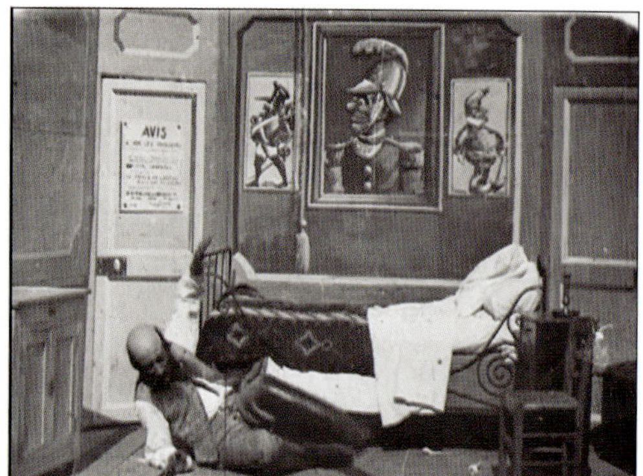

Illustrations 44-45 : films n° 102 *L'École des gendres* (1897) et n° 122-123 *L'Auberge ensorcellée* (1897), le décor du flip book *Le Bain* est utilisé dans ces deux films.
Films No. 102 *The School for Sons-in-law* (1897) and No. 122-123 *The Bewitched Inn* (1897), the decor of the flip book *Le Bain* is used in both these films.
© Cinémathèque Française / © Collection Lobster films.

 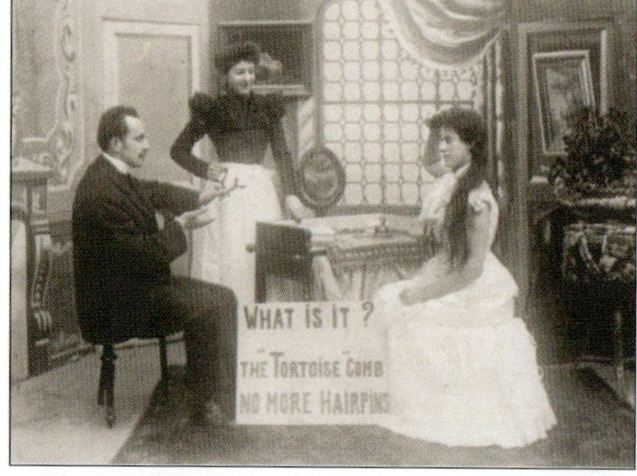

Illustrations 46-47 : films n° 128 *Après le bal, le tub* (1897), avec Jehanne d'Alcy et vue publicitaire *Le Tortoise Comb* (ca 1900), on retrouve ce décor qui a subi quelques transformations.
Films No. 128 *After the ball* (1897), with Jehanne d'Alcy, and publicity image for *The Tortoise Comb* (ca 1900). The set is the same but it has undergone some transformations.
© Collection Lobster films / © Cinémathèque Française.

Illustrations 48-49 : Flip books *Le Voyeur* et *Le Coucher de la mariée*.
Flip books *The Voyeur* and *The Bridegroom's Dilemma*.
© Onno Petersen – Collection Pascal Fouché.

Illustrations 50-51 : films n° 183 *L'Illusionniste fin de siècle* et n° 309-310 *Nouvelles luttes extravagantes*, le muret du flip book *Le Voyeur* est réutilisé.
Films No. 183 *An Up-to-Date Conjurer* (note the stool) and No. 309-310 *The Wrestling Sextette*, the wall of the flip book *Le Voyeur* is reused.
© Collection Lobster films.

Illustrations 52-53 : films n° 102 *L'École des gendres* (1897) et n° 177-178 *Le Coucher de la mariée* (1899), le lit en bois est celui du flip book *Le Coucher de la mariée* (présumée première version du film 177-178).
Films No. 102 *The School for Sons-in-law* (1897) and No. 177-178 *The Bridgegroom's Dilemma* (1899), the wooden bed is that of the flip book *Le Coucher de la mariée* (presumed first version of the movie 177-178).
© Cinémathèque Française.

Illustrations 54 à 56: Elise de Vère (ca 1897) portant un tutu comparable à celui du flip book. La carte postale datée du 18 mai 1901 montre qu'il s'agit d'une photographie correspondant au début de sa carrière. On constate le changement de morphologie de l'actrice au sortir de l'adolescence (55-56).
Elise de Vère (ca 1897) wearing a tutu similar to the one in the flip book. In the postcard dated May 18, 1901 we see that the photograph corresponds to the beginning of her career. There is a change in the actress's morphology when she is no longer an adolescent (55-56).
© Collection Thierry Lecointe.

Illustrations 57-58 : le baquet du flip book *Lutte de cuisiniers* est assez comparable à celui du film n° 95 *L'Hallucination de l'alchimiste*(1897).
The wooden tub from the flip book *Lutte de cuisiniers* is quite similar to the one in film No. 95 *An Hallucinated Alchemist* (1897).
© Onno Petersen – Collection Pascal Fouché / © Collection Lobster films.

 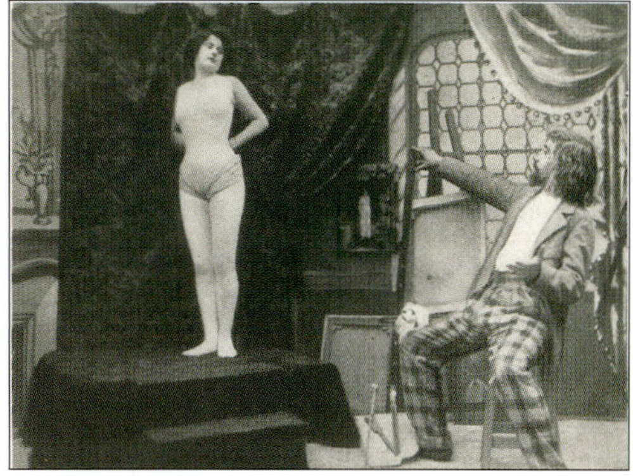

Illustrations 59–60

Illustration 60 : *Le Peintre et son modèle,* titre attribué par Maurice Bessy et Lo Duca, *Georges Méliès, mage,* Prisma, Paris, 1945, p. 147. Méliès porte le même pantalon à carreaux dans le flip book *Pose chez l'artiste. Vénus* (59).
Le Peintre et son modèle [*The Painter and his model*], title attributed by Maurice Bessy and Lo Duca, *Georges Méliès, mage,* Prisma, Paris, 1945, p. 147 (60). Méliès wears the same plaid pants as in the flip book *Pose chez l'artiste. Vénus* (59).
© Onno Petersen – Collection Pascal Fouché / © Collection particulière.

Illustration 61 : « *Le Modèle narcissique* (1896) » [selon les vendeurs], tirage argentique (11,5 x 16 cm), ayant servi à la publication. *"The Narcissistic Model* (1896)"* [according to the publishers], silver print (11.5 x 16 cm), was used for publication.
© Collection Particulière.

Illustrations 62-63 : films n° 112 *Entre Calais et Douvres* (1897) et n° 312-313 *Le Déshabillage impossible* (1900), Méliès porte le pantalon à carreaux dans le film n° 312-313 visible dans le flip book *Pose chez l'artiste. Vénus* et un modèle similaire dans la vue n° 112.
Films No. 112 *Between Dover and Calais* (1897) and No. 312-313 *An Increasing Wardrobe* (1900), Méliès is still wearing the plaid pants in the movie No. 312-313 (note the iron bed) seen in the flip book *Pose chez l'artiste. Vénus* and a similar one in the film No. 112.
© Collection Lobster films.

Illustrations 64-65 : films n° 78-80 *Le Manoir du diable* (1896) et n° 96 *Le Château hanté* (1897), La table basse, accessoire récurrent visible dans le flip book *Pose chez l'artiste. Vénus.*
Films No. 78-80 *The Devil's Castle* (1896) and No. 96 *The Haunted Castle* (1897),
The coffee table, reccursary accessory seen in the flip book *Pose chez l'artiste. Vénus.*
© Collection Lobster films.

Illustration 66 : flip book *La Puce.*
Flip book *The Flea.*
© Onno Petersen – Collection Pascal Fouché.

 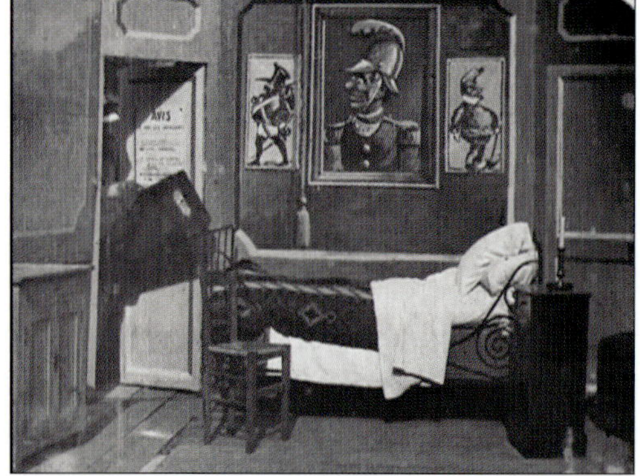

Illustrations 67-68 : films n° 82 *Le cauchemar* (1897) et n° 122-123 *L'Auberge ensorcellée* (1897), Le couvre-lit, accessoire récurrent visible dans le flip book *La Puce.*
Films No. 82 *A Nightmare* (1897) and No. 122-123 *The Bewitched Inn* (1897),
The bedspread, a recurrent accessory seen in the flip book *La Puce (The Flea).*
© Collection Lobster films.

Illustrations 69-70 : film n° 1 *Une Partie de cartes* (1896) et confection de décors dans le studio de Montreuil. On remarquera le canotier que Méliès porte régulièrement dans la vie comme à l'écran.
Film No. 1 *Playing Cards* (1896) and building sets in the Montreuil studio. Note the boater that Méliès wears regularly, both on and off screen.
© Collection Lobster films / © Cinémathèque Française.

Illustrations 71-72-73 : La machine à vapeur de la classe Teutonic et la voiture de 42 pied modèle 1888 en service sur la London and North Western Railway visibles sur le flip book *Train en marche*.
The Teutonic class steam engine and the 42 feet passenger carriage, model 1888, operational on the London and North Western Railway seen in the flip book *Train en Marche*.
© Collection particulière.

3

Flip Books frames /
photogrammes des flip books

Images 37 à 41 : un homme s'avance vers le chef de quai et le salue en soulevant son canotier puis sort du champ à droite (image 48) - images 37 to 41: a man walks towards the station master and greets him by lifting his boater, then leaves the screen on the right (image 48).

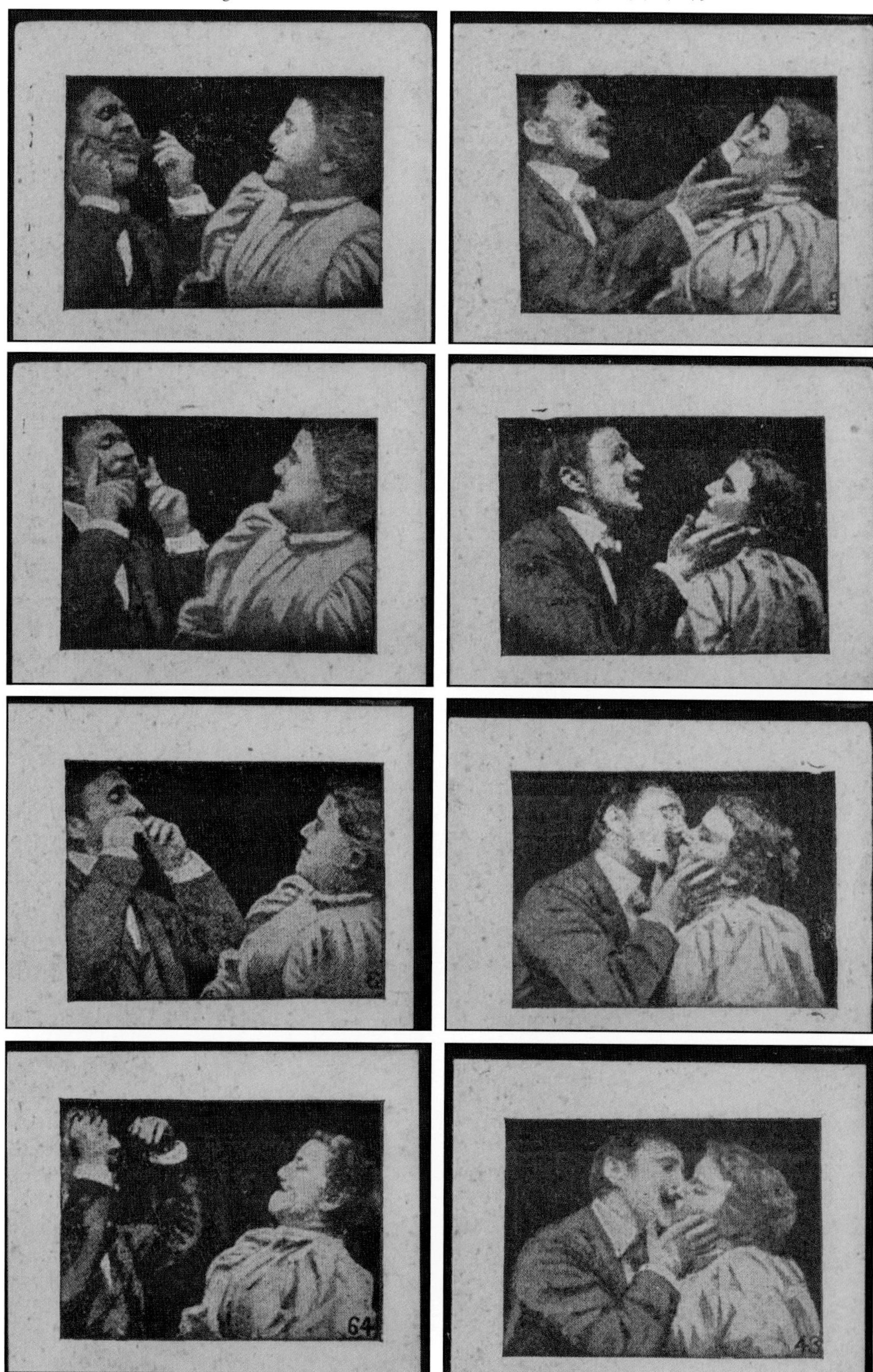

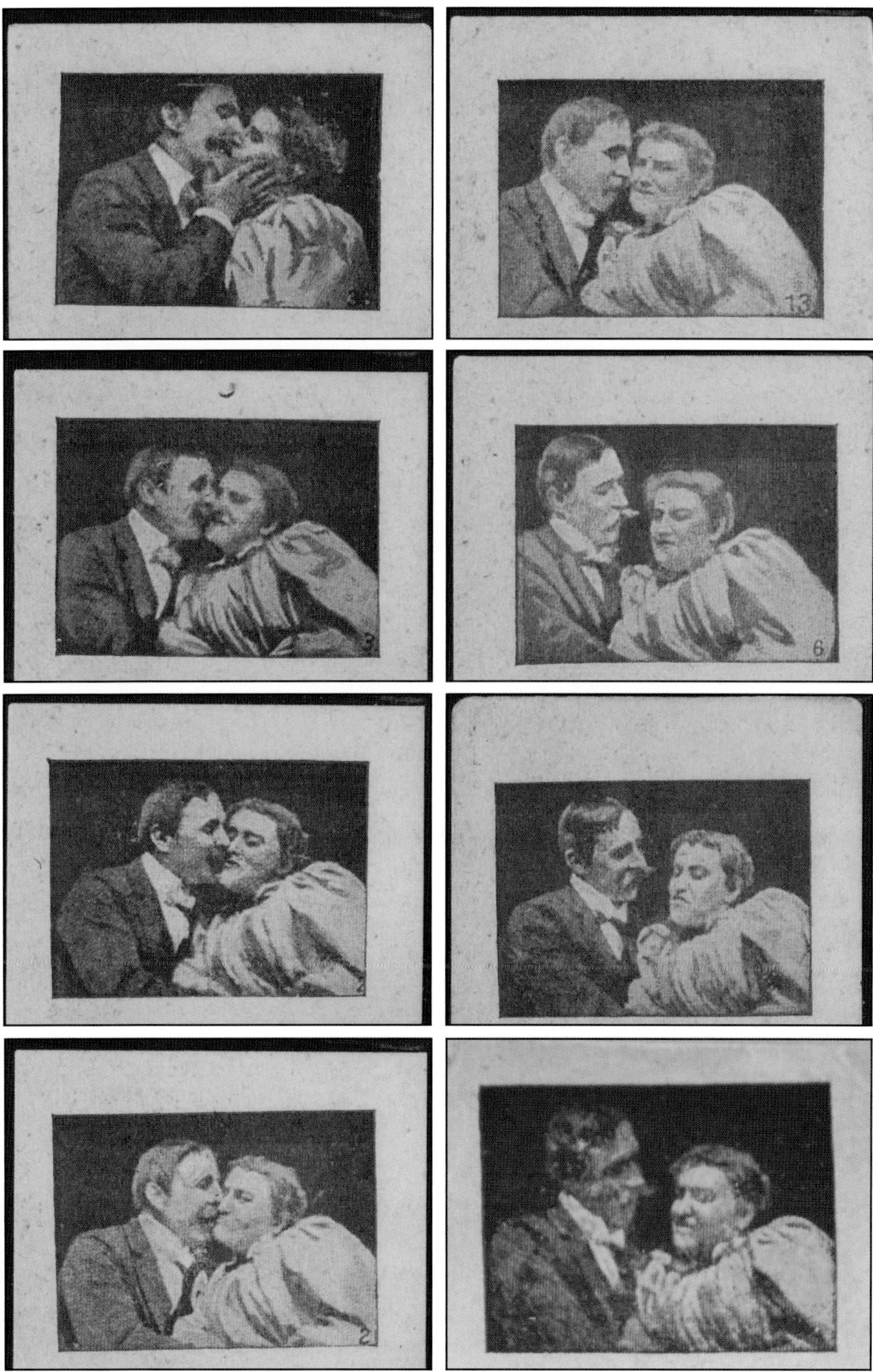

Nuit agitée ou *La Nuit terrible*, (121/121 photogrammes), édité par / edited by Beaulieu [ca juin / jun 1898 - janvier / January 1900, possible réédition].
Photogrammes / Frames : 1-2-11-20-29-38-47-56-65-74-83-93-104-114-120-121.

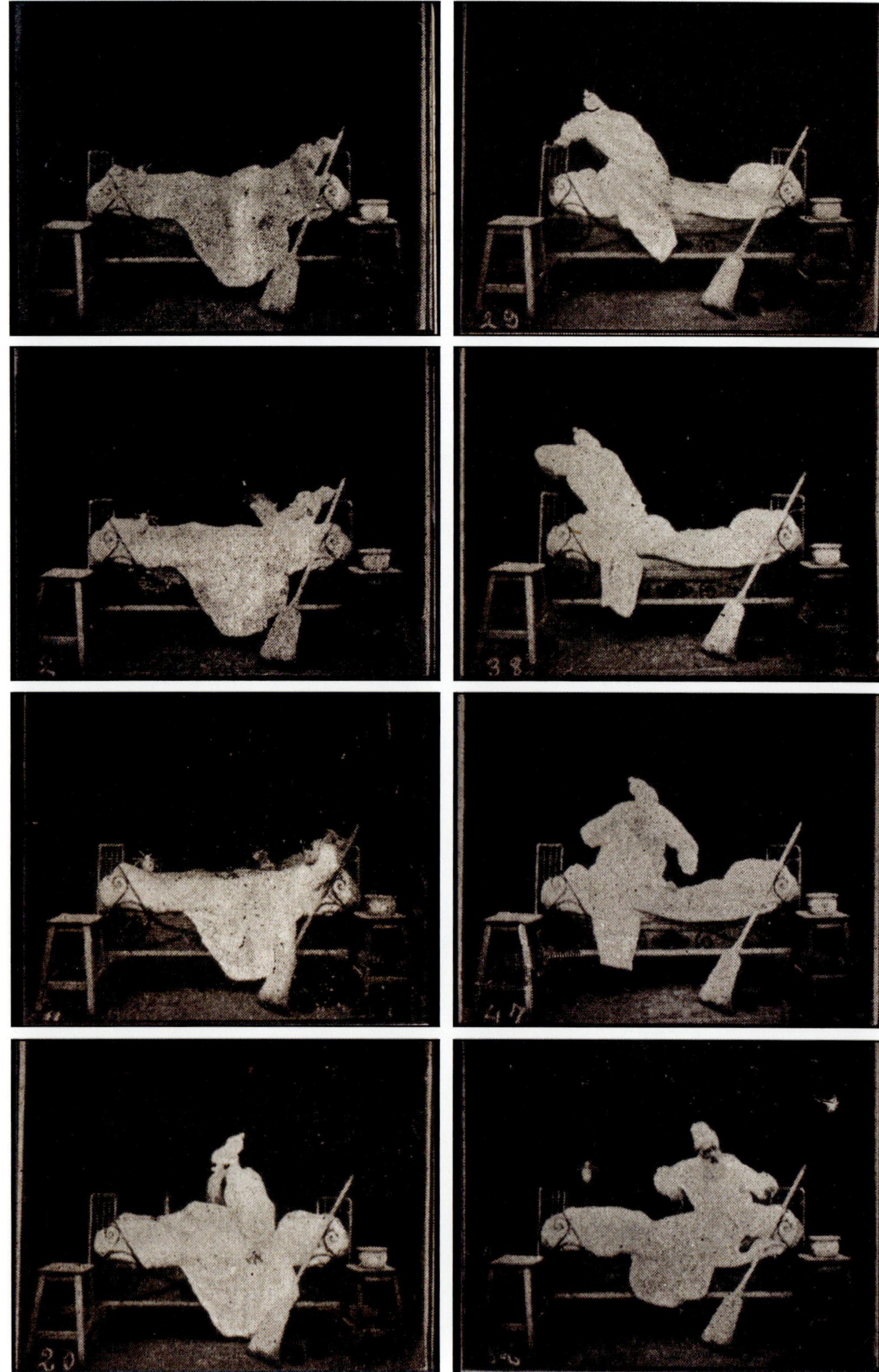

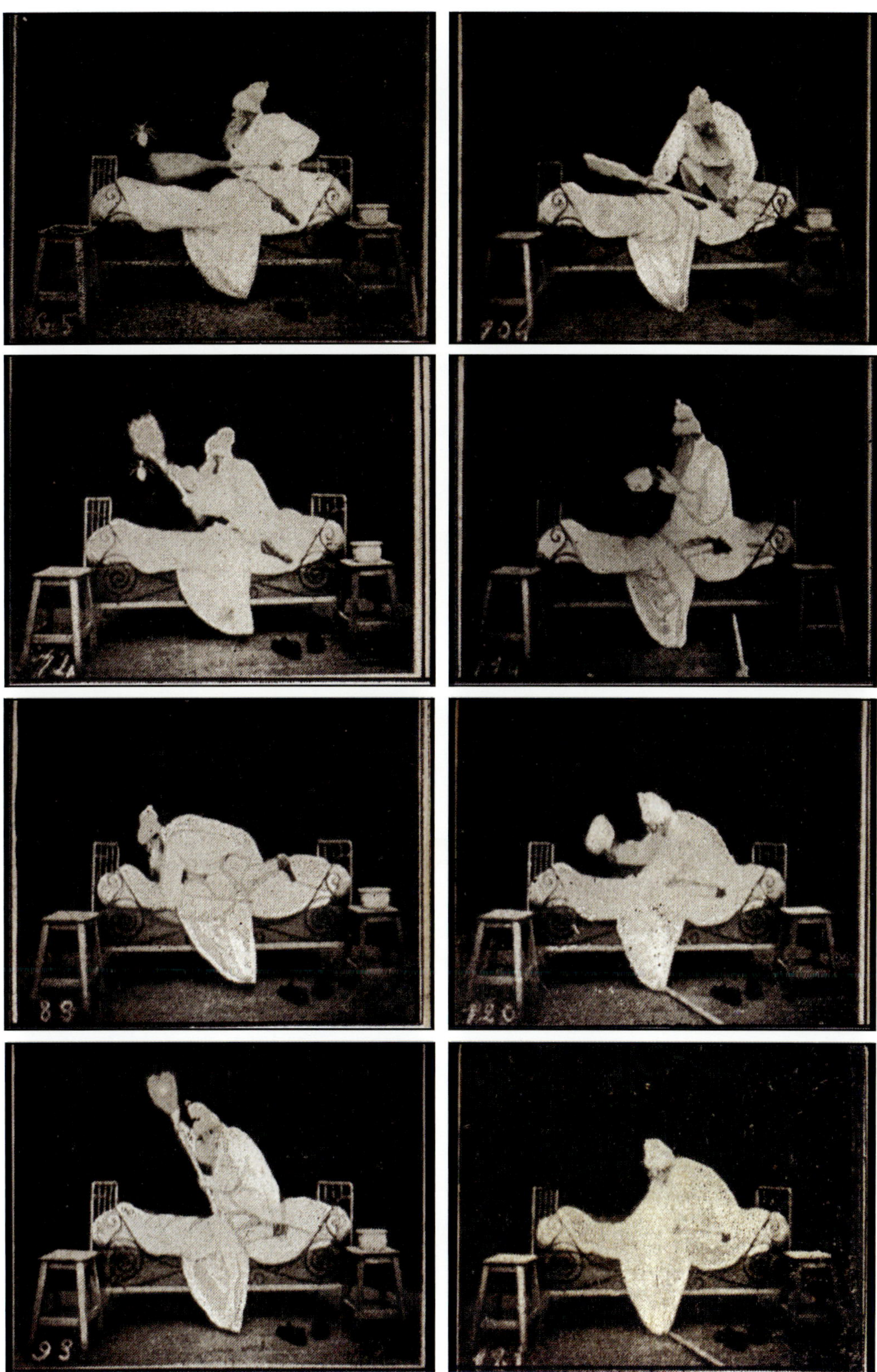

Le Bain, (80/80 photogrammes), édité par / edited by Beaulieu [ca octobre / October 1897 - mai / may 1898].
Photogrammes / Frames : 1-2-8-14-20-26-32-38-44-50-56-62-68-74-79-80.

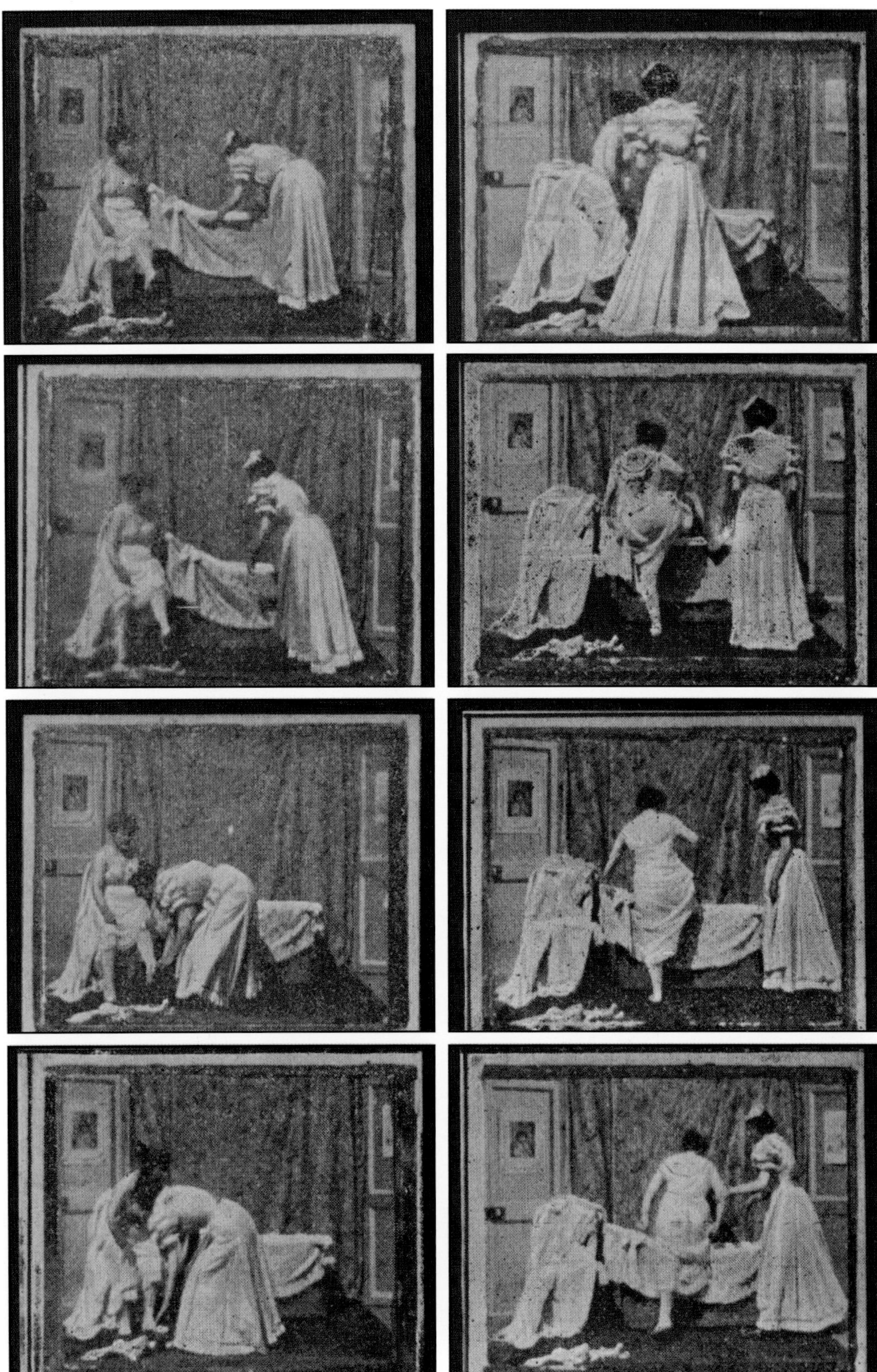

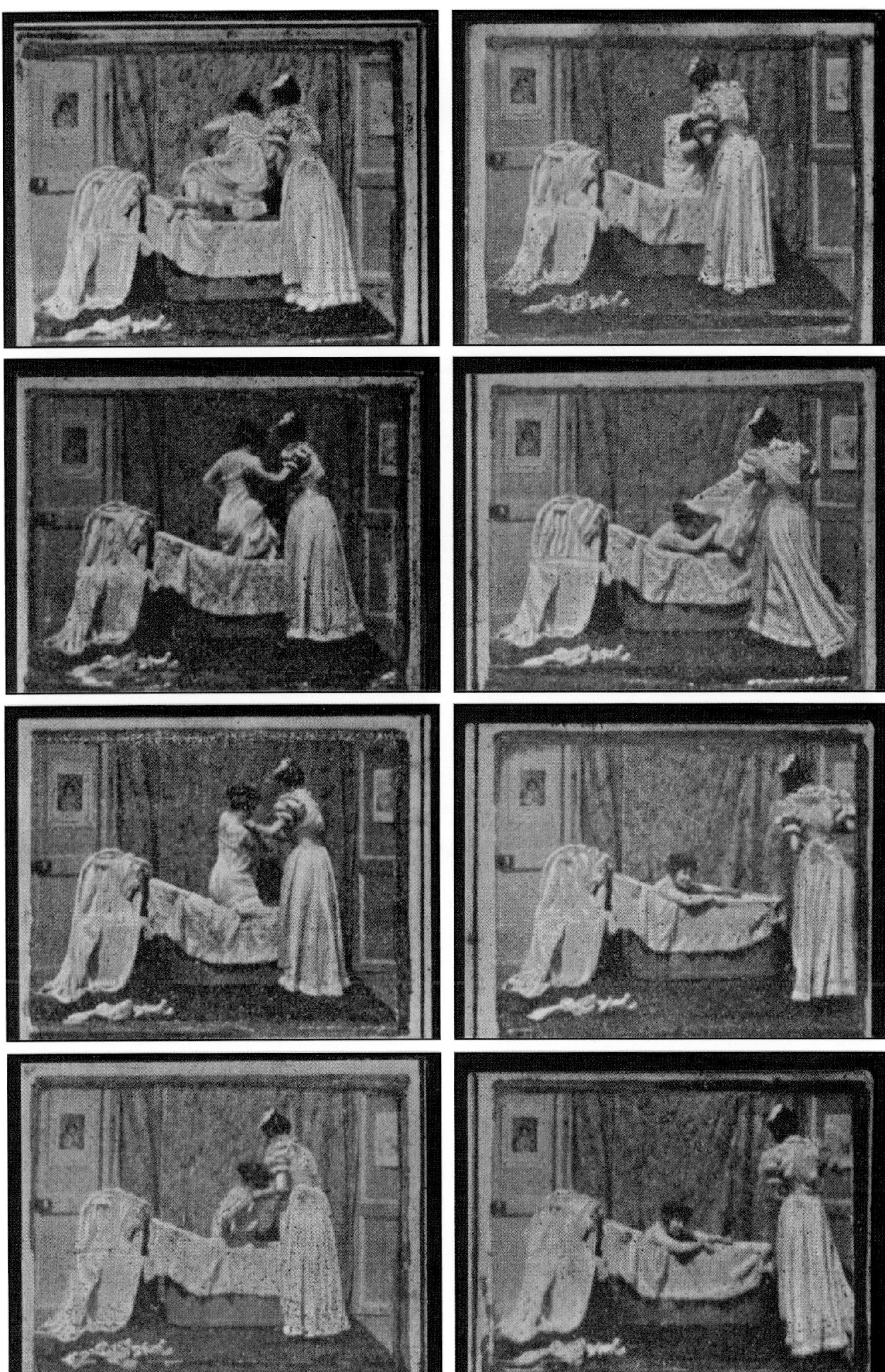

Le Voyeur, (80/80 photogrammes), édité par / edited by Beaulieu [ca avril/April 1897 - septembre / September 1897]. Photogrammes / Frames : 1-2-8-14-20-26-32-38-44-50-56-62-68-74-79-80.

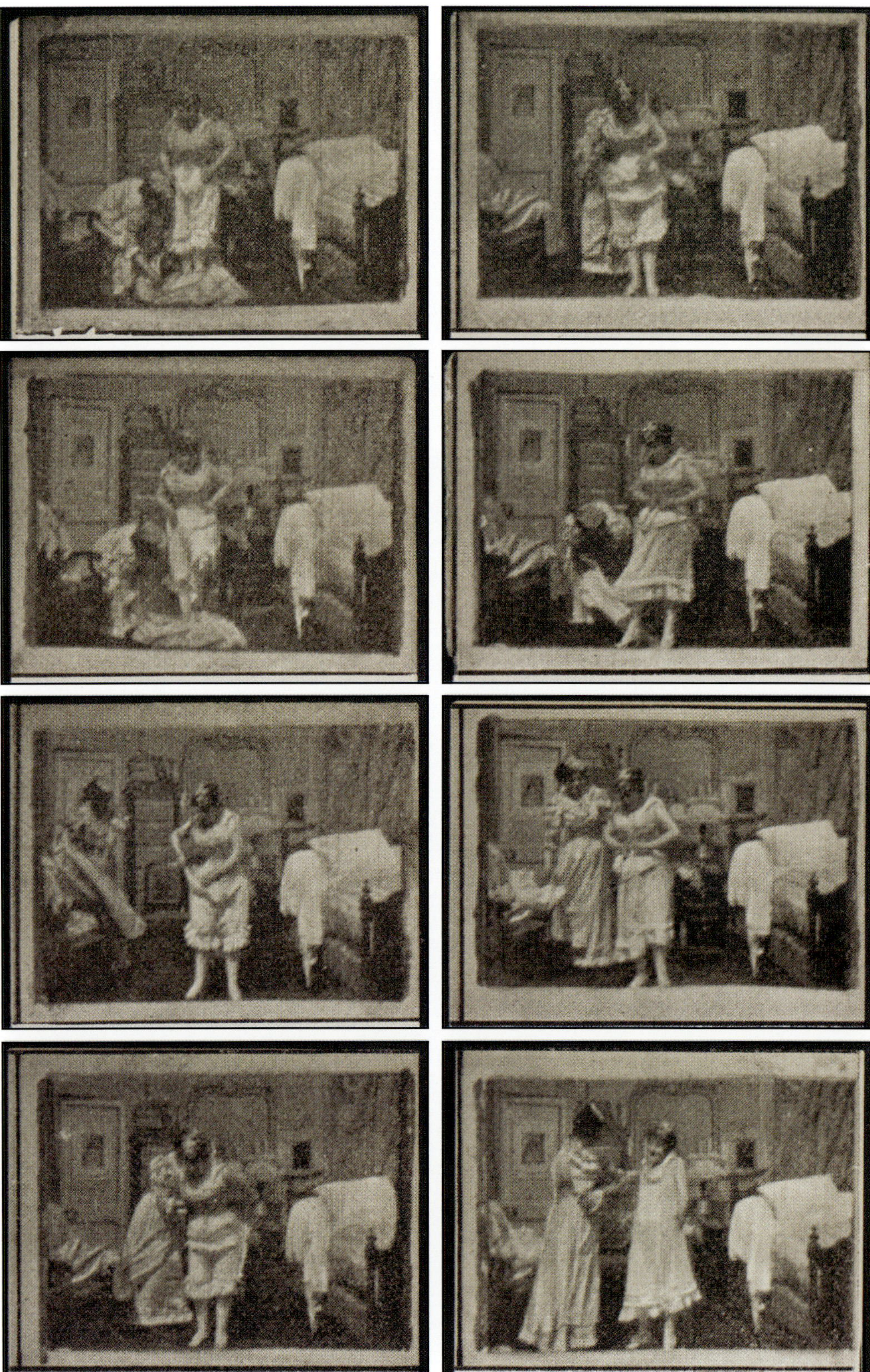

L'Amant surpris, (90/90 photogrammes), édité par / edited by Beaulieu [ca octobre / October 1897 - mai / may 1898].
Photogrammes / Frames : 1-2-8-15-21-28-41-48-55-61-65-69-76-82-89-90.

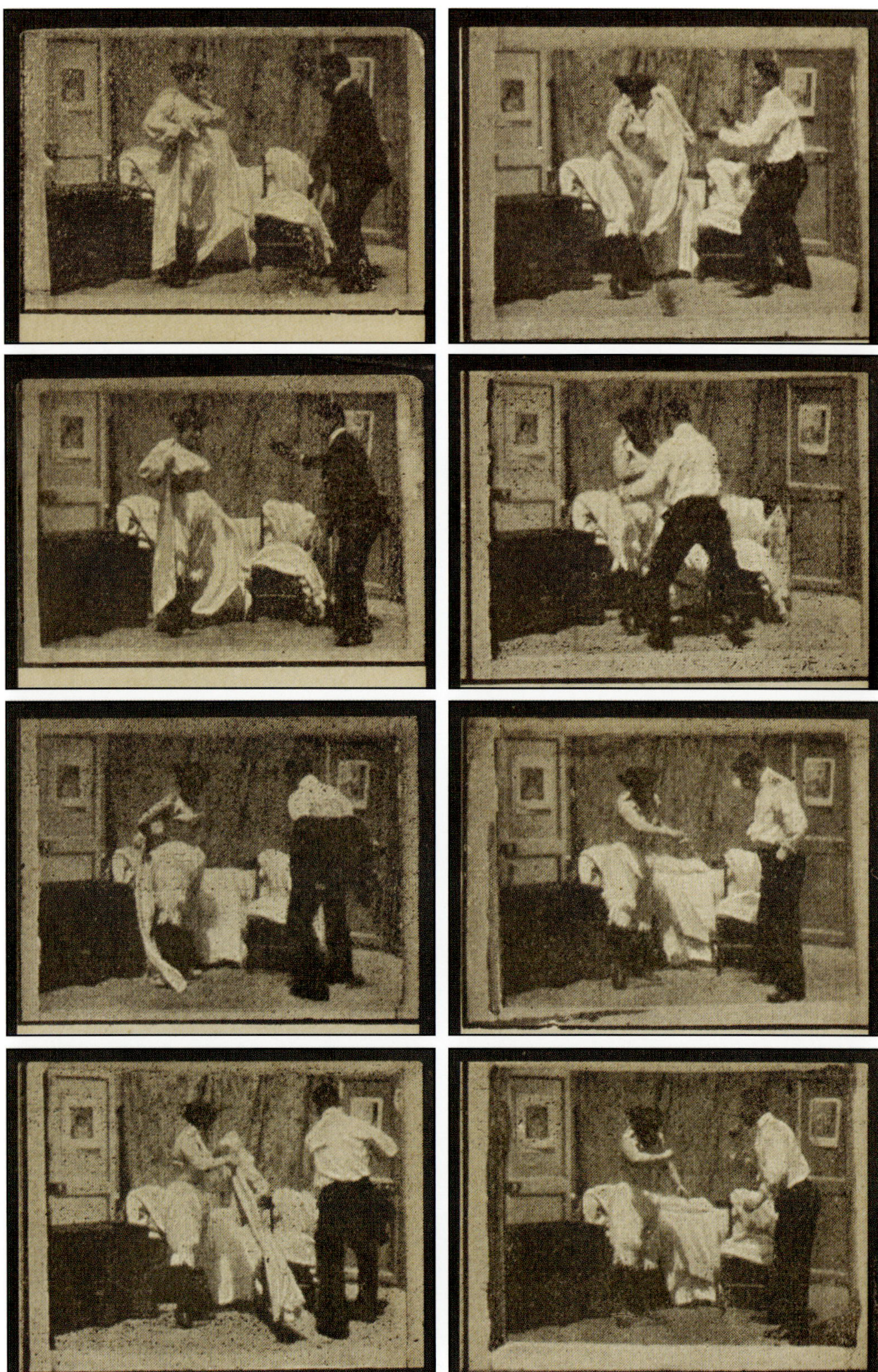

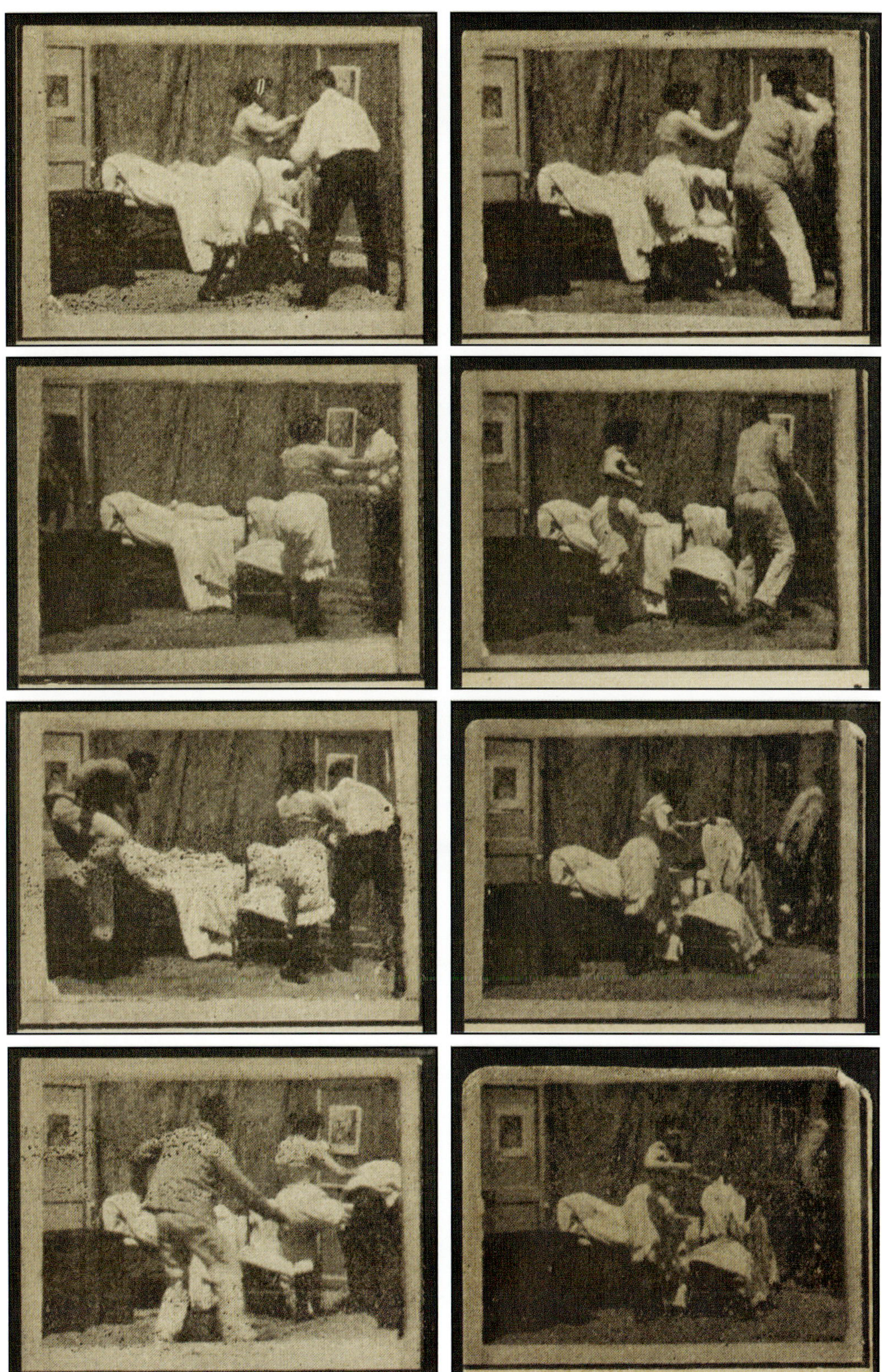

Prestidigitation, (121/121 photogrammes), édité par / edited by Beaulieu [ca octobre / October 1896 - mars / March 1897].
Photogrammes / Frames : 1-2-11-20-29-38-47-56-65-74-83-92-101-110-120-121.

La Danse, Danseuse ou ***La Danseuse***, (121/121 photogrammes), édité par / edited by Beaulieu [ca octobre / October 1896 et
mars / March 1897]. Photogrammes / Frames :
1-2-7-11-15-20-21-22-23-24-25-29-34-38-48-57-62-64-73-79-84-93-95-98-104-108-112-117-118-119-120-121.

La Danse.
Elise de Vère esquisse des pas de gigue (images 20 à 34)
Elise de Vère sketches of jitter/jig steps (images 20 to 34).

Lutte de cuisiniers, (121/121 photogrammes), édité par / edited by Beaulieu [ca février / February 1900 - février / February 1901, possible réédition].
Photogrammes / Frames : 1-2-11-20-29-38-47-56-62-74-83-92-101-111-120-121.

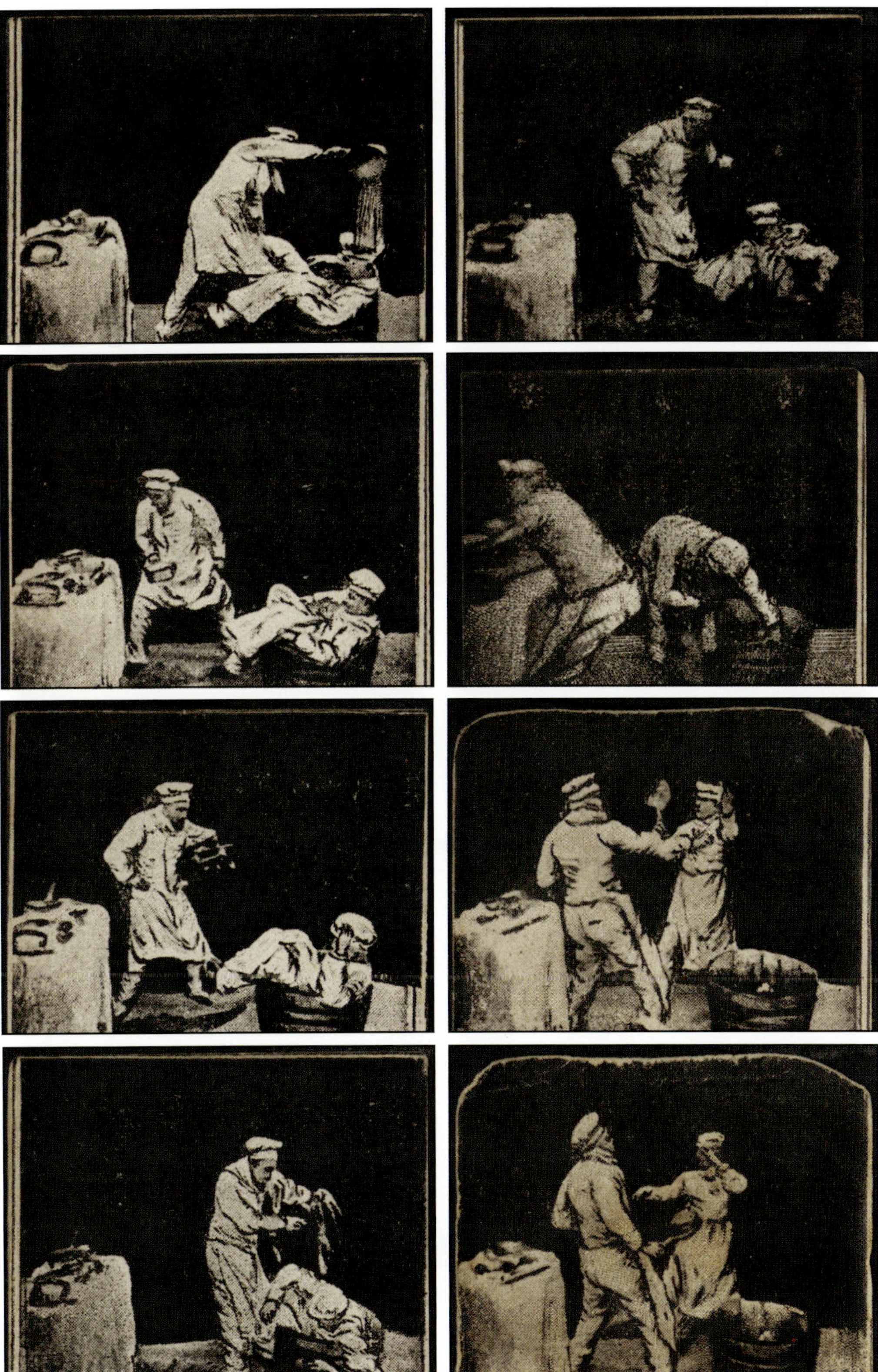

Le Duel, (121/121 photogrammes), édité par / edited by Beaulieu [ca juin / june 1898 - janvier / January 1900, possible réédition].
Photogrammes / Frames : 1-2-11-20-29-38-47-56-65-74-83-92-101-110-120-121.

Le Bâton, (121/121 photogrammes), édité par / edited by Beaulieu [ca juin / June 1898 - janvier / January 1900, possible réédition].
Photogrammes / Frames : 1-2-11-20-29-38-47-56-65-74-83-92-101-110-120-121.

Boxe, (121/121 photogrammes), édité par / edited by Beaulieu [ca octobre / October 1897 - mai / May 1898].
Photogrammes / Frames : 1-2-9-19-29-33-43-53-63-73-83-92-106-117-120-121.

Duel au sabre ou *Escrime*, (121/121 photogrammes), édité par / edited by Beaulieu [ca juin / June 1898 - janvier / January 1900, possible réédition].
Photogrammes / Frames : 1-2-11-20-29-38-47-56-65-74-83-92-101-110-120-121.

Pose chez l'artiste. Vénus, (90/90 photogrammes), édité par / edited by Beaulieu [ca octobre / October 1897 - mai / May 1898]. Méliès identifié des images 9 à 16; Méliès identified in images 9 to 16. Photogrammes / Frames : 1-2-9-10-11-12-13-14-15-16-20-23-27-30-34-37-41-44-48-51-55-58-61-64-68-71-75-78-82-85-89-90.

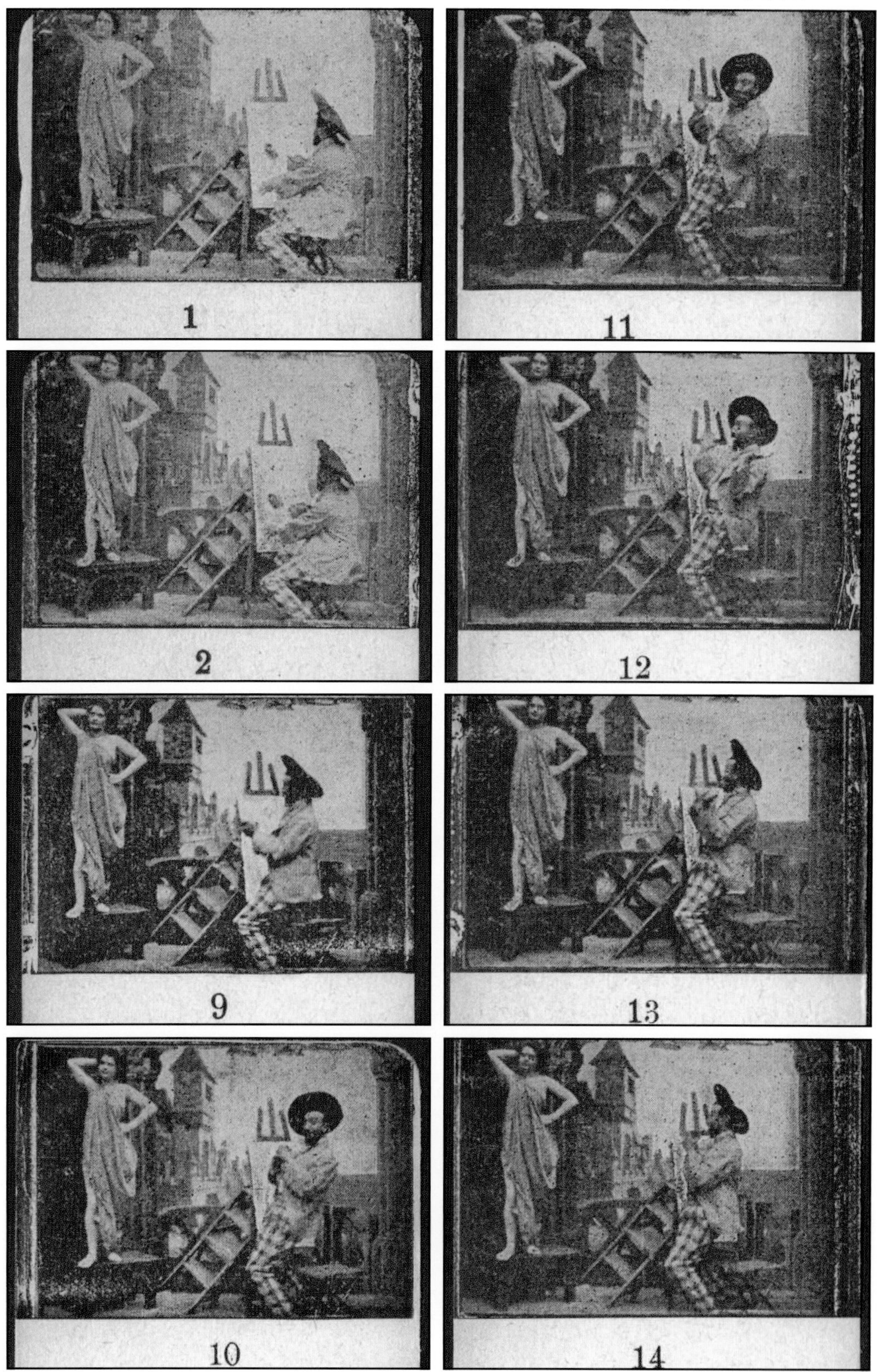

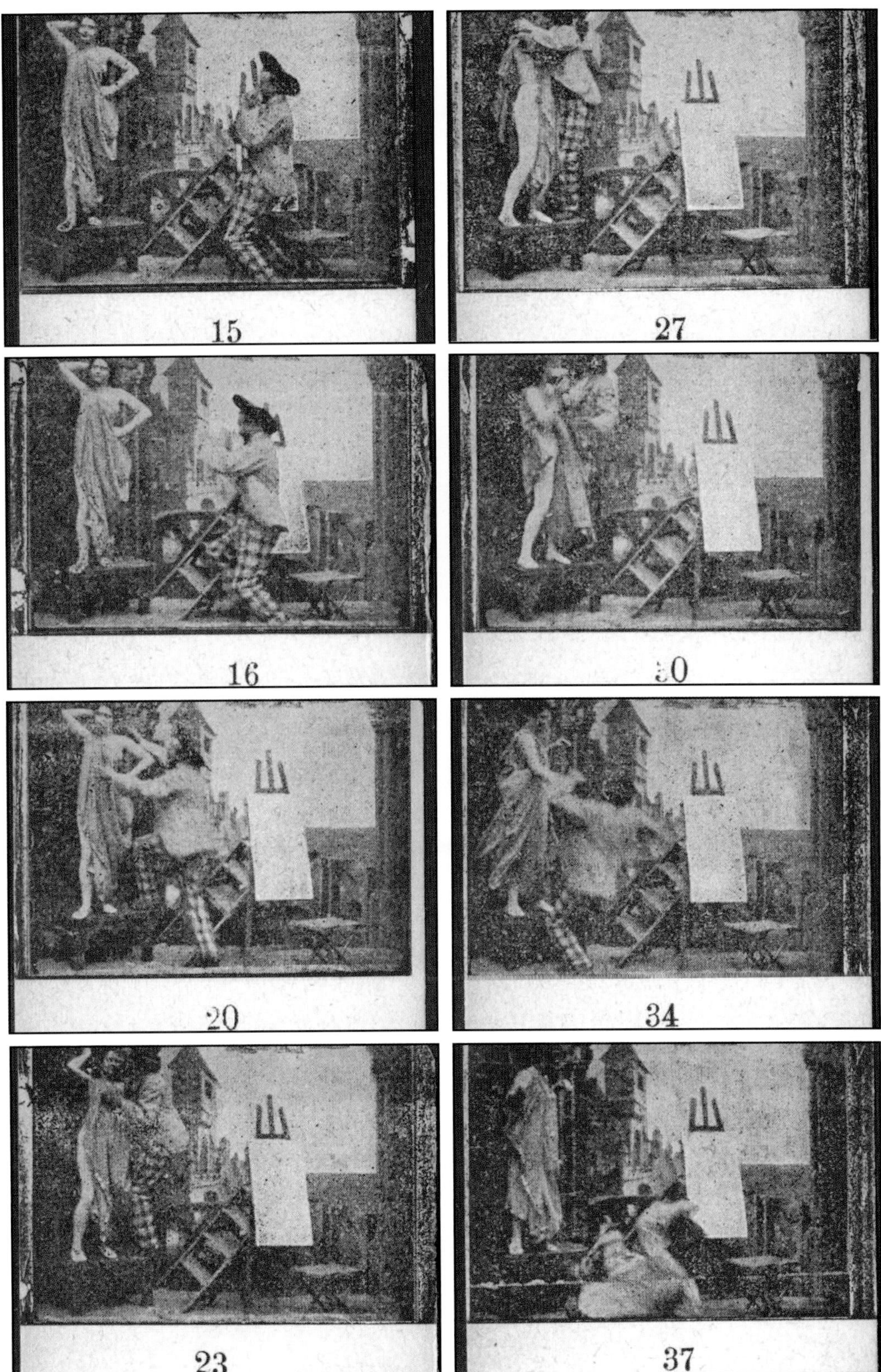

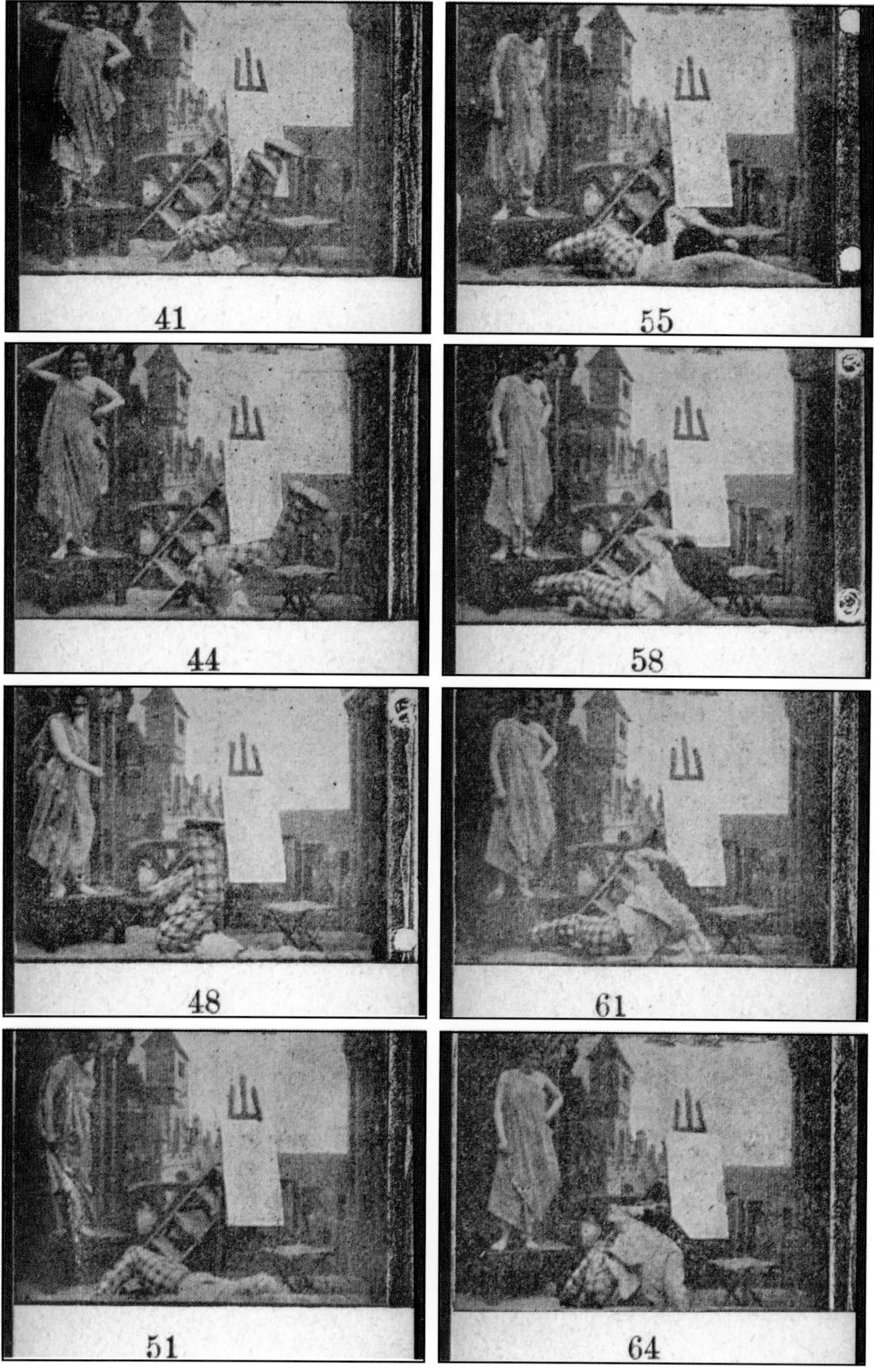

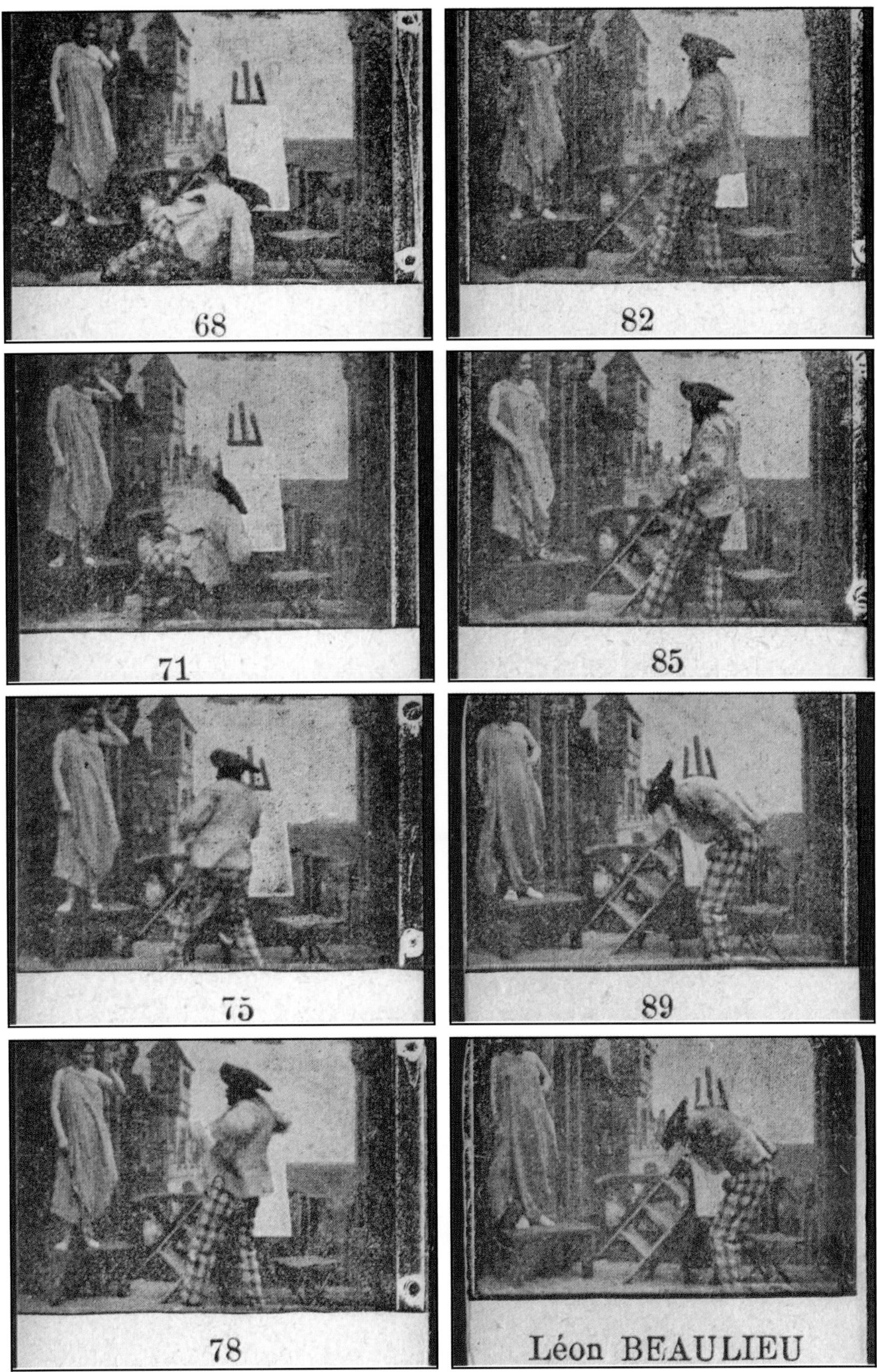
68
82
71
85
75
89
78
Léon BEAULIEU

La Puce ou *Madame cherche ses puces*, (90/90 photogrammes), édité par / edited by Beaulieu [ca juin / June 1898 - janvier / January 1900, possible réédition].
Photogrammes / Frames : 1-2-9-16-23-30-35-43-51-58-65-72-79-86-89-90.

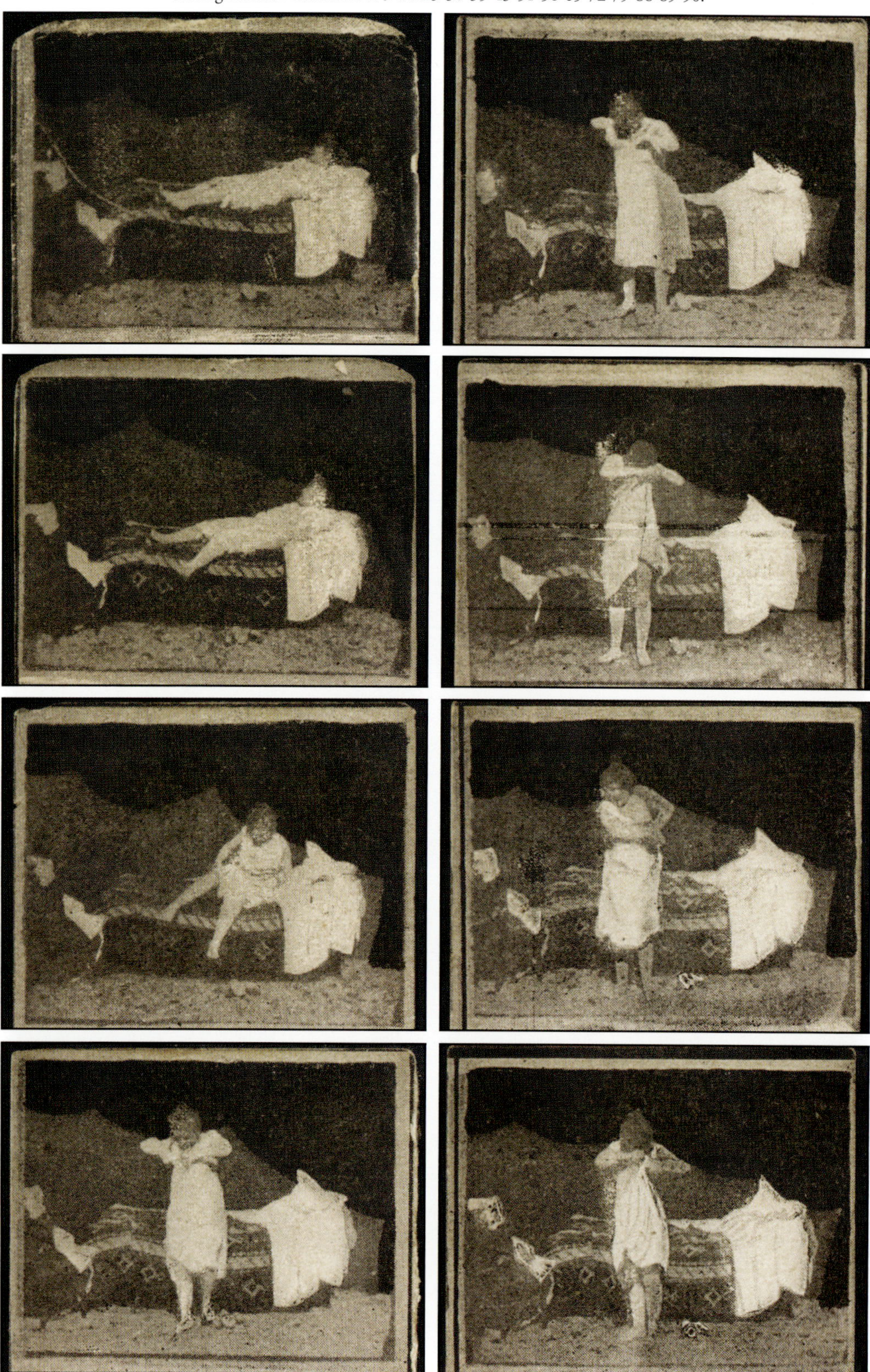

La Méprise ou *Méprise*, (89/90 photogrammes), édité par / edited by Beaulieu [ca février / February 1900 - février / February 1901, possible réédition].
Photogrammes / Frames : 1-2-8-14-20-26-32-38-44-50-56-62-68-75-82-89.

M. TÉTARD
MODES
MODES

Le Coup du père François, (90/90 photogrammes), édité par / edited by Beaulieu [ca avril / April 1897 - septembre / September 1897].
Photogrammes / Frames : 1-2-9-16-23-30-37-44-51-58-65-73-79-86-89-90.

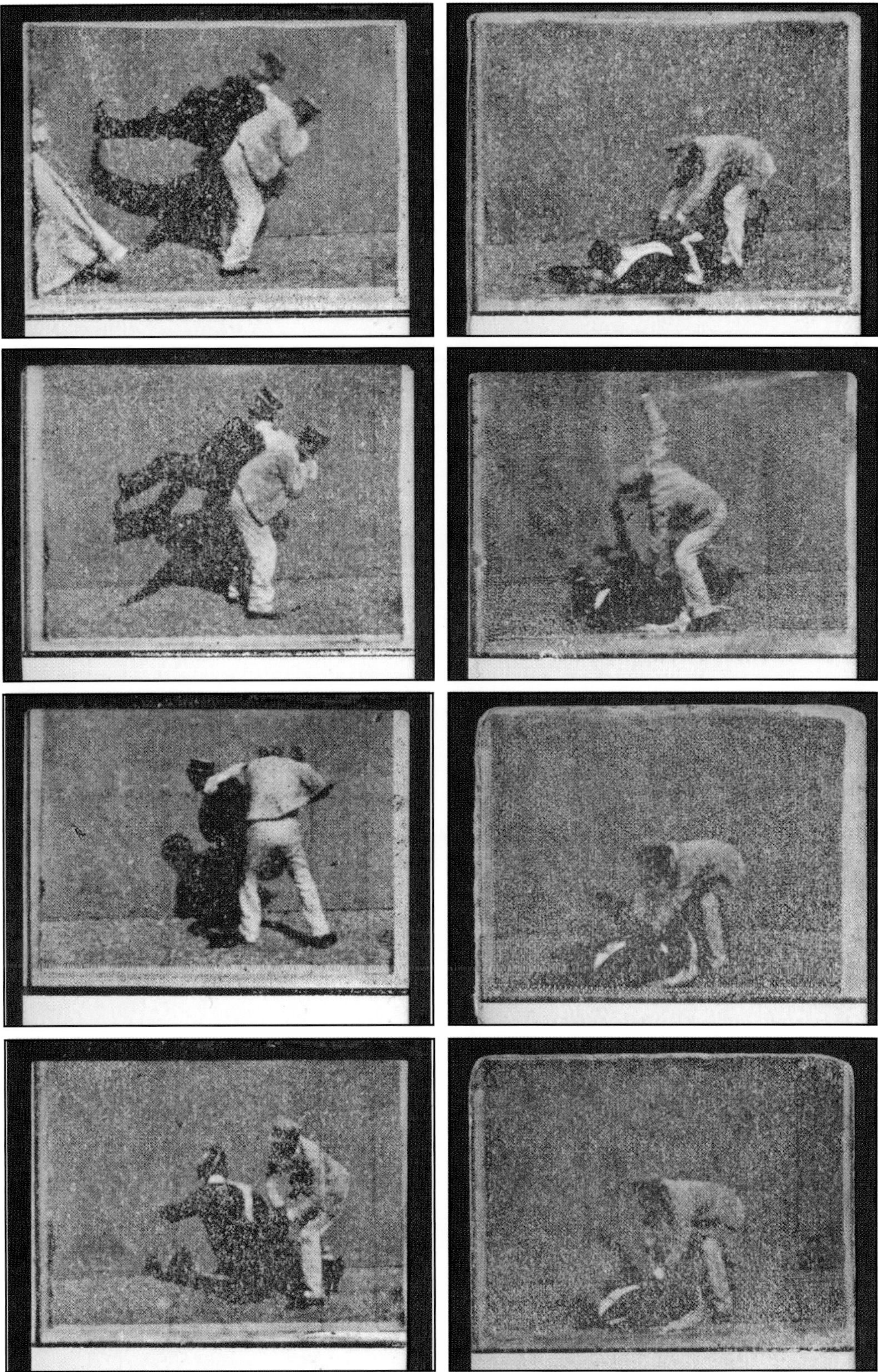

« *Partie de cartes à trois* », (2 x 48/96 photogrammes), édité par / edited by Beaulieu [ca juin / June 1898 - janvier / January 1900, possible réédition].
Photogrammes / Frames : 1-3-11-17-25-31-39-45-53-59-67-73-81-87-94-96.

« Partie de cartes à trois ».

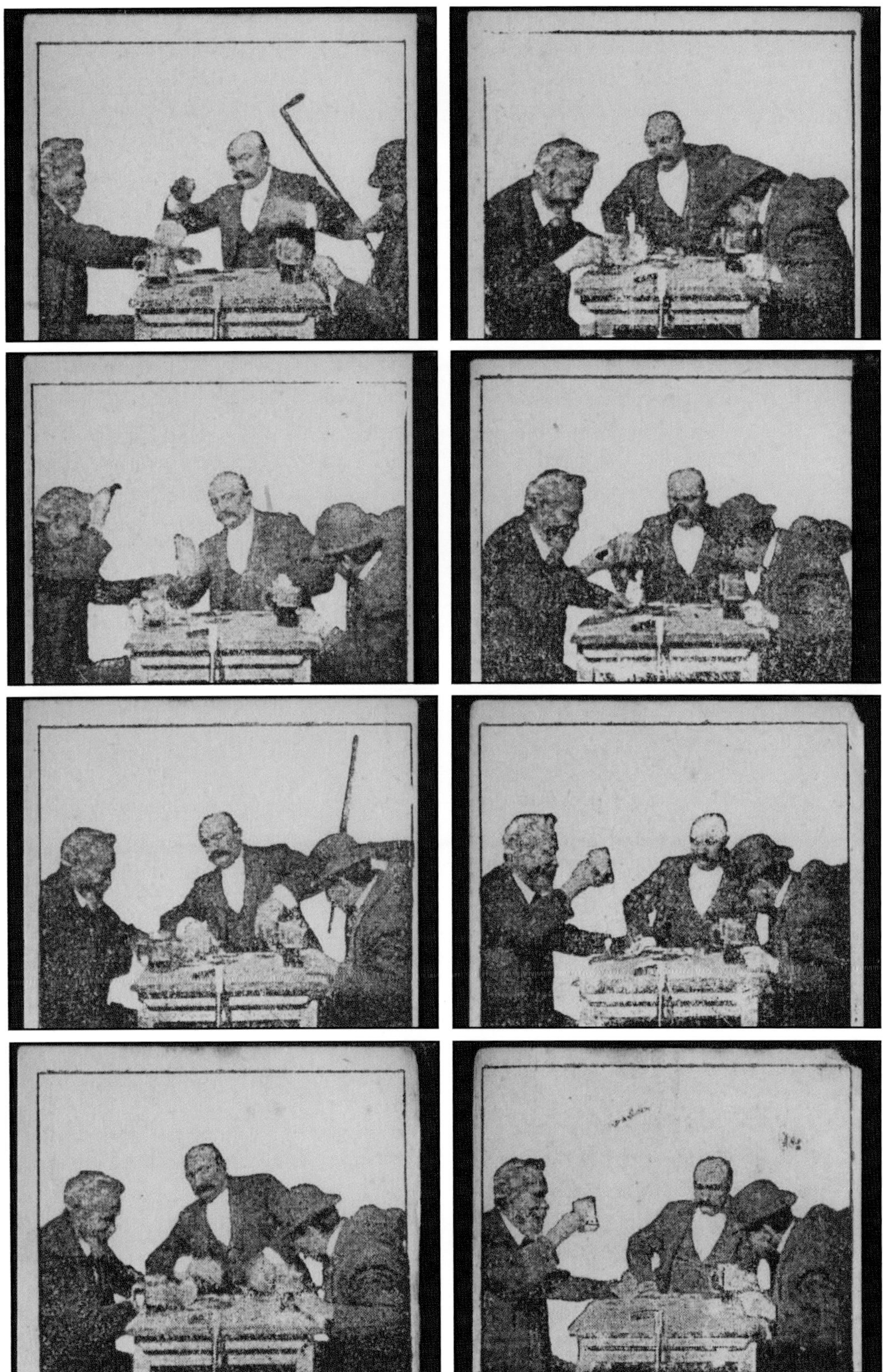

Loïe Fuller, (90/90 photogrammes), édité par / edited by Prissette [ca août / August 1896 – 1899].
Photogrammes / Frames : 1-2-8-15-21-28-34-41-47-54-60-67-73-78-89-90.

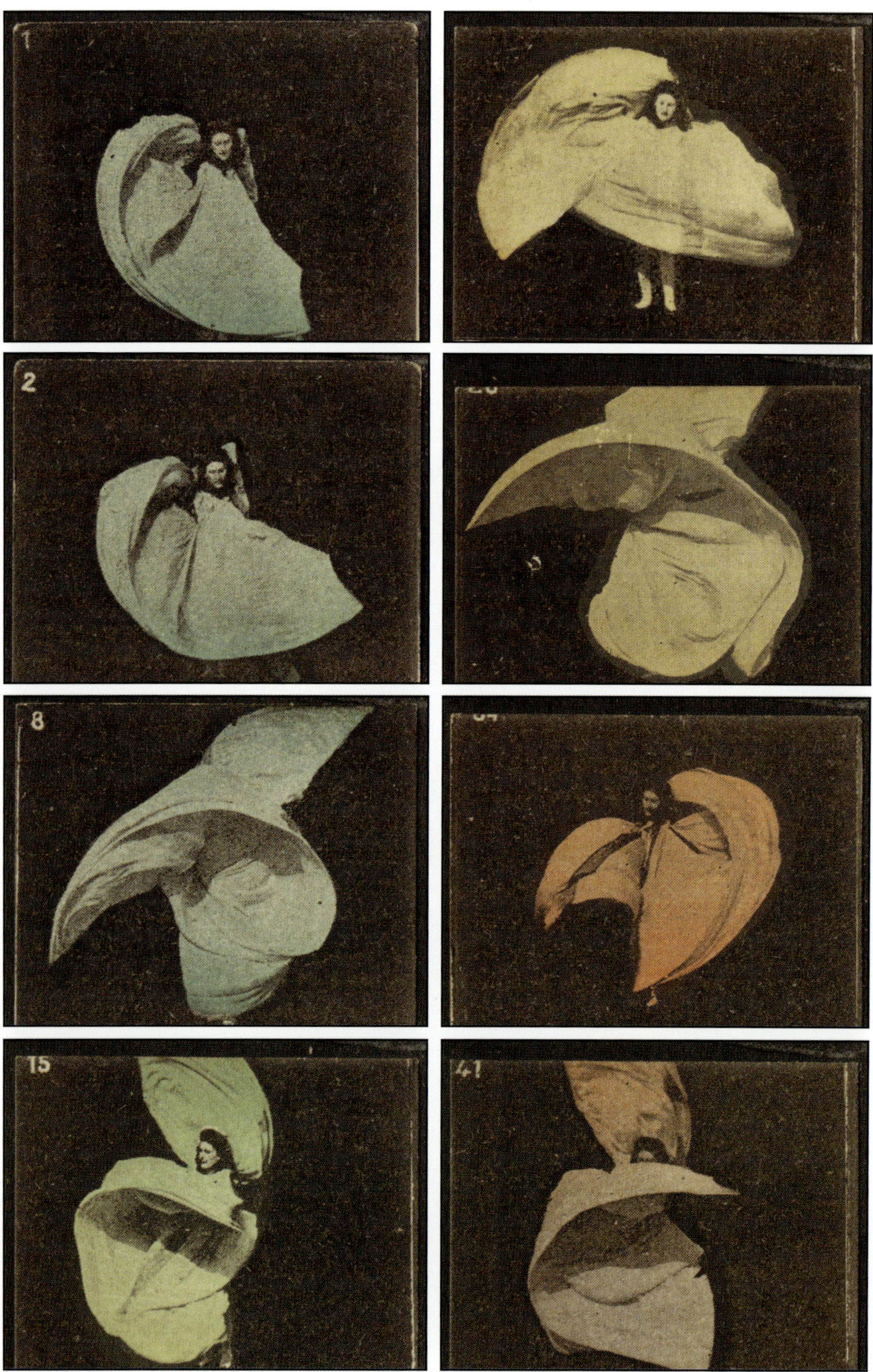

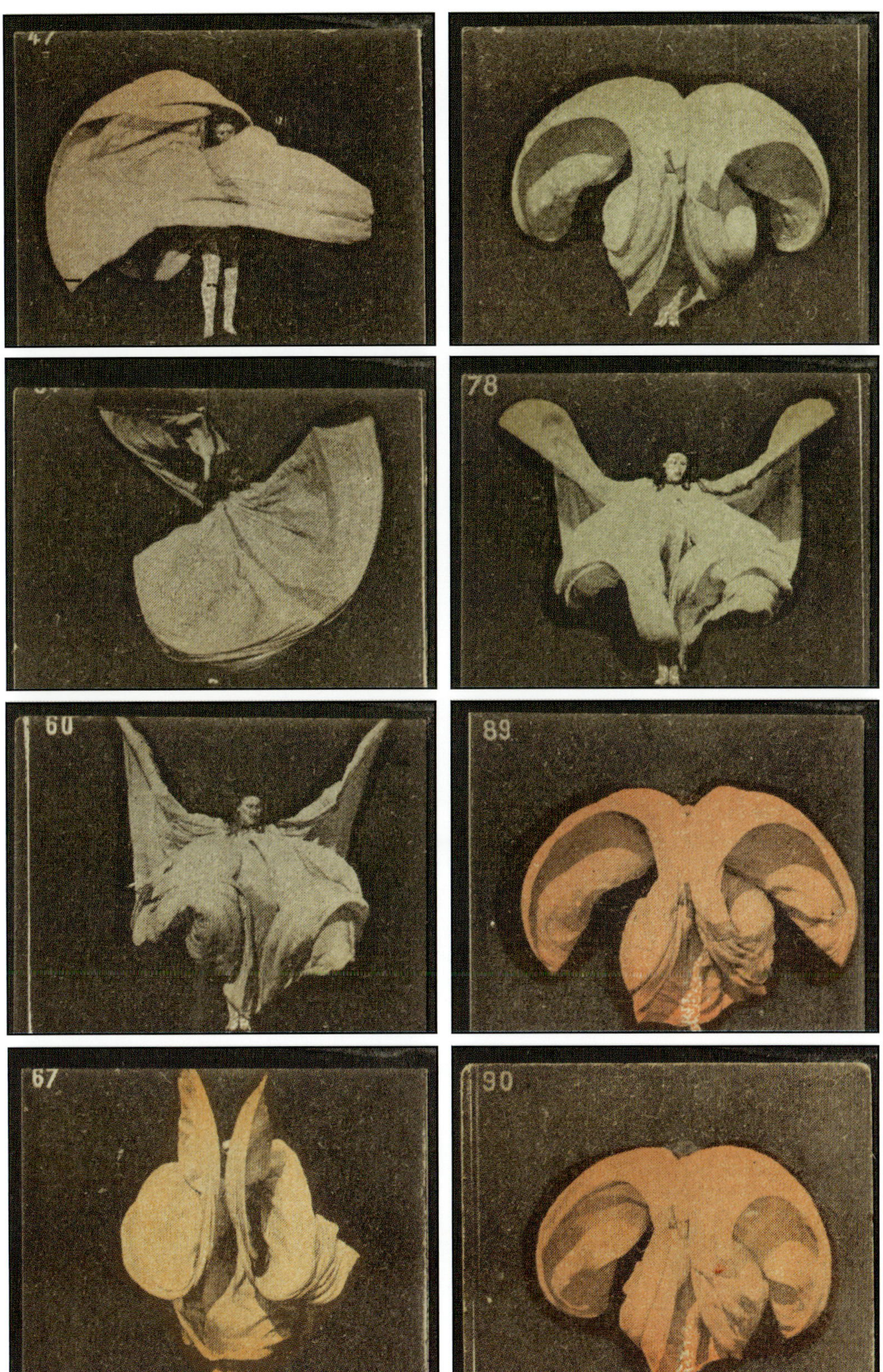

1
21
2
28
15
34
41

La Danse du Cancan, (84/84 photogrammes), édité par / edited by Prissette [ca juillet / July 1896 – 1899].
Photogrammes / Frames : 1-2-9-15-22-28-35-42-48-54-61-67-74-80-83-84.

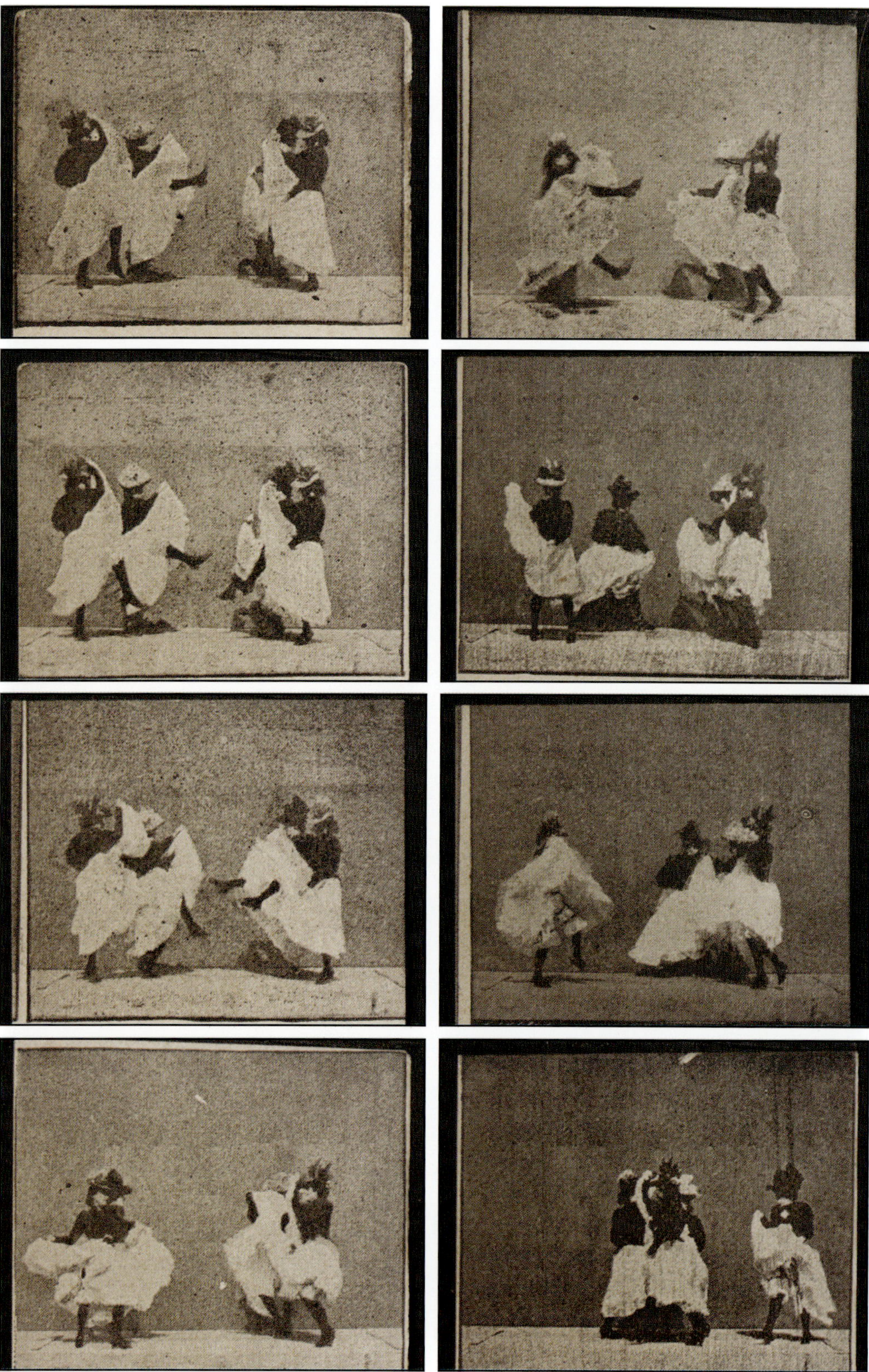

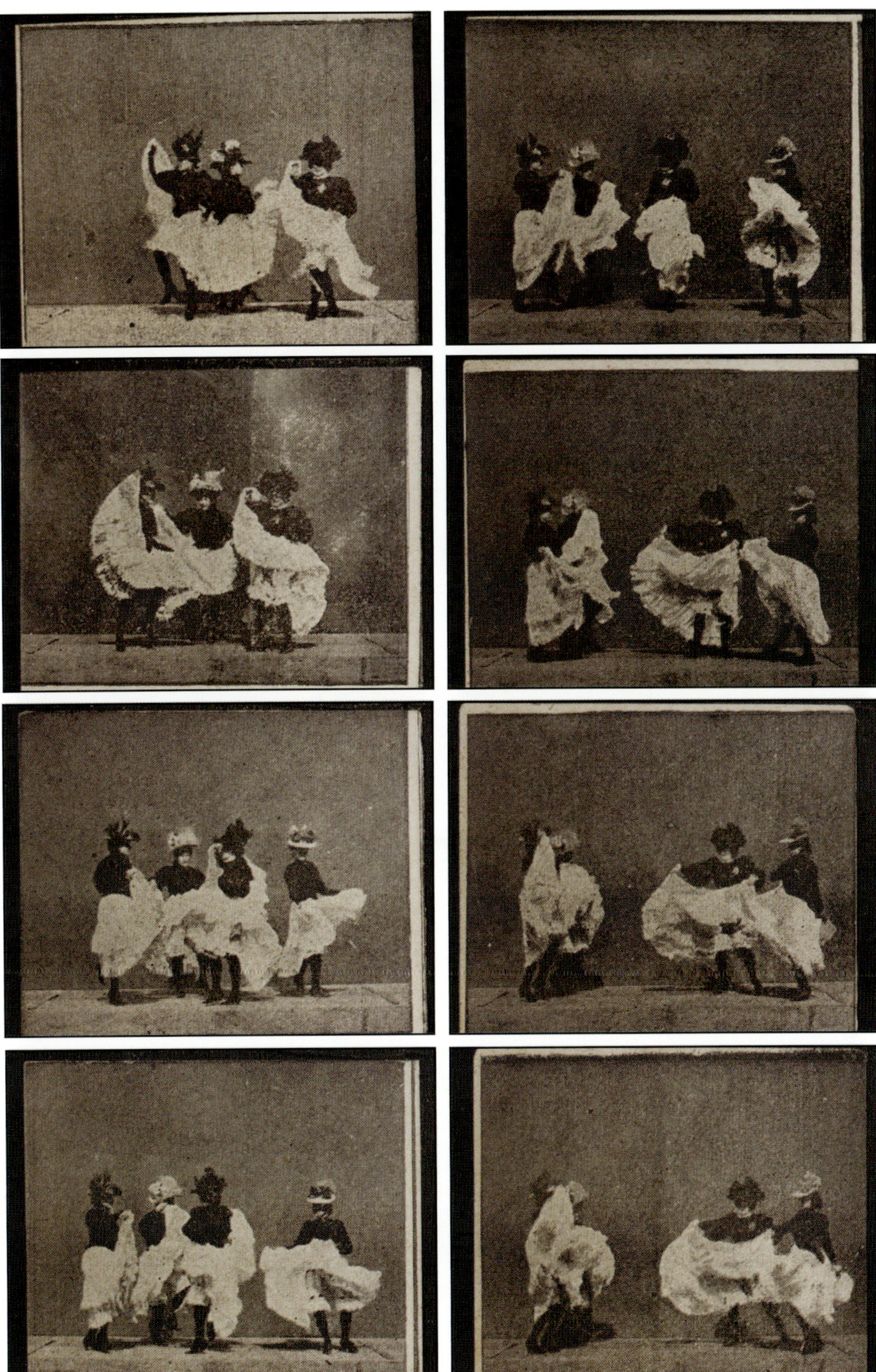

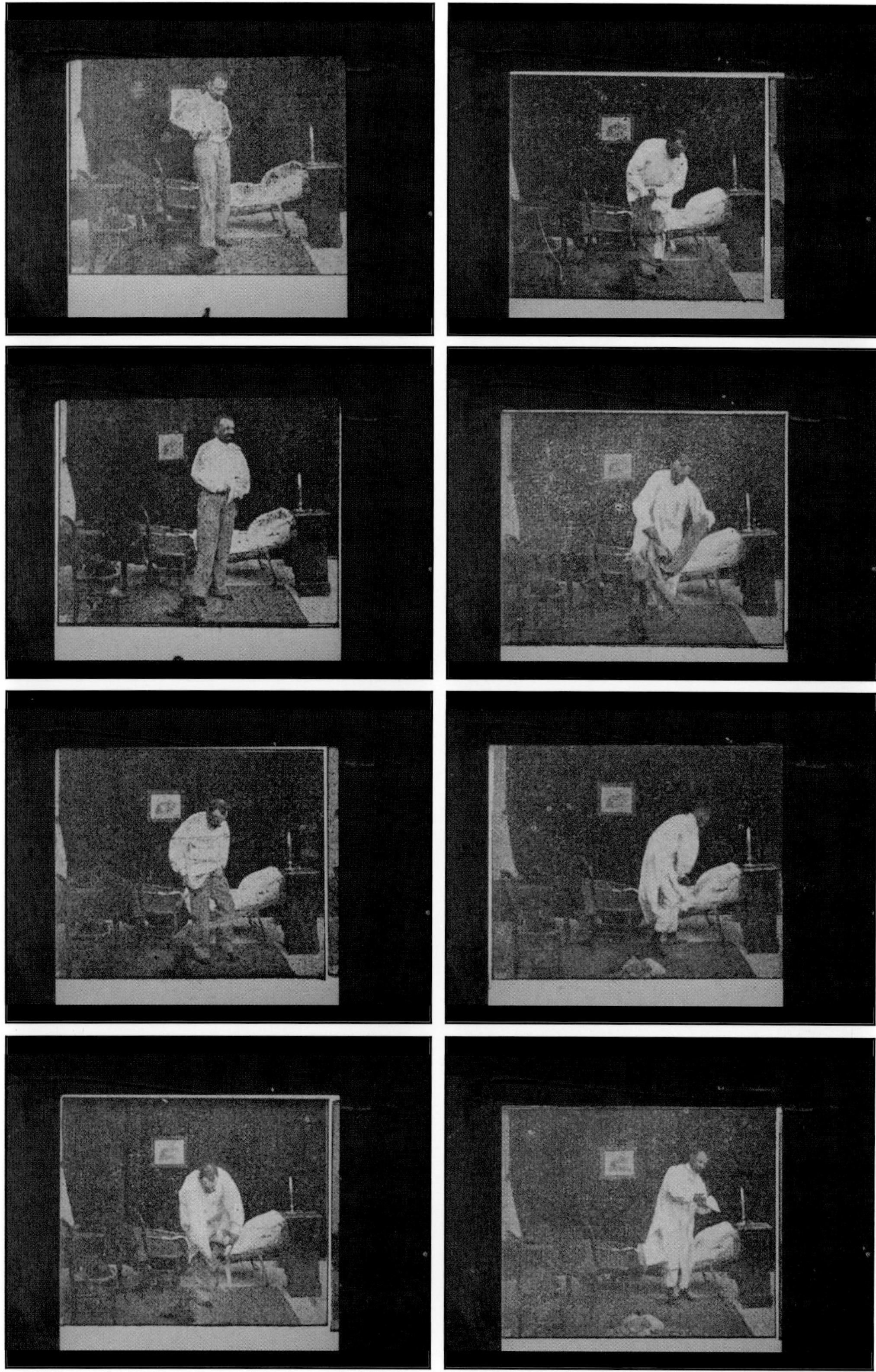

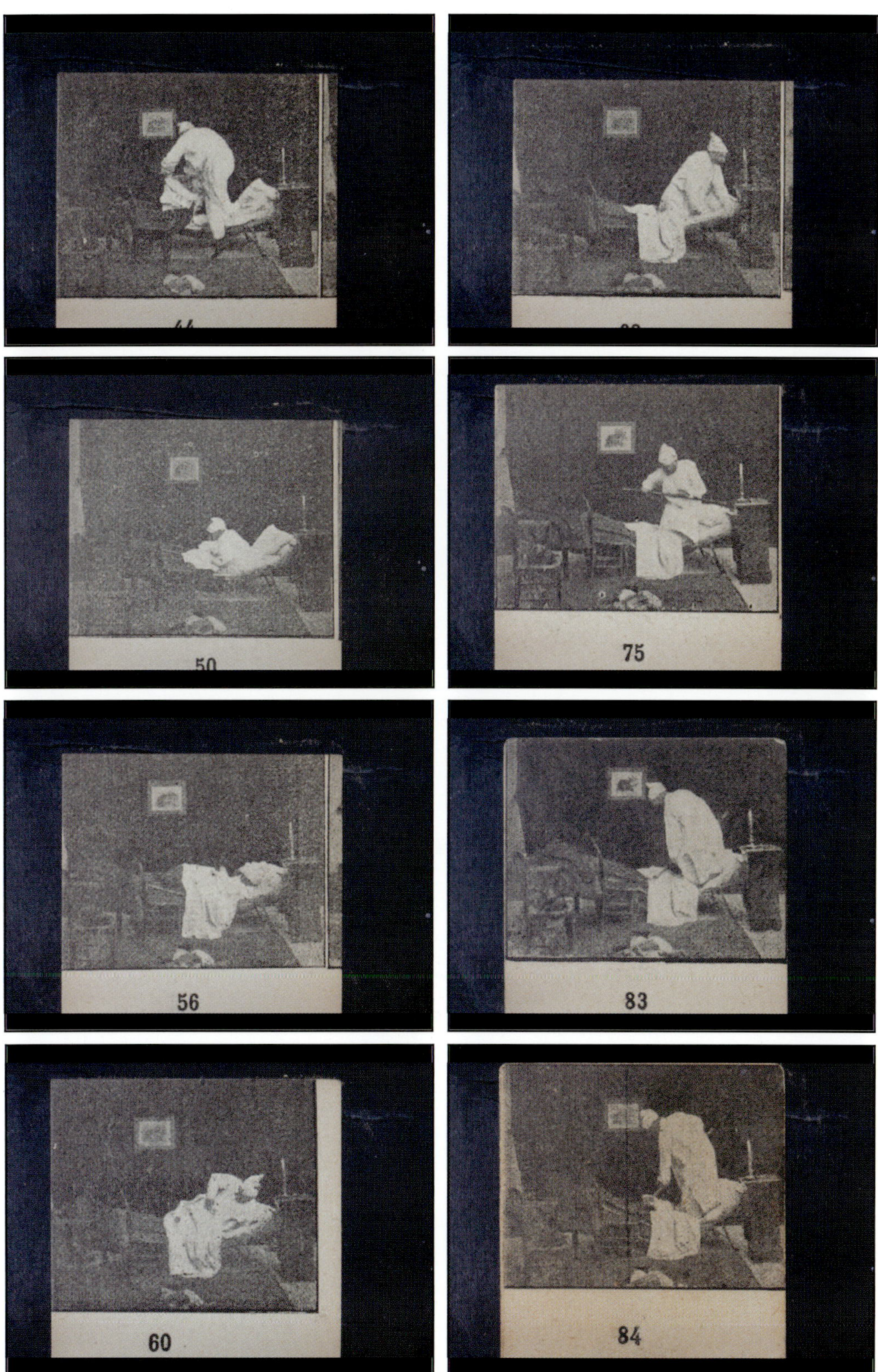

« *Train en marche* », (2 x 32/64 photogrammes), édité par / edited by [Beaulieu], [ca juillet / July 1897 - février / February 1901].
Photogrammes / Frames : 1-2-5-7-9-11-13-15-17-19-21-23-25-29-31-32.

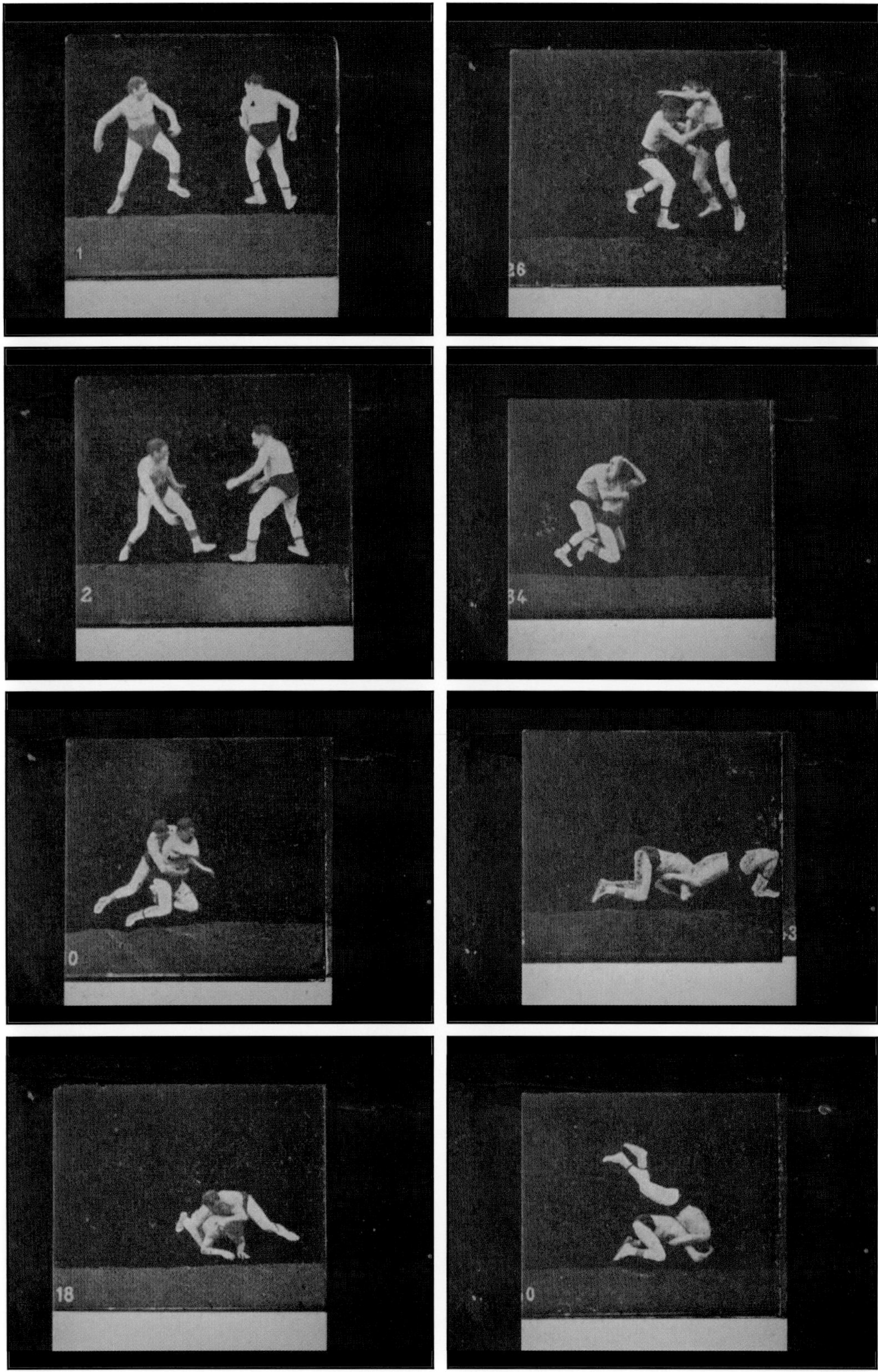

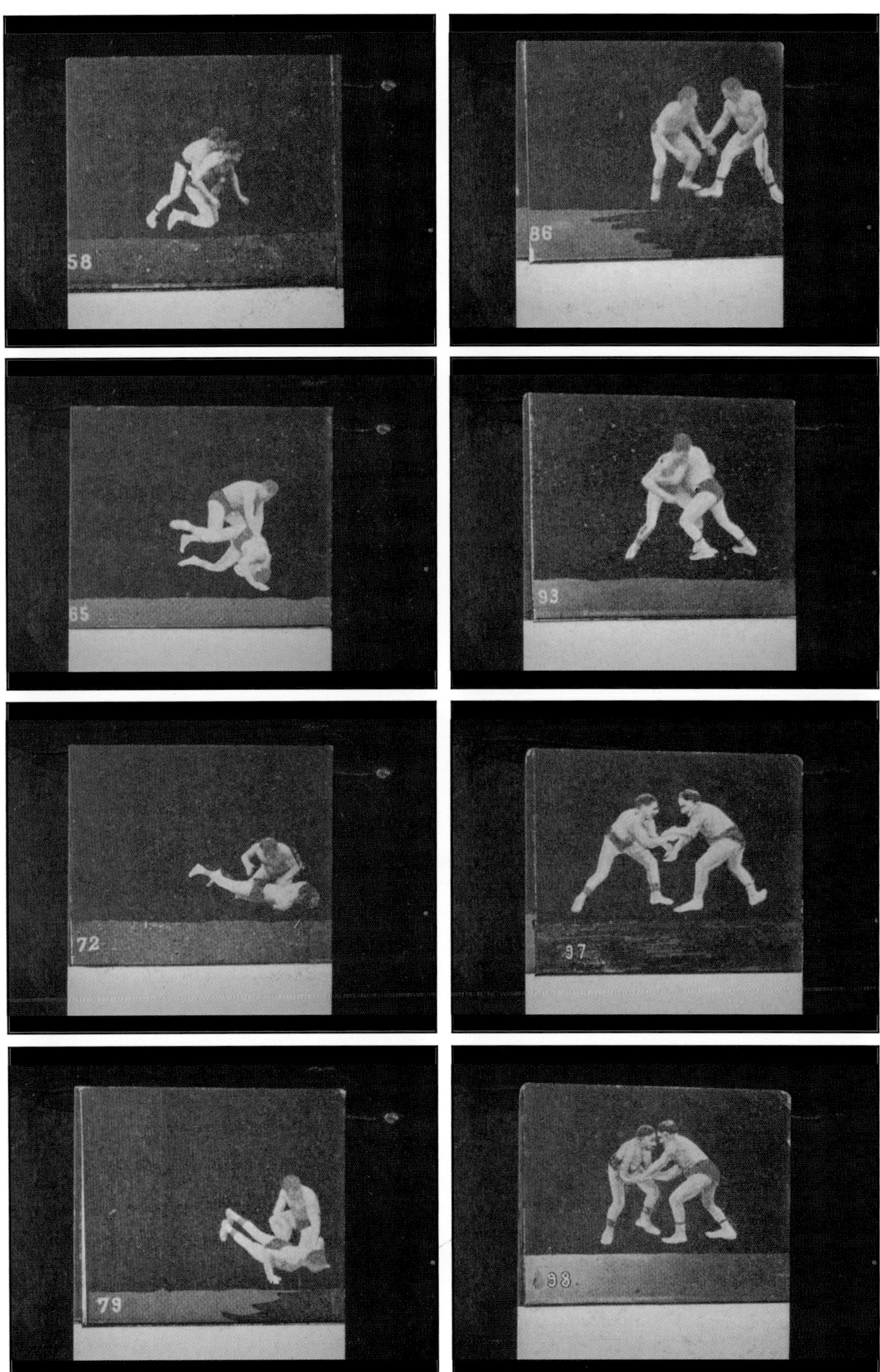

D'entre les morts…

André Gaudreault

À la mémoire de Madeleine Malthête-Méliès, grâce à qui
Georges Méliès a connu une deuxième naissance.

Au contraire des frères Lumière, ces spécialistes des images immobiles[1] dont la réputation tient au fait qu'ils ont eu le don de les *mobiliser*, ces images, Thierry Lecointe a, lui, le don d'*immobiliser* les images animées, de les arrêter. Et ce, dans le but de nous permettre de mieux voir ce qu'elles cèlent et recèlent. Ainsi nous a-t-il proposé, il y a près d'une vingtaine d'années déjà, des panoramas composites d'arènes où s'étaient déroulées des corridas captées par le Cinématographe[2], panoramas composés à partir d'arrêts sur image qu'il utilise pour rabattre la temporalité sur un espace qu'il « augmente » en le dépliant, en quelque sorte, pour lui donner une extension qui lui permet de produire des vues panoramiques spectaculaires, tel ce panorama d'une corrida filmée aux arènes de Nîmes reconstitué à partir de onze cadrages différents (voir l'illustration ci-dessous) qui, n'eût été son ingéniosité, n'existerait qu'à l'état virtuel, et morceau par morceau, dans la série des vues Lumière tournées en ce lieu.

« Panorama de la corrida filmée aux arènes de Nîmes, le 24 septembre 1899 par deux techniciens de la maison Lumière »
(Thierry Lecointe, *Le Cinématographe-Lumière dans les arènes*, Montpellier, UBTF, 2007, p. 107).

Il s'agissait pour lui, ce faisant, de repérer des indices pour établir une chronologie précise des tournages « à partir de la position de l'ombre de l'architecture des arènes dans la *plaza*[3] ». L'ombre des bâtiments comme « indice » pour établir une chronologie… Une astuce digne d'un fin limier, à laquelle Lecointe aura une nouvelle fois recours, ici même, à propos du folioscope *Arrivée d'un train*. J'y reviendrai.

L'« enquêteur » Lecointe a plus d'un don, comme le lecteur pourra s'en rendre compte en consultant (si ce n'est en dévorant) le présent ouvrage. Il a l'art, comme tout bon détective, de faire parler ses sources, entre autres les personnages « de papier » qui figurent sur les images (elles aussi arrêtées) du « cinématographe de poche » de Léon Beaulieu – et qui sont des personnages « de papier » tout simplement parce que les « films » dont il est ici question ne sont pas couchés sur *film* mais sur *papier*, destinés qu'ils sont à être « visionnés » par feuilletage.

Des « films sur papier »… L'expression ne peut faire autrement que d'évoquer, pour tout spécialiste de la cinématographie des premiers temps, les fameux *paper prints* de la Library of Congress, ces images « réanimées » dans les années 1950 grâce à cet ancien détective (tiens, tiens…) qu'était Kemp Niver[4].

Je n'aurai pas besoin d'entrer ici dans le détail des multiples autres talents de Lecointe – qui conduit de main de maître l'« enquête » à laquelle il s'adonne dans le présent ouvrage, sur des « documents » qui sont, comme il l'écrit ici, « à la croisée des chemins entre film celluloïd, paper-print et livre » – puisque l'arrière-petit-fils de Méliès lui-même, Jacques Malthête, s'en charge dans l'« Introduction », lui qui, à l'instar notamment de sa mère Madeleine Malthête-Méliès, petite-fille du magicien de Montreuil, a tant fait pour restituer Méliès à l'histoire.

Ce qu'accomplit ici Lecointe (pareillement à Niver qui a su redonner vie à des images inertes), c'est une sorte de miracle qui consiste à ressusciter sous nos yeux, comme si c'était d'« entre les morts » – pour évoquer une œuvre littéraire dont la lecture donne froid dans le dos, jusqu'à en avoir le vertige (pour ne pas dire le « vertigo » ainsi que des sueurs (« froides » bien entendu[5]) –, des vues qui n'avaient justement pas été *vues* depuis longtemps, depuis très longtemps même, et dont (du moins pour une partie d'entre elles) nous ne soupçonnions même pas l'existence. Qui plus est, le travail de l'enquêteur Lecointe permet de révéler, de mettre au jour, une activité artistique et commerciale bien singulière du magicien de Montreuil. Oui, l'enquêteur Lecointe est un fin limier, mais au contraire du Scottie de Hitchcock, il n'a pas le vertige… C'est plutôt lui, et la spirale frénétique de son questionnement, qui donnent le vertige. Nous ne sommes malheureusement pas habitués à lire des ouvrages dont l'auteur – comme le fait ici Lecointe – affine constamment ses hypothèses, au fur et à mesure que nous avançons dans la lecture des résultats qu'il nous livre, sans hésiter surtout à y renoncer – ce pour quoi il mérite tout notre respect – lorsque ces mêmes résultats les invalident.

Combien d'« entre les morts » se retourneront d'ailleurs dans leur tombe à la sortie du présent ouvrage, je ne saurais le dire, mais ils seront nombreux. Car Thierry Lecointe nous fait part ici d'une découverte fabuleuse : il a en effet *arraché à l'oubli* les plus anciens « films » de Méliès ! Rien que cela ! Non pas qu'il ait découvert lui-même les *flip books* en question (c'est à Pascal Fouché que l'on doit dire merci pour cela). Ce n'est pas cela l'exploit de Lecointe. Le véritable tour de force de Lecointe, c'est d'avoir réussi à transformer ces témoins muets en informateurs loquaces, en allant même jusqu'à les « démonter […] pour en extraire d'éventuelles informations[6] », et en utilisant mille et une astuces pour leur faire rendre gorge, pour les forcer à lui rendre… Georges. Au nombre de ces astuces, certains types d'opérations que nous avions oubliées depuis l'école primaire et le collège : triangulation géométrique, plus petit commun multiple, mais aussi calcul de la focale, repérage et mesure des ombres portées pour déterminer la date et l'heure des tournages, j'en passe et des meilleures[7]. Tel un démiurge qui donne dans la transsubstantiation, Lecointe nous montre la recette qu'il faut suivre pour transformer progressivement une masse d'images arrêtées en des incunables incontournables, qui viennent se loger dans la filmographie du magicien de Montreuil. Avant Lecointe, on ignorait généralement que Méliès avait produit et réalisé des folioscopes, maintenant on le sait.

Lecointe n'est jamais à court de ressources pour satisfaire sa curiosité et son besoin d'aller au bout de ses intuitions. Qui plus est, il est – un peu comme Méliès – adepte d'une certaine forme de transformisme : il pratique lestement, lui aussi, substitutions, métamorphoses, apparitions et disparitions. Ainsi se saisit-il, en 2013, de la pièce à conviction n° 1, un *flip book* qui est connu sous le titre d'*Arrivée d'un train gare de Vincennes* et dont on pense qu'il POURRAIT ÊTRE la reproduction pour le folioscope, par Dieu sait qui (Méliès N'AYANT JAMAIS, pour autant qu'on sache, produit de folioscopes) d'une vue cinématographique qui, elle, POURRAIT ÊTRE de Méliès.

Après quelques-uns de ces tours de passe-passe dont il a le secret, il ébranle ces incertitudes. Et l'*Arrivée d'un train gare de Vincennes* se métamorphose subitement (rien dans les mains, rien dans les poches !) en… *Arrivée d'un train (gare de Joinville)*. D'un coup de baguette magique, la gare de Vincennes disparaît et c'est la gare de Joinville qui apparaît. Comme dans tout bon film de Méliès, un élément se substitue à un autre… et on peut désormais affirmer que cette vue EST de Méliès, que C'EST, bel et bien, une reproduction PAR Méliès pour le folioscope d'une de ses vues, PAR un Méliès dont on sait désormais qu'il A produit des folioscopes. Et pourtant, on ne cessait de dire sur toutes les tribunes que les images de ce *flip book* étaient trop mauvaises, qu'on n'arriverait jamais à prouver qu'elles étaient de Méliès. Conservateurs, archivistes et même une arrière-arrière-petite-fille de Méliès s'accordaient à considérer la tâche comme impossible[8]. Mais Lecointe, comme Méliès, était manifestement prêt à « réaliser l'impossible[9] ».

Les allusions à Hitchcock que j'ai faites jusqu'à maintenant pouvaient avoir l'air gratuites, mais n'est-il pas troublant de songer que Lecointe pense reconnaître Méliès qui ferait « une furtive apparition à la Hitchcock » sur le quai de la gare de Joinville-le-Pont, dans les premières secondes du même folioscope *Arrivée d'un train* ? En paraphrasant la terminologie de Lecointe, je dirais que j'attribue un degré de « confiance élevée » à la probabilité que ce pseudo-quidam qui ne se comporte pas du tout comme quelqu'un « attendant son train ou un passager » soit bel et bien Méliès lui-même, qui apparaît sur l'« écran » virtuel de ce « petit livre qu'on feuilletait très vite[10] » qu'est le folioscope montrant le quai de la gare de Joinville.

Je sais que dorénavant, quand je verrai un folioscope dans une brocante, la séquence suivante surgira immédiatement dans mon esprit : Lecointe/Proust/madeleine/Méliès. Un seul de ces quatre mots commence par une minuscule, mais il aurait pu tout aussi bien prendre lui aussi la majuscule… En effet, il y a, nous le savons tous, une Madeleine chez notre *fabricant de photographies animées* de prédilection, mais il y en a une aussi chez le *fabricant de suspenses angoissants* dont j'ai évoqué plus haut l'une des œuvres.

Dans *Vertigo*, la vue de Judy a sur Scottie le même effet que le goût des madeleines sur Proust : voir Judy ramène au souvenir de Scottie sa Madeleine à lui (fût-elle une fausse Madeleine puisqu'elle s'appelle en fait Judy Barton et qu'elle a naguère personnifié – autre substitution – Madeleine Elster, que son mari a assassinée et qui semble être revenue d'*entre les morts* sous l'apparence de Judy).

Jacques et les autres proches de Madeleine me pardonneront de dire ici que notre Madeleine « à nous », les férus de Méliès, si elle était encore parmi nous, aurait peut-être pu – elle qui, ayant été élevée par lui, le connaissait jusque dans ses mouvements les plus subtils – garantir à Lecointe que c'était bien son grand-père qui jouait au quidam sur le quai de la gare de Joinville…

Ce qui aurait pu permettre à Lecointe, qui considère l'*Arrivée d'un train* comme un « probable Méliès – confiance élevée », de passer ainsi à un « confirmé Méliès ». Et de lever le voile sur un Méliès qui est un « transformiste » impénitent, lui qui substitue tout à son contraire et inversement et qui n'a pas à revenir d'entre les morts pour continuer à nous jouer de sacrés tours. On en découvre régulièrement, et la liste est longue des trucs qu'on réussit à « débiner[11] » au fur et à mesure des années qui égrènent les décennies qui nous séparent de la disparition de Georges, et dont le plus récent, à ce que je sache, concerne un film qui n'a pas subsisté, et qui (s'il a vraiment existé) daterait de 1896. En effet, en transformiste impénitent, qui veut constamment nous faire prendre des vessies pour des lanternes, Méliès nous fait croire depuis des lustres que c'est sur la place de l'Opéra, à Paris, qu'il aurait été frappé d'une illumination soudaine[12] :

> Veut-on savoir comment me vint la première idée d'appliquer le truc au cinématographe ? Bien simplement, ma foi. Un bloquage de l'appareil dont je me servais au début […] produisit un effet inattendu, un jour que je photographiais prosaïquement la place de l'Opéra : une minute fut nécessaire pour débloquer la pellicule et remettre l'appareil en marche. Pendant cette minute, les passants, omnibus, voitures, avaient changé de place, bien entendu. En projetant la bande […], je vis subitement un omnibus Madeleine-Bastille changé en corbillard et des hommes changés en femmes. Le truc par substitution, dit *truc à arrêt*, était trouvé […]

Or, tel ne serait peut-être pas le cas, comme je l'ai annoncé en 2018[13]. Certains indices nous permettent en effet de penser, Jacques Malthête et moi, que ce serait en effet plutôt sur la *place Saint-Augustin* que Méliès aurait vécu son fameux épisode du blocage de l'appareil, si tant est que l'événement soit vraiment survenu[14]. Dans la chaîne des paroles que prononce Méliès, la « place Saint-Augustin » disparaît et c'est la « place de l'Opéra » qui apparaît, la plus connue des deux places (la plus *glamour* aussi) se substituant ainsi à une place parisienne qui a eu, elle aussi, le privilège d'apparaître dans le catalogue de Méliès et, tenez-vous bien, pas n'importe où dans ce catalogue, puisqu'elle « apparaît » tout juste avant (au n° 69) le tout premier film à trucs de Méliès, *Escamotage d'une dame chez Robert-Houdin* (au n° 70)… Ceci pouvant peut-être expliquer cela.

Un dernier mot concernant l'ouvrage de Lecointe sur les folioscopes : cet ouvrage n'est pas un *flip book* – ce « petit livre qu'on feuillet[te] très vite » –, ce qui n'empêche pas qu'on puisse le qualifier de « flippant[15] » et qu'il se lise du début à la fin « comme un roman », comme un… *page-turner* captivant.

J'ajouterai pour finir une simple remarque : son travail de détective ès *paper prints* a valu à Kemp Niver un Oscar d'honneur, qui lui a été remis en 1955 pour avoir mis au point un procédé qui a permis de « ressusciter » les films sur support papier déposés auprès de la Library of Congress[16]. Peut-être la France devrait-elle rendre à César ce qui lui appartient, et honorer Madeleine (à titre posthume), ainsi que, dans un même mouvement, Jacques et Thierry, qui se sont tant évertués à faire revenir Georges d'entre les morts...

Notes

1. Cf. leur production, dans les années 1880, de millions de plaques photographiques de la marque « Étiquette bleue ».

2. On trouve notamment trois exemples de ces panoramas dans son article intitulé « Les tournages multi-caméras chez Lumière », publié dans François Albera, Marta Braun et André Gaudreault (dir.), *Arrêt sur image, fragmentation du temps. Aux sources de la culture visuelle moderne/Stop Motion, Fragmentation of Time: Exploring the Roots of Modern Visual Culture*, Lausanne, Payot Lausanne, 2002, p. 271–296.

3. *Ibid.*, p. 282.

4. Selon Paul Spehr et Erik Barnouw, qui signent respectivement l'avant-propos et l'introduction de l'ouvrage de Kemp Niver publié en 1985 ; voir Paul Spehr, « Foreword », et Erik Barnouw « Introduction », dans Kemp R. Niver, *Early Motion Pictures: The Paper Print Collection in the Library of Congress*, Washington, Library of Congress, 1985, p. vii et xv.

5. Je fais évidemment allusion ici au livre écrit par Pierre Boileau et Pierre Ayraud, dit Thomas Narcejac (Boileau-Narcejac, *D'entre les morts*, Paris, Denoël, 1954), dont le film d'Hitchcock *Sueurs froides* (*Vertigo*, 1958) est l'adaptation.

6. Ainsi démonte-t-il page par page un exemplaire abîmé et incomplet d'un folioscope d'*Arrivée d'un train* qui lui appartient, afin de « confirmer que le flip book est constitué chez l'imprimeur de bandes de onze photogrammes juxtaposés, parfaitement alignés de gauche à droite ».

7. Amis lecteurs, le saviez-vous, vous, que l'ombre portée par un élément d'architecture donne deux dates, et seulement deux, de tournage possibles au cours d'une même année civile ? Saviez-vous que l'orientation et la longueur d'une ombre permettent même de connaître l'heure approximative d'un tournage ?

8. « [...] film preservationists, archivists, and even a Méliès' descendant thinks *it's an almost impossible task* » (Maane Khatchatourian, « George Melies Flip Book Sets off Crowdsourcing », *Variety*, 24 juillet 2013, https://variety.com/2013/film/global/george-melies-flip-book-sets-off-crowdsourcing-1200564564).

9. « [...] il n'y a pas à dire, il faut absolument *réaliser l'impossible* [...] » (Georges Méliès, dans André Gaudreault, *Cinéma et attraction. Pour une nouvelle histoire du cinématographe*, suivi de *Les vues cinématographiques* (1907) de Georges Méliès, éditées par Jacques Malthête, Paris, CNRS Éditions, 2008, p. 203 ; souligné dans le texte).

10. *Dixit* la seconde épouse de Méliès, Jehanne d'Alcy, citée ici même par Jacques Malthête dans l'Introduction.

11. On sait que Méliès était partisan du secret des magiciens et que, à son avis, un véritable professionnel de la magie se devait d'être discret à cet égard. Il veillait donc à ne jamais « débine[r] le truc » (Georges Méliès, dans André Gaudreault, *op. cit.*, p. 217).

12. *Ibid.*, p. 213–214.

13. Dans une communication intitulée « Que n'a-t-on pas dit sur le fameux épisode du blocage de l'appareil sur la place de l'Opéra (point d'interrogation et point d'exclamation) » présentée à Paris, en mars 2018, au colloque *Truquer, créer, innover. Les effets spéciaux français* (dont les actes paraîtront en 2021).

14. Découverte faite avec la complicité de Stéphane Tralongo, que je remercie.

15. Au sens de « [q]ui étonne, voir[e] frappe de stupeur » (https://dicocitations.lemonde.fr/dico-mot-definition/62704/flippant.php).

16. « Long months of effort finally established the feasibility of the project. New negatives – then projection prints – *could* be made from the paper rolls. The old films could, in short, be brought back from the dead. [...] For his mutiple role in the restoration miracle, Niver received an Oscar » (Erik Barnouw, « Introduction », dans Kemp R. Niver, *Early Motion Pictures, op. cit.*, p. xv–xvi) ; on remarquera ici le recours à l'expression « back from the dead », qui évoque le titre du livre de Boileau-Narcejac et celui du présent article...

Le flip book, un objet singulier entre livre et cinéma

Pascal Fouché

Il est fort probable que nos ancêtres aient depuis longtemps effeuillé une suite de dessins pour les voir s'animer, mais ce n'est qu'en 1868 que le premier brevet qui industrialise le flip book a été déposé par un imprimeur anglais, John Barnes Linnett. D'autres suivront dans différents pays, mais le principe variera peu et les flip books édités de nos jours sont encore très proches de ce qu'ils étaient au XIXe siècle : un carnet de petit format qui se tient d'une main et se feuillette de l'autre pour donner aux images reproduites en séquence l'illusion du mouvement.

Les premiers sont illustrés de dessins mais la photographie et le cinéma vont être rapidement exploités. Les découvertes d'Etienne-Jules Marey et d'Eadweard Muybridge autour de la chronophotographie et la naissance du cinéma deviennent des sources inépuisables pour la production de nouveaux flip books.

Des extraits des films des pionniers du cinéma sont déclinés en flip books dès le XIXe siècle, notamment de l'américain Thomas Edison et de l'allemand Max Skladanowsky, qui les éditent eux-mêmes, ou du français Léon Gaumont dont on connaît des exemplaires possédant son copyright. Le flip book est muet comme ces premiers films, il en est donc un reflet parfait. Par la suite on utilisera plus facilement des scènes cultes où on se servira du flip book comme produit dérivé ou objet promotionnel pour accompagner le lancement d'un film. C'est ainsi qu'il existe des flip books pour pratiquement tous les films produits par Disney.

Mais le cinéma n'est qu'un des nombreux sujets que le flip book couvre. Souvent considéré comme un jouet, il vise alors un public d'enfants avec fréquemment un dessin assez épuré et un format qui facilite le feuilletage. Pour les adultes, il sert rapidement de cadeau publicitaire pour vanter les marques ou les produits et de

© Onno Petersen – Collection Pascal Fouché.

155

manuel d'apprentissage pour de très nombreux sports afin de montrer le swing idéal ou la meilleure façon de réussir un home run… Tous les sportifs mythiques ont au moins un flip book qui célèbre leurs exploits.

Les sujets d'actualité, les anniversaires d'événements marquants servent aussi souvent de prétextes à la réalisation de flip books et l'érotisme, exploitant notamment le dévoilement progressif du corps, a également inspiré les fabricants.

En outre, depuis la fin du XIXe siècle, de nombreux ouvrages de tous les genres comportent aussi en bord de pages des dessins ou des photos qui peuvent être feuilletés comme un complément d'illustration sur le sujet du livre ou un atout supplémentaire pour séduire son public.

Dès les années 1950, les artistes se sont à leur tour appropriés le flip book rivalisant d'imagination quant aux techniques, aux formats ou aux reliures de leurs œuvres. Enfin l'Internet a, cent ans après l'invention du cinéma, ouvert de nouvelles possibilités en permettant à tout un chacun de placer des dessins ou des photos qu'il suffit d'imprimer pour les assembler et constituer son flip book.

L'ensemble constitue un univers extrêmement varié car le flip book a la particularité d'être intemporel et universel. On en trouve dans tous les pays sous divers noms (flick ou flicker book au Royaume-Uni, daumenkino en Allemagne, para para book au Japon, etc.) où, comme ils ne comportent le plus souvent que très peu de textes, ils sont compris par tous. Les québécois et parfois les français ont adopté le terme folioscope qui est à l'origine une marque inventée par un marchand de jouets français à la fin du XIXe siècle. Ce terme a l'inconvénient, étymologiquement, de n'avoir aucun rapport avec l'objet qu'il veut nommer.

Les enfants apprécient les ateliers qui leur permettent d'en fabriquer eux-mêmes ce qui constitue une excellente introduction aux mystères de l'animation et du cinéma. Parfois informatif, toujours ludique, le flip book est fait pour surprendre ; en quelques secondes il doit raconter une histoire et, selon qu'on le feuillette plus ou moins rapidement, il peut aussi révéler des détails qui ont échappé au premier coup d'œil.

Le flip book est un objet fragile, de ceux que l'on qualifie d'éphémères, car plus il a été feuilleté plus il est potentiellement abîmé, c'est pourquoi il est difficile de trouver les plus anciens en bon état ; c'est aussi le signe qu'ils ont été très utilisés. C'est le cas de nombre de ceux de la fin du XIXe siècle et particulièrement de ces extraits de films qui, pour une bonne part, ne sont pas identifiés et peuvent constituer la trace unique de films aujourd'hui disparus.

Cette première tentative, menée conjointement par Thierry Lecointe et Robert Byrne, pour en identifier certains ouvre peut-être la voie à des découvertes inestimables.

Introduction

Jacques Malthête

Au tournant du siècle dernier, un marchand de bimbeloterie, Léon Beaulieu (1857–1901), faisait commerce de petits carnets de photographies dont le feuilletage faisait bouger, comme au cinéma, les trains et les personnages qui y figuraient. Cela se passait à Paris, disons entre 1896 et 1901. Beaucoup de ces folioscopes (Beaulieu les avait baptisés *cinématographes de poche*, Pascal Fouché préférant le terme *flip book*) se trouvent aujourd'hui dans des collections privées, dont celle de Pascal Fouché, auteur ici d'une biographie de Beaulieu. La présente étude, menée principalement et brillamment par Thierry Lecointe, porte sur 27 folioscopes Beaulieu appartenant à cette collection, à laquelle viennent s'ajouter quelques exemplaires du même fabricant issus des collections de François Binétruy, Carlo Montanaro et Thierry Lecointe.

En analysant un tel corpus, outre quelques folioscopes dont les images sont attribués à Pathé, Edison, Skladanowsky et Gaumont, Lecointe a cru reconnaître une vingtaine de films de Georges Méliès après un long et minutieux cheminement, et au prix d'une analyse serrée et systématique, pour ne pas dire scientifique, qui l'a conduit à des hypothèses très solidement argumentées. Par exemple, en classant les folioscopes en plusieurs catégories selon le nombre de feuillets – avec un maximum de 121 – et suivant le sens de feuilletage – d'avant en arrière ou inversement –, Lecointe est arrivé à cerner certaines des caractéristiques essentielles de la production de Beaulieu.

Cela dit, comme on le sait, administrer la preuve n'est pas toujours chose facile quand il s'agit d'attribuer, comme ici à Méliès, par exemple, ce qui de prime abord pourrait être une reproduction partielle d'un de ses films.

Lecointe est un chasseur d'indices très talentueux : une carte postale lui fait découvrir une vue de la gare où s'arrête le train qu'un folioscope anime, l'orientation et la longueur d'une ombre lui donnent la saison et l'heure approximative d'une prise de vue en plein air, un élément de décor, un costume vus dans un folioscope se retrouvent dans un film sauvegardé de Méliès ou dans une photographie de promotion d'un de ses films perdus ...

Malheureusement, la mauvaise qualité des photogrammes reproduits par photogravure (présence d'un gros tramage et d'un renforcement à l'encre de certains contours) rend l'identification des personnages un peu hasardeuse. Grâce à la remise en mouvement des photogrammes – numérisés par Onno Petersen et réanimés par Robert Byrne –, on peut néanmoins arriver à estomper l'effet du tramage et espérer ainsi reconnaître la gestuelle sinon le visage d'un acteur ou d'une actrice connus, comme Georges Méliès, Jehanne d'Alcy ou Élise De Vère.

Une vingtaine de folioscopes ont pu être ainsi considérés comme provenant de films de Méliès jusque-là inconnus. On mesure évidemment l'énorme intérêt de cette découverte. Les arguments sont nombreux pour étayer ce postulat, mais, pour ma part et en ce qui concerne précisément les personnages, je crois ne vraiment reconnaître Méliès que dans un seul flip book, *Pose chez l'artiste. Vénus*. Dans *Nuit agitée*, c'est apparemment aussi lui (avec une fausse barbe blanche) qui joue, dans un costume similaire à celui du film sauvegardé correspondant, *Une nuit terrible*. Par sa taille et sa gestuelle, Jehanne d'Alcy est à peu près sûrement présente dans *Le Coucher de la mariée* et très probablement dans *La Puce* et *Le Bain*. Pour le reste, on retrouve ici un lit, là un élément de décor, ailleurs encore une pièce d'habillement présents dans un film sauvegardé de Méliès ou sur l'une de ses photographies de promotion conservées dans un fonds d'archives.

À présent se pose la question du statut matériel de la source filmique. Concernant la vingtaine de folioscopes supposés provenir d'un film de Méliès, il se trouve qu'aucun d'entre eux ne correspond précisément à un film sauvegardé. S'appuyant sur un certain nombre de considérations, Lecointe fait l'hypothèse que certains proviendraient d'une première version dont ils ne constitueraient bizarrement que la seule trace.

L'exemple du folioscope *Nuit agitée* fait partie d'un des rares doublons qui permettent d'illustrer toute la démarche de Lecointe, car son frère jumeau, le film de Méliès, *Une nuit terrible*, est sauvegardé. Les scénarios sont certes identiques, mais avec toutefois des différences notables. D'abord les durées : *Une nuit terrible* mesure 20 mètres, soit une minute à 16 images par seconde, alors que le folioscope est constitué de 121 photogrammes seulement, ce qui correspond à une longueur de pellicule de 2 m 30, soit 10 secondes selon la cadence du folioscope restituée (12 images par seconde). Déjà, il est assez remarquable d'arriver à faire tenir dans un temps aussi court l'essentiel d'une action développée en 60 secondes dans le film. Comme si Méliès tourné cette version en s'arrangeant pour ramasser l'action principale, le gag, en une dizaine de secondes en vue d'une version folioscope. Cette bande spéciale mesurait peut-être également 20 mètres, peut-être même un peu moins, dans laquelle a été prélevé le fragment destiné au folioscope.

L'autre différence notable (sans parler de la caméra moins proche du sol dans le film, de la tête de lit à gauche dans le film, à droite dans le flip book, la table de nuit et la chaise du film transformées en tabourets dans le folioscope, avec le pot de chambre posé sur le tabouret de droite alors qu'il est à gauche dans le film) est la présence d'un fond noir, comme dans les vues de Marey et d'Edison. Cette caractéristique particulière est pour Lecointe un argument en faveur de l'antériorité de la version folioscope. On peut en effet comprendre l'usage du fond noir pour faire ressortir les personnages lorsque l'éclairage est moyen et la pellicule peu sensible, mais alors pourquoi Méliès aurait-il refait le même film la même année (1896), et peut-être même à quelques jours d'intervalle, en abandonnant le fond noir ? Toujours est-il que, si l'on se fie à ses films sauvegardés, il ne l'emploiera que dans ses films à surimpressions. Par ailleurs, dans les films à fond noir qu'on lui attribue à partir des folioscopes, il n'y a paradoxalement aucune surimpression, ni, du reste, aucun trucage. Était-ce un choix délibéré de sa part, si tant est que le corpus étudié ici est représentatif de la production des folioscopes Méliès ?

Il est étonnant qu'aucun texte connu de Méliès, ni aucun de ses entretiens retranscrits, ne mentionne cette activité singulière. Nous disposons d'un seul témoignage, celui de sa seconde épouse, Jehanne d'Alcy, qui a déclaré lors d'une séance de la Commission de recherches historiques de la Cinémathèque française (17 juin 1944) :

> M. Langlois.– Il [Méliès] a fait toutes les choses de Lumière, d'après le catalogue, et il a commencé à faire toutes les scènes jouées très vite.
>
> [...].
>
> Mme Méliès.– Il a fait *Le Bain de la Parisienne* et le petit livre qu'on feuilletait très vite.

On aura compris que ces folioscopes issus du cinéma naissant sont loin d'avoir livré tous leurs secrets. C'est un dossier complet et passionnant qui attend à présent le lecteur, avec ses trouvailles, ses interrogations, ses hypothèses séduisantes et ses conclusions hardies.

Le « cinématographe de poche » de Léon Beaulieu (1896–1901) : des fragments de films Méliès (et autres) disparus ressuscités par des flip books

Thierry Lecointe avec la collaboration de Pascal Fouché

À l'origine, il y en avait vingt-quatre…
© Onno Petersen – Collection Pascal Fouché.

En cherchant bien, ils sont vingt-sept !
© Onno Petersen – Collection Pascal Fouché.

Préambule :
comment la recherche est née

Bernhard Richter et sa fille Sara ont découvert en Allemagne, dans une librairie spécialisée en livres anciens, un flip book[1] montrant l'arrivée d'un train en gare. Il s'agit d'un petit livret composé d'une succession de pages, constituées de photographies, lesquelles, se feuilletant avec le pouce ou un appareillage adapté restituent les mouvements d'un train arrivant en gare, des passagers descendant des voitures et de ceux déambulant sur le quai. Bernhard Richter, co-fondateur avec Kobold d'une société d'animation – Kobold CharakterAnimation – pris contact avec Mme Maane Khatchatourian, journaliste au magazine Variety de Los-Angeles, afin de diffuser l'information selon laquelle ce flip book, réalisé à partir de photographies, serait peut-être issu d'un film Méliès réputé disparu. Il s'agissait à ce moment-là de lancer un appel à recherches collaboratives via le web. Selon les Richter, ce film pourrait être *Arrivée d'un train (gare de Vincennes)*. Mme Khatchatourian prit soin de contacter, préalablement à l'édition de son article, les spécialistes français de Méliès les plus connus, des archivistes américains ainsi qu'une association internationale – Domitor[2] – regroupant essentiellement des universitaires spécialistes du cinéma dit « des premiers temps ». Son objectif était de valider ou à défaut de préciser les hypothèses émises par les propriétaires du flip book. Les contacts par e-mail avec Domitor eurent lieu le 16 juillet 2013 pour une parution en webmagazine prévue dès le lendemain, mercredi 17 juillet. L'article en question est accessible en version électronique, daté *in fine* du 24 juillet 2013 à 12:28 PM PT (Pacific Time, fuseau horaire de Los-Angeles).[3] En tant que membre de Domitor, j'ai eu accès au problème posé. La communauté des chercheurs de Domitor fut très active pendant les deux à trois mois suivants au sein de son réseau. Malgré cette euphorie autour de nouvelles perspectives en matière de recherches, il n'en ressortait que très peu d'éléments pragmatiques supposés établir au moins des pistes d'investigation, faute de pouvoir apporter quelques certitudes. L'exaltation retomba face aux difficultés d'identification et sans avoir accès au livret lui-même. À la lecture de l'article de Maane Khatchatourian les avis, impressions et en fin de compte la perplexité des spécialistes qu'elle interrogea furent analogues à celles des Domitorians. Elle écrivait donc en préambule qu'en matière d'identification, « les conservateurs, les archivistes et même un descendant de Méliès pensent que c'est une tâche presque impossible ». Ainsi, Jan-Christopher Horak, directeur de UCLA Film & Television Archive, a déclaré « qu'il ne pouvait attribuer le film avec confiance ni aux frères Lumière ni à Méliès en raison de l'absence de signalisation, du quai indiscernable et du fond flou des images ». Pauline Duclaud-Lacoste, une arrière-arrière-petite-fille de Méliès a mentionné « qu'elle était sceptique quant à l'attribution du film à Méliès car il était un partisan convaincu de la nouveauté » (supposant que cette arrivée de train s'inscrivait dans une déjà très longue liste d'arrivées de trains filmées par de nombreux producteurs dont Lumière entre autres [il y a pourtant deux arrivées de train dans la filmographie Méliès]). Serge Bromberg, producteur de Lobster films, éditeur du remarquable coffret Méliès en six DVD, restaurateur d'une version couleur, parmi d'autres qui n'ont pas survécu, du *Voyage dans la Lune* et récemment des *Contes merveilleux de Méliès en couleurs*,[4] a déclaré « qu'il n'y avait qu'une chance sur cent d'identifier avec précision l'origine du livre parce que sa qualité d'image était médiocre, ainsi que l'absence d'indice de contexte et des marques traditionnelles Méliès ». Quant à Jacques Malthête, répondant à Maane Khatchatourian dans un mail du 27 juillet 2013, il expliqua :

> À ma connaissance, ces films [les deux arrivées de train] ne sont pas conservés et il ne semble pas qu'il en existe encore des copies. Par conséquent, il est impossible de comparer la version flip book avec un document incontestablement identifié parmi la production de Méliès.
>
> De plus, il faut savoir que, parmi les premiers cinématographistes, beaucoup ont pris de telles arrivées de trains (Lumière, Pathé, Normandin...), donc – encore une fois – il est assez difficile, voire même impossible, d'attribuer ce flip book à Méliès.
>
> Peut-être deux pistes possibles : 1 – Présence de Méliès sur le quai ? En fait, il apparaît souvent dans ses films, mais la qualité optique de la vidéo YouTube n'est pas suffisante pour vérifier cette possibilité. 2 – Photographies et cartes postales éditées autour de 1900 montrant les gares de Vincennes et de Joinville afin de les comparer avec ce que l'on voit dans le flip book, mais ces gares ont très bien pu être filmées par d'autres cinéastes.
>
> Cela dit, il n'est pas assuré que ces deux gares mentionnées dans le catalogue Méliès soient réellement celles de Vincennes et de Joinville. Par exemple, il est pratiquement certain qu'un autre film de 1896, *Les Quais de Marseille*, n° 29, n'a pas été tourné à Marseille, mais sur la côte normande.[5]

Malgré un contexte compliqué et le scepticisme général, trois personnes continuèrent à s'intéresser à la question au-delà des premières difficultés rencontrées. Pascal Duclaud-Lacoste installé à Bruxelles, le père de Pauline, prit contact avec les Richter afin de numériser et animer les images du flip book pour en extraire quelques éventuels indices. Jean-Pierre Sirois-Trahan, membre de Domitor, professeur titulaire au département de littérature, théâtre et cinéma de l'université Laval à Québec, historien de Méliès,[6] continua à entretenir des échanges sur le sujet avec les quelques Domitorians encore impliqués. En ce qui me concerne, chercheur indépendant, au regard des images révélées par le flip book, je déterminais de prime abord que plusieurs indices permettraient sans doute de localiser la gare.

Mais plus encore, au-delà de cette arrivée de train, j'imaginais que ce flip book (dont le fabricant, Léon Beaulieu, était d'ores-et-déjà connu car mentionné par les Richter) devait appartenir à une production plus complète. Et si c'était le cas, peut-être allions-nous découvrir et identifier d'autres films appartenant à un corpus Méliès ou autres. Je me mis en quête de rechercher sur internet d'autres flip books Beaulieu. Le moteur de recherche aidant, avec des mots clés sélectionnés, m'amena sur le blog de Pascal Fouché,[7] collectionneur de flip books, historien, installé à Paris, propriétaire d'autres exemplaires de Léon Beaulieu. Je diffusais cette information me paraissant capitale à la communauté Domitor le 15 août 2013. Pour des raisons de visibilité professionnelle et institutionnelle, ce fut Jean-Pierre Sirois-Trahan qui prit contact avec Pascal Fouché. Pascal Duclaud-Lacoste eut de son côté la même idée, se focalisant sur l'arrivée du train, désirant ainsi obtenir une meilleure version du flip book que celle détenue par les Richter. Il entra donc également en contact avec lui, le premier d'ailleurs. Pascal Fouché et le réseau Domitor fédérèrent en quelque sorte la relation entre nous quatre. Nous ne remercierons jamais assez Pascal Fouché pour sa collaboration, le prêt de ses très rares livrets et la confiance qu'il a témoignée envers des personnes qui lui étaient complètement inconnues. C'est aussi à l'ensemble de la communauté des collectionneurs privés que vont nos remerciements car sans eux bon nombre de recherches ne pourrait avoir cours tant la conservation et la préservation des matériaux sont capitales pour les chercheurs.

La coopération ainsi établie, Pascal Duclaud-Lacoste procéda à la numérisation et à l'animation d'une version complète de cette *Arrivée du train*, prêtée par Pascal Fouché, de manière remarquable (il numérisa trois autres flip books par la suite de cette collection). Par ailleurs, des recherches documentaires furent effectuées par Pascal Fouché sur le personnage Beaulieu, Jean-Pierre Sirois-Trahan et moi-même nous chargeant de celles sur la filmographie Méliès. Nos échanges allaient durer deux années produisant quelques avancées. Cependant, les liens tissés se dénouèrent d'eux-mêmes sans heurt. Des positions professionnelles peu compatibles en terme de calendrier et de disponibilité, de futures attentes éditoriales s'avérant divergentes et des orientations dogmatiques trop discordantes entre certains sont sans doute à l'origine de la clôture de notre groupe de travail en été 2015.

En octobre 2017, lors du festival du film muet de Pordenone, au hasard des discussions entretenues avec divers historiens, j'allais établir un contact, grâce aux relations et l'intervention de Sabine Lenk, avec Robert Byrne, directeur du San Francisco Silent Film Festival. Cette aventure, alors en sommeil, allait peut-être de nouveau être relancée. Après une première rencontre à Paris entre Pascal Fouché, Robert Byrne et moi le mardi 14 novembre 2017, l'étude du corpus Beaulieu pris un nouveau départ. C'est ainsi que 13 flip books numérisés par le photographe hollandais Onno Petersen et réanimés par Robert Byrne furent projetés pour la toute première fois au public lors du 24ème San Francisco Silent Film Festival le 2 mai 2019. Du 5 au 12 octobre 2019, 24 flip books, qui composaient alors l'intégralité du corpus, furent projetés à Pordenone lors des 38èmes Giornate del cinema muto.

Notes

1. Comme le rappelle Pascal Fouché, nous utiliserons le terme « flip book » pour désigner les matériaux étudiés malgré la récente position ou recommandation émise par la Commission d'enrichissement de la langue française concernant des équivalents français à utiliser pour des termes ou expressions en langue étrangère dans le domaine de la culture (édition, médias et mode), préconisant le nom masculin « folioscope ». Voir « Avis et communications, avis divers », dans le *Journal officiel* du 25 juin 2019, texte 103. Pascal Fouché précise que « folioscope » (une marque à l'origine, tout comme « frigidaire » ou « mobylette ») est composé d'une racine latine « folio », ablatif de *folium*, « feuille » et du terme « scope », du grec *skopein*, « observer » et veut donc dire littéralement « observer une feuille », ce qui ne rend pas du tout compte de l'objet qu'on a entre les mains contrairement aux autres mots en scope comme stéthoscope (observer la poitrine) ou périscope (observer autour). On consultera la page du blog de Pascal Fouché sur ce point : http://www.flipbook.info/blog.php publiée le 30 juin 2019 à 23:51:53.

2. Domitor, The International Society for the Study of Early Cinema : https://domitor.org/fr/

3. https://variety.com/2013/film/global/george-melies-flip-book-sets-off-crowdsourcing-1200564564/ Cf. annexe 1.

4. Sortis respectivement en septembre 2010, mai 2011 et janvier 2019.

5. Il n'y a effectivement aucune trace d'un passage de Méliès à Marseille à ses tout débuts de tourneurs. Par ailleurs, il s'agit de l'unique vue de Marseille, ce qui paraît pour le moins étonnant. Néanmoins, l'intitulé de cette vue est récurrente dans les différents catalogues (encore identifiée dans le catalogue américain 1905 comme *The Docks at Marseille*). Jacques Malthête se veut moins affirmatif aujourd'hui à la relecture des « Mémoires » de Georges Méliès rédigés en 1936 (voir, par exemple *Georges Méliès, la vie et l'œuvre d'un pionnier du cinéma*, établie et présentée par Jean-Pierre Sirois-Trahan, Les Éditions du Sonneur, 2012, p. 101). En effet, Méliès y cite « les docks de Marseille » parmi ses vues de 1896, qu'on rangera plus tard dans la catégorie de la *cinématographie éducative*. Jacques Malthête ajoute que si Méliès « prend la peine de citer ce film dans cette catégorie, après 40 ans, c'est probablement parce qu'il avait été tourné sur place, à Marseille ». Un tournage en septembre-octobre 1896 (par un représentant, voire un client de Méliès) est peut-être envisageable, à une époque où les kinétographes fabriqués par Méliès et son associé Reulos commencent à être vendus mais dont les développements et tirages des épreuves semblent revenir à l'entreprise de Méliès. Méliès aurait pu intégrer cette vue dans son catalogue comme c'est le cas chez d'autres producteurs. Rappelons que le brevet français n° 259.444 délivré le 4 septembre 1896 pour MM. Korsten, Méliès et Reulos est libellé : « *Appareil destiné à prendre et à projeter les photographies animées* », *l'appareil se voulait donc réversible*. De la même manière, j'ai toujours eu l'intuition que la vue n° 91 *Défilé de pompiers* a été enregistrée à Nîmes (diffusée le 28 décembre 1896 dans cette ville) par un tourneur indépendant Ferdinand Itier, photographe, qui utilisait dès décembre 1896 un kinétographe Méliès (sa filmographie est constituée de vues Méliès et de vues locales dont les tirages positifs ne semblent pas avoir été de son ressort).

6. – Georges Méliès, *La vie et l'œuvre d'un pionnier du cinéma*, coll. « La petite collection », édition établie et présentée par Jean-Pierre Sirois-Trahan, Paris, Les Éditions du Sonneur, 2012 ;

   – Georges Méliès, *Écrits sur la magie et le cinéma*, édition établie et présentée par Jean-Pierre Sirois-Trahan, Paris, P.U.F., 2013 ;

   – « Les relations entre Pathé et Méliès : aux sources du cinéma industriel et du cinéma indépendant (1908–1913) », *Cinéma & Cie. International Film Studies Journal*, nouvelle série, vol. XIII, n° 21, automne 2013, pp. 95–107 ;

   – « La scène réfractée au travers de la lentille de Georges Méliès », *Méliès, carrefour des attractions, suivi de Correspondance de Georges Méliès (1904–1937)*, André Gaudreault et Laurent Le Forestier (dir.) et Stéphane Tralongo (coll.), Cerisy-la-Salle/Rennes, Colloque de Cerisy/Presses Universitaires de Rennes, 2014, pp. 189–199.

7. Voir « Le blog de Pascal Fouché – Flipbook.info » : http://www.flipbook.info/index.php

Arrivée du train [collection P. Fouché] ou *Arrivée d'un train en gare* [collection F. Binétruy], (121 photogrammes) : enquête, analyse et résultat

© Onno Petersen – Collection Pascal Fouché.

C'est une relative méconnaissance de l'histoire du cinéma des premiers temps qui amena les Richter sur la piste de Méliès. En effet, sur leur page YouTube du 12 juillet 2013,[1] parmi l'argumentaire développé en onze points, l'un d'eux annonce : « à l'époque en question entre 1895–1898 il y a seulement deux fameux films connus montrant une arrivée de train. Un par Lumière et l'autre par Méliès. Nous savons que ce n'est pas l'arrivée du train par les Lumière ». Ils ajoutèrent que « parmi d'autres films, Méliès montra "Arrivée d'un train gare de Vincennes" en 1896 ». La piste Méliès avec son « arrivée en gare de Vincennes » ne tenait donc qu'à cela.

Le flip book des Richter mis en ligne sur YouTube et simplement feuilleté avec le pouce montrait d'emblée des images dont quelques détails allaient orienter mes recherches. La locomotive à vapeur paraissait être assez facilement identifiable. Les wagons à double étages étaient à priori d'un modèle très spécifique susceptible de ne pas être utilisé sur toutes les lignes de chemin de fer. La géographie des lieux (forme du quai, courbure de la voie, nombre de voies, architecture et mobilier urbain du quai en vis-à-vis, urbanisation réduite, feston d'un toit au niveau du quai, position de la gare par rapport aux voies) allait permettre – au moins – d'exclure quelques gares de nos investigations. L'ombre portée au sol par le toit allait être capitale pour trouver l'orientation géographique de la voie ferrée.

La numérisation en haute résolution et l'animation des flip books étaient indispensables dans notre entreprise de recherche. La numérisation des images allait nous permettre de visualiser des détails par agrandissement des photogrammes. L'animation du film à partir des images numérisées, recadrées afin d'être stabilisées, allait permettre d'obtenir une lecture visuelle mieux définie du lieu (selon le principe de la persistance rétinienne). Par ailleurs un défilement régulier des images allait peut-être révéler des indices imperceptibles lors d'un feuilletage ou d'une exploitation unitaire des photogrammes.

Parallèlement à ces orientations techniques, il convenait aussi de lister les films des premiers temps montrant diverses arrivées de train filmés par les producteurs cinématographiques afin de comparer films, ou à défaut lieux, et les images du flip book. Ainsi, nous savons que :

> - Lumière filma deux arrivées, l'une à Lyon-Perrache, l'autre à La Ciotat ;
>
> - Pathé en filma deux voire trois, l'une en gare de Bel-Air à Paris, une autre en gare de Saint-Mandé (selon des comptes rendus de presse uniquement) et une autre sur la ligne d'Auteuil de la compagnie des chemins de fer de l'Ouest ;[2]
>
> - Gaumont filma *Station du Pont Marcadet, chemin de fer du Nord - Le Chemin de fer de ceinture, station de Ménilmontant – Arrivée d'un train en gare d'Auteuil – Entrée d'un train en gare de Juvisy* ;
>
> - Joly-Normandin enregistra deux vues *Arrivée d'un train en gare d'Asnières – Arrivée d'un train en gare de Paris Bel-Air* ;
>
> - G. W. De Bedts en proposa deux selon des comptes rendus de presse, la première *Arrivée en gare de Vincennes* et la seconde « en gare des chantiers de Versailles » ;
>
> - Pipon-Pressecq avec leur cinographoscope filmèrent *Arrivée en gare de Passy* ;
>
> - Pirou enregistra *Arrivée et départ du train de Menton à Monte-Carlo* ;[3]
>
> - Ferdinand Itier, un tourneur régional du sud de la France (Nîmes) tourna *Arrivée d'un train en gare de Saint-Cézaire* [petite gare en banlieue de Nîmes] ;
>
> - Charles Arambourou, un autre tourneur régional de Châtellerault filma *Arrivée à Châtellerault du train venant de Senillé* ;
>
> - on recense aussi des projections d'arrivées de train en gare de Moulins et Commentry (c'est en fait le même exploitant itinérant qui, pour des raisons publicitaires, arrivant de Moulins, projette à Commentry une vue dite « arrivée d'un train en gare de Moulins » puis, arrivant de Commentry, projette à Clermont-Ferrand une soi-disant « arrivée de train en gare de Commentry ») ;
>
> - Méliès filma deux vues répertoriées n° 8 *Arrivée d'un train (gare de Vincennes)* et n° 35 *Arrivée d'un train (gare de Joinville)* ;[4]
>
> - Auguste Baron filma une *Arrivée d'un train à wagons à étages*. De toute évidence ce train identique à celui du flip book arrive dans la même gare que celle visible sur le flip book.[5]

Les tournages d'arrivée de train étaient presque aussi nombreux que les prises de vues photographiques éditées en cartes postales, la locomotive était sans doute un symbole majeur de la révolution industrielle.

Pourquoi circonscrire la recherche autour de vues cinématographiques des années

1896–1898 ? Ce positionnement, à priori subjectif, renvoie d'ailleurs aux interrogations développées par Roland Cosandey (mail du 16 août 2013) :

> 1. La séquentialité de flip books à images photographiques est-elle toujours issue d'un enregistrement filmique ?

> 2. Si c'est le cas, se pouvait-il que l'enregistrement cinématographique ne fût qu'un moyen sans autre finalité (ce qui supposerait une certaine inversion hiérarchique)

> 3. Ou alors, le film préexistait-il toujours comme film autonome, secondairement utilisé pour une sélection de photogrammes animables par le pouce ou la manivelle ?

> 4. Ou encore trouverait-on les deux cas de figure ?

> [...] Et ces questions renvoient à l'interrogation de Lecointe (courriel du 16 août) : à quoi ressemble le corpus connu des flip books de Beaulieu ?

> [...] Quand on voudra bien nous montrer les autres images de cette collection, que le « catalogue » [blog de Pascal Fouché] donné sur le site dissimule, hélas, je suis persuadé que l'identification positive de leur source filmique pourra être faite pour certaines d'entre elles.

> Et je suis certain qu'une cohérence s'esquissera. Nous pourrons alors à nouveau nous occuper de l'ombre de notre train…

> Je pose une autre question : quelles archives à votre connaissance conservent un lot quantitativement significatif de « cinémas de poche » produits par Beaulieu ?

Sans occulter la possibilité d'une captation chronophotographique[6] (à différencier de cinématographique) par Léon Beaulieu lui-même ou autres (par d'éventuels associés ?), l'étude physique du flip book en tant qu'objet reflète une qualité assez modeste de l'ensemble par les matériaux utilisés, la qualité du tirage des photogrammes (en ce qui concerne une absence de normalisation des formats d'images) et la rigueur apportée à la découpe. Dès lors, notre analyse commune nous a conduit à envisager une structure commerciale de Beaulieu probablement sommaire, dénuée de gros moyens financiers. Ce constat privilégia nos recherches pour l'identification des photogrammes du flip book vers des sources préexistantes, donc filmiques (sans renoncer à d'autres pistes), issues d'une ou plusieurs productions identifiées. Il nous semblait plus cohérent de croire en une récupération par Beaulieu de bandes cinématographiques éventuellement déclassées, c'est-à-dire inutilisables par le cinématographe compte tenu de leur état (soit d'un exploitant, soit directement d'un producteur). La raison d'une limitation temporelle ciblée sur 1896-1898 est quant à elle liée au sujet – arrivée d'un train en gare – dont l'ensemble des vues sont principalement circonscrites sur ces premières années de l'exploitation cinématographique.

La numérisation et l'animation du flip book par Pascal Duclaud-Lacoste nous fut d'une aide capitale. Après l'animation du flip book des Richter ne comportant que cent-neuf (109) images, la version complète de Pascal Fouché avec ses cent-vingt et un (121) photogrammes s'anima à son tour et restitua l'ensemble d'un mouvement très similaire à celui du train filmé par les Lumière arrivant en gare de La Ciotat. La locomotive devint particulièrement bien discernable à tel point que des inscriptions typographiques devenaient visibles : une mention « EST » sur l'avant à droite de la machine à vapeur, une seconde mention identique sur le flanc gauche et un numéro, « 634 » ou « 654 », sur le même flanc. On distingue également sur ce côté d'autres marques trop mal définies pour en décrypter une indication typographique (l'esquisse de « Série 8 »). S'agissant d'un train des chemins de fer de l'Est, la locomotive était donc identifiée comme une 031T (T pour tender) série 8, modèle utilisé par cette compagnie ferroviaire sur la ligne dite de « Vincennes ». Des photographies de ce type de locomotive permettront de confirmer les positions et types d'inscriptions discernables sur celle du flip book [ill. 1-2-3]. Les voitures à double étage étaient également identifiées : un modèle surnommé « Bidel » (inspiré par la forme des roulottes de la Grande Ménagerie Bidel) utilisé sur cette ligne [ill. 4-5-6].[7] Notre fameux train roulait donc sur la ligne de Vincennes, partant de Paris-Bastille (km 0) jusqu'à Verneuil-l'Étang (km 54,130). Au total, vingt-trois gares étaient desservies par cette ligne. Mon attention allait plus particulièrement s'arrêter sur certaines : Paris-Bel-Air (km 3,140), Saint-Mandé (km 4,280), Vincennes (km 5,415), Fontenay-sous-Bois (km 7,711), Nogent-sur-Marne (km 8,661) et Joinville-le-Pont (km 10,608). La seule logique préalable reposait sur mon intuition que la bonne gare serait l'une de celles filmées par l'un des producteurs cinématographiques connus et sans doute à proximité de Paris, soit : Pathé (Paris-Bel-Air ou Saint-Mandé), De Bedts (Vincennes), Méliès (Vincennes ou Joinville-le-Pont). Les images Joly étant à priori exclues car les photogrammes de ce fabricant ont un format carré. Néanmoins, la lecture des photogrammes Joly allait me permettre d'exclure définitivement la gare Paris-Bel-Air tout en confirmant mes premières pistes[8] [ill. 7-8-9]. Le dernier indice était les ombres du toit très marquées sur de nombreux photogrammes ainsi que celles de quelques personnages sur le quai. Sans une connaissance géographique précise du lieu (ses coordonnées géographiques : latitude et longitude), il est bien sûr impossible de déterminer avec précision l'azimut du soleil – même si sa hauteur est évaluable par l'ombre portée par un élément d'architecture visible sur le site – et donc de déterminer les deux dates de tournage possible au sein d'une année civile. Cependant, dans notre cas, les ombres sont extrêmement courtes, la hauteur du soleil était donc particulièrement élevée. Or, à la latitude moyenne allant de Paris (48° 51' 24" N) à Verneuil-l'Étang (48° 38' 40" N), la seule saison possible pour une telle culmination de l'astre ne pouvait être que l'été (début mai à mi-août pour les bornes extrêmes).[9] D'ailleurs, la densité des feuillages de la végétation visible confirme la saison estivale (on ne trouve pas dans cette région d'arbres à feuillage persistant). Plus encore, non seulement le tournage est estimé autour du solstice d'été mais à une heure proche de midi (entre 10 et 14 heures). Ainsi, deux hypothèses pouvaient être envisagées. Si le tournage a eu lieu le matin (entre 10h et 12h TU), le soleil était au Sud-Sud-Est et les ombres portées au sol orientées au Nord-Nord-Ouest. Dans ce cas, compte tenu de l'angle perceptible entre la direction des ombres et des rails, on peut en déduire une orientation sensiblement Nord-Sud de la voie ferrée (à plus ou moins 20 degrés d'incertitude), le train provenant du Nord. Par ailleurs, si on considère que le tourneur est sur le quai côté gare (en raison d'une structure architecturale visible – le toit avec ses festons), le village se situerait donc à l'Est des voies (une gare se situant quasiment toujours du côté du village sauf quand celle-ci est souterraine ou aérienne implantée au-dessus des voies comme c'était le cas à Vincennes et Saint-Mandé). Si le tournage a eu lieu l'après-midi (entre 12h et 14h TU), le soleil était alors au Sud-Sud-Ouest et les ombres portées au sol orientées au Nord-Nord-Est. Dans ce cas, on peut en déduire une orientation sensiblement Est-Ouest de la voie ferrée (à plus ou moins 20 degrés), le train provenant de l'Est. Selon la même hypothèse quant à la position du tourneur, le village desservi se situerait donc au Sud des voies. Sur la ligne dite de « Vincennes », les voies sont Est-Ouest à Fontenay-sous-Bois (je ne compte pas les gares de Paris-Reuilly et Paris-Bel-Air trop urbanisées, Saint-Mandé et Vincennes d'une architecture incompatible avec les images du flip book). Elles le sont aussi à Saint-Maur-des-Fossés, au Parc Saint-Maur et Champigny-sur-Marne. Or, ces trois villages (Fontenay, Saint-Maur et Champigny) se trouvent au Nord des voies. Cette hypothèse était donc à exclure de nos résultats. Par ailleurs, la courbure des voies me permettait de rejeter comme hypothèse les gares de Fontenay, du Parc Saint-Maur et de La Varenne Saint-Maur. À l'exception des quatre gares s'étendant entre les kilomètres 16,783 et 23,692 (trop éloignées de Paris et jamais filmées) dont les voies sont sensiblement Nord-Sud, nos recherches iconographiques du lieu à identifier allaient s'orienter dans un premier temps sur les gares de Nogent-sur-Marne et Joinville-le-Pont (même si la courbure des voies à Nogent ne correspond pas) dont les villages sont situés à l'Est des voies.

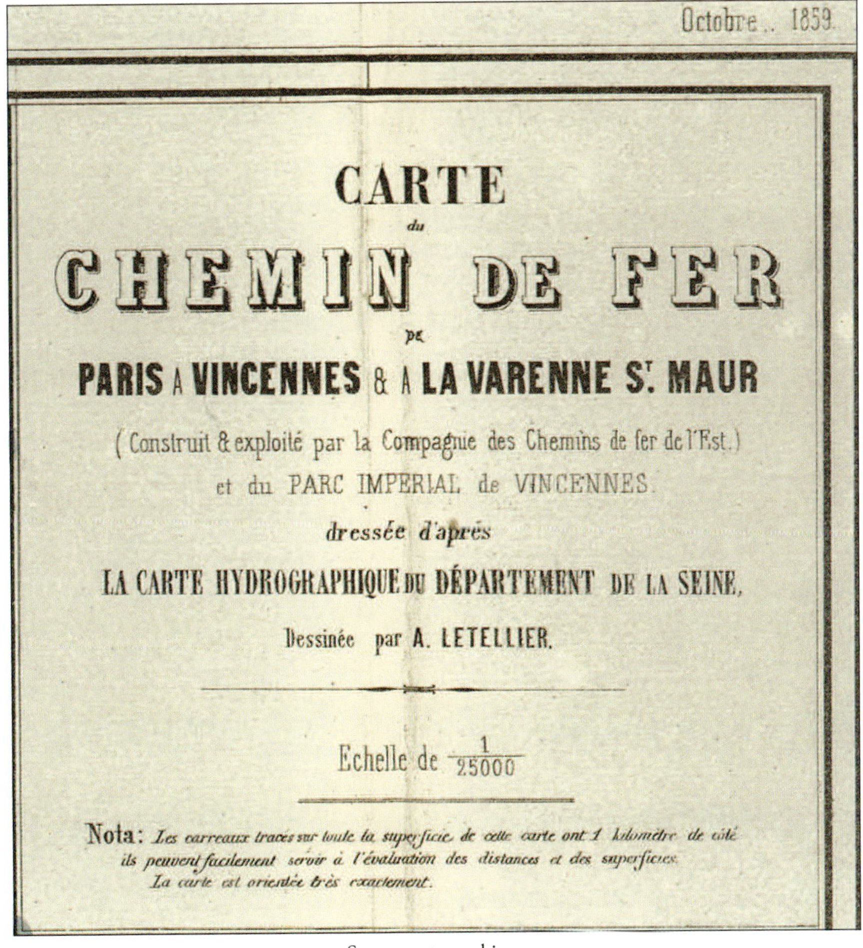

Source cartographique.

Focus sur les trois gares de Fontenay-sous-Bois, Nogent-sur-Marne et
Joinville-le-Pont.
Les lignes verticales du quadrillage matérialisent le Nord Vrai.

Focus sur les voies Est-Ouest de Saint-Maur-les-Fossés, du Parc-de-Saint-Maur et
Champigny-sur-Marne. © Collection particulière.

Nous allions donc parcourir les sites internet proposant des photographies des gares, trains, wagons de cette ligne. Assez rapidement, de mon côté, j'avais pu exclure les gares urbanisées de Paris-Bel-Air, Saint-Mandé, Vincennes et même Nogent-sur-Marne [ill. 13 à 15]. Des éléments concordants commencèrent à se profiler sur la gare de Joinville-le-Pont. Pascal Duclaud-Lacoste trouva une carte postale de la gare, une « vue prise à vol d'oiseau » selon la légende. Cette représentation aérienne globale du site (nous n'avons d'ailleurs trouvé aucune autre vue aérienne d'une gare des années 1900 ! la chance du chercheur…) a levé les dernières ambiguïtés qui subsistaient encore pour l'identification formelle du lieu. Ainsi, nous pouvons dire avec 100% de certitude que le train du flip book arrive en gare de Joinville-le-Pont en provenance de Paris, en été, un peu avant midi [ill. 16 à 25].[10]

Les photogrammes du flip book proviennent-ils du film de Méliès n° 35 *Arrivée d'un train (gare de Joinville)*, qui aurait été tourné deuxième quinzaine de juillet 1896 ?[11] C'est l'hypothèse la plus probable puisque Méliès est le seul à nommer, dans toutes les filmographies nationales de l'époque, cette scène avec précision. Bien sûr, si Auguste Baron filme une arrivée dans la même gare, sans citer le nom de la gare, nous savons qu'il ne s'agit pas des mêmes images que celles du flip book [ill. 10 à 12].

L'animation du flip book et l'étude de ses photogrammes révèlent une particularité que l'on retrouve sur l'ensemble des exemplaires que nous possédons de cette arrivée du train en gare de Joinville. La matrice qui a servi à la reproduction des photogrammes a été partiellement renforcée au tire-ligne : les contours du pantalon blanc d'un personnage sur le quai et les festons du toit ont été renforcés à l'encre. Les photogrammes de la bande cinématographique originelle étaient-ils à ce point usés qu'une retouche devenait indispensable ? C'est selon toute vraisemblance la raison le plus rationnelle. En revanche, l'analyse technique des épreuves papiers du flip book par Pascal Duclaud-Lacoste montre que la retouche fut effectuée à l'échelon de l'imprimeur et non au niveau du photogramme celluloïd.

Par ailleurs, l'animation m'a interrogé sur les mouvements de deux personnages. D'abord celui dont les contours du pantalon blanc ont été renforcés. Au regard de sa tenue vestimentaire (pantalon blanc et couvre-chef), il pourrait s'agir d'un chef de gare (sans aucune certitude) [ill. 26]. Quoi qu'il en soit, les déplacements sur le quai de ce personnage sont particulièrement erratiques et ne répondent à aucune autre logique que celle de créer du mouvement. Mouvement global qui se termine à la fin des vingt secondes de film par une sortie hors champ sur la gauche en rapprochement. J'en ai conclu que ce personnage jouait comme un acteur, ce qui attesterait d'une mise en scène de l'action. Ensuite, nous avons dès les premières images un couple de personnages sur la droite au niveau de l'ombre de l'appentis. L'un d'eux se détache en s'avançant vers le chef de gare en pantalon blanc. À la seconde 6, il se fléchit pour saluer le chef de gare en soulevant son canotier (nous reviendrons plus loin sur cet accessoire de costume récurrent). Deux secondes plus tard, il disparait en sortant du champ par la droite en rapprochement. Quelle étrange attitude pour un personnage attendant son train ou un passager ! Puisse-t-il s'agir de Georges Méliès dans une furtive apparition à la Hitchcock ? C'est notre intuition.

Enfin, les animations effectuées par Robert Byrne à différentes vitesses de défilements montrent que la plus juste se situe à 5 images/seconde (6 parait légèrement rapide). Même si à cette vitesse le mouvement général est saccadé, les déplacements des personnages sont plus cohérents qu'aux vitesses supérieures. L'analyse cinématique du train, surtout au moment où une passagère descend de la voiture « Bidel » alors que le convoi n'est pas encore stoppé, conforte davantage cette vitesse de défilement. N'oublions pas que la 031T tracte son convoi en 1896 à 45 km/h (12,5 m/s) sur le plat en moyenne (la vitesse maximale d'exploitation étant établie à 75 km/h). Dans notre cas de figure, ce train est en pleine décélération pour s'arrêter définitivement en gare. Ainsi, le flip book a sans doute été conçu avec un photogramme sur deux de la bande cinématographique. Le film originel aurait été tourné à 10-12 images/seconde, ce qui parait conforme à l'une des pratiques décrites par Méliès (les cinématographes enregistrent à cette époque environ entre 12 et 16 images/seconde).[12] Nous avons également remarqué de légères ruptures de continuité chronologique attestant que des morceaux de bande cinématographique n'ont pas été utilisés.[13] Il est difficile d'en établir la raison (dégradation trop importante à ces endroits et ce qui justifierait les retouches sur les autres photogrammes ?). Ainsi, à raison d'une image retenue sur deux photogrammes, la longueur totale de la bande cinématographique dont ont été extraites les images s'établit à 4,84 mètres (hors hiatus chronologiques) d'une bande mesurant originellement 20 mètres.[14]

Les images montrent également un arrêt d'un train au niveau de la caméra au sixième wagon après la locomotive, le début du septième étant face à l'appentis dont on distingue les festons. La photographie aérienne de la gare avec le convoi à l'arrêt permet de confirmer la position du tourneur, légèrement en amont du corps principal de la gare vers Paris.[15] Evidemment, aucune autre preuve ne vient compléter notre analyse et donc, en l'absence de certitude, nous avons décidé de classifier ce flip book comme la survivance d'un film donné comme : « probable Méliès – confiance élevée » (nous reviendrons plus loin sur cette notion de critères de classification).

L'étude complémentaire de la production Beaulieu et le rapprochement de ce flip book avec d'autres matériaux de ce corpus allaient par la suite confirmer le lien probable entre ce flip book et Méliès.

Notes

1. https://www.youtube.com/watch?v=UTqQeCJLHdE, voir annexe 2.

2. Film visible dans DVD 2 dans Camille Blot-Wellens, *La colección Sagarmínaga (1897–1906) Érase una vez el cinematógrafo en Bilbao*, Filmoteca Española, 2011, p. 172. La locomotive est une 030 T série 3500.

3. On pourra notamment consulter la base de données développée par Jean-Claude Seguin : https://www.grimh.org/index.php?option=com_content&view=article&id=4465&Itemid=717&lang=fr.

4. Nous ne listerons pas les diverses arrivées de train retranscrites dans les listes des trois distributeurs de films qui commercialisent des vues des producteurs cités dans le corps du texte. Ils sont tous aussi fabricants ou revendeurs de cinématographes. Il s'agit de Georges Mendel (Cinétographe et Cinématographe Parisien), Clément-Gilmer (Vitagraphe) et Mazo (Héliographe) [son catalogue est plus succinct que les deux premiers].

5. Film visible dans DVD 2 dans Camille Blot-Wellens, *La colección Sagarmínaga (1897–1906) Érase una vez el cinematógrafo en Bilbao*, *op. cit.*, p. 181. La locomotive n° 642 est une 031 T des chemins de fer de l'Est.

6. Il existe des flip books américains de 1897 (« Living Photograph » éditées par Gies & Co, copyright de M. Kingsland)

conçus à partir de captations photographiques : « Pictures are taken by Special Photographic Machinery invented by us », mention notée en première page.

7. Ils circulent aussi sur la ligne d'Auteuil mais il s'agit d'une ligne opérée par la compagnie des chemins de fer de l'Ouest.

8. Mes remerciements vont à Camille Blot-Wellens, rencontrée au festival de Pordenone où elle présenta le 11 octobre 2013, lors des 32èmes Giornate del cinema muto l'ensemble des films à cinq perforations réalisés entre 1896 et 1897 provenant essentiellement de trois collections, espagnole, portugaise et suisse. Elle me communiqua des photogrammes de l'arrivée du train qui allaient me confirmer que la gare du flip book n'était pas Paris-Bel-Air mais aussi que la locomotive et les voitures étaient identiques à celles du livret Beaulieu.

9. A la latitude de Paris, la hauteur du soleil culmine, à midi, au solstice d'hiver à seulement 18° par rapport à l'horizon. La hauteur s'élève à 41° aux équinoxes de printemps et automne. Au solstice d'été, la hauteur est maximum avec 64°. Le 1er mai, le soleil à midi atteint 56° ; le 1er septembre il atteint 49°.

10. Les 23 gares ont été photographiées quasiment toujours dans les deux sens de circulation et systématiquement avec une 031T et sa série de wagons « Bidel ». Il a donc été assez facile par comparaison avec les images du flip book de confirmer mes hypothèses en excluant une à une chacune de 22 autres gares en dehors de Joinville-le-Pont.

11. La date de la fermeture annuelle du théâtre Robert-Houdin de Méliès a eu lieu du 15 juillet au 1er août 1896. Il est probable qu'une majorité de ses premiers films ait été tournés à cette époque. La mention la plus ancienne de ce titre « *Chegada de um expresso à estaçao de Joinville-le-Pont* » apparaît dans la presse de Lisbonne, dans *A Vanguarda*, le 15 août 1896, source Jean-Claude Seguin. En outre, nous n'avons pas trouvé, pour le moment, trace dans la presse de titres de la filmographie Méliès antérieurs au 13 août 1896, Cf. *L'Express de Mulhouse* pour *Arrivée d'un train en gare de Vincennes*, dans Jacques et Chantal Rittaud-Hutinet, *Dictionnaire des cinématographes en France (1896–1897)*, Honoré Champion, Paris, 1999, pp. 317 et 517, y compris pour les projections au sein du théâtre Robert-Houdin de Méliès qui débutèrent à partir du 5 avril 1896. Première mention dans *Le Soleil, Petite Gazette des Théâtres*, 3 avril 1896, citée dans Jacques et Chantal Rittaud-Hutinet, *ibid.*, p. 357.

12. Méliès parle de 12, 16 ou 18 images par seconde : « En général, les images sont prises à une vitesse de 12, 16, 18 à la seconde », dans Georges Méliès, « Les vues cinématographiques. Causerie par Geo. Méliès », *Annuaire général et international de la photographie*, Paris, Librairie Plon, 1907, pp. 362–392, reproduit dans André Gaudreault, *Cinéma et attraction. Pour une nouvelle histoire du cinématographe*, Paris, CNRS Éditions, p. 197, texte présenté et annoté par Jacques Malthête. Chez Lumière, la vitesse théorique est 15 images/seconde.

13. Rupture très ténue entre les photogrammes 42 et 43, beaucoup plus marquée entre les photogrammes 81 et 82, 85 et 86.

14. Nous avons retenu la valeur moyenne de 20 mm par photogramme : 19 mm pour l'image et 1 mm d'inter-image.

15. Nous signalerons que Baron installa sa caméra au même endroit mais plus haute. Baron était sans doute installé sur une sorte d'échafaudage.

Mais qui est Léon Beaulieu ?
Quid de son entreprise ?

Son parcours de vie

Avec de la ténacité, l'habitude de ce type de recherches, mais aussi pas mal de chance il faut bien le reconnaître (mais la chance fait aussi partie du plaisir du chercheur), j'ai [Pascal Fouché][1] trouvé des informations biographiques sur le fabricant de flip books Léon Beaulieu.

Ayant constaté qu'on ne trouvait plus de trace de lui après 1900, je me suis dit qu'il était peut-être mort à la fin ou au tout début du siècle. Grâce aux archives numérisées de la Ville de Paris, j'ai pu retrouver son acte de décès et par déduction sa date de naissance.

La chance c'est d'une part qu'il soit décédé à Paris, ce qui n'était pas évident même pour quelqu'un qui exerce son activité à Paris, mais c'est aussi qu'il soit mort en 1901 alors que les archives n'étaient, au moment de ma recherche, numérisées que jusqu'en 1902... S'il était mort ailleurs et plus tard, il y aurait eu très peu de chance de retrouver quoi que ce soit sur lui car les généalogistes et les historiens savent qu'il est pratiquement impossible de faire toutes les circonscriptions pour retrouver un décès.

L'élément qui permet de l'authentifier avec certitude, alors qu'il ne s'appelle pas exactement Léon Beaulieu mais Joseph Léon Beaulieu, c'est l'adresse de son domicile, où il est décédé, le 257, rue Saint-Denis. C'est l'une des cinq adresses qui figurent sur les flip books que j'ai dans ma collection. La probabilité qu'un autre Léon Beaulieu ait vécu à cette adresse à cette même époque est à peu près nulle.

Voici la transcription de l'acte de décès (ci-desous) : « L'an mil neuf cent un, le vingt-trois février à deux heures du soir, acte de décès de : Joseph Léon Beaulieu, Bimbelotier, âgé de quarante-trois ans, né à Paris ; fils de Louis Beaulieu, et de Marie

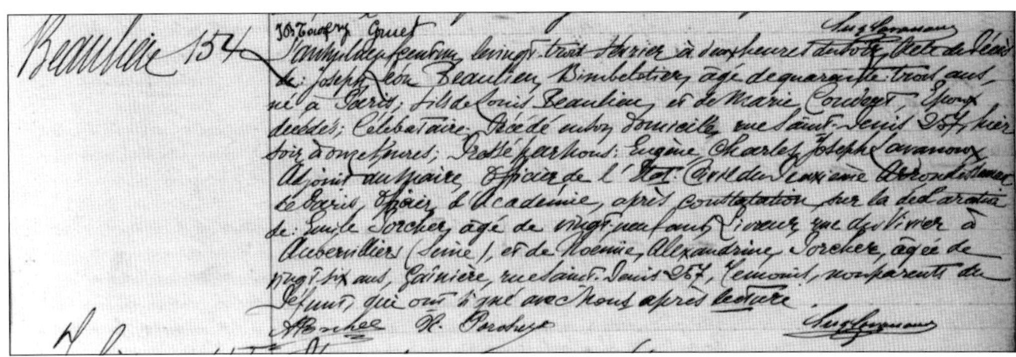

© Collection particulière.

Coudert, Epoux décédés ; Célibataire ; Décédé en son domicile, rue Saint-Denis 257, hier soir à onze heures ; [...] ».

Quels sont les éléments les plus importants de cet extrait des actes de décès du 2ᵉ arrondissement de Paris ? Joseph Léon Beaulieu, né à Paris, est mort à l'âge de 43 ans le 22 février 1901 (veille de l'acte) à son domicile 257, rue Saint-Denis. Sa profession : bimbelotier.

Puisqu'il n'y a pas de registre du commerce à cette époque (il est créé en France en 1919 mais il existe par ailleurs des annuaires professionnels), on ne peut pas en savoir davantage sur son activité que cette profession notée sur son acte de décès. Marchand de bimbelots ou de bibelots ; les bimbelots (terme aujourd'hui disparu) sont des jouets d'enfants, catégorie dans laquelle on range sans doute les flip books. On peut déjà en tirer la conclusion qu'il n'a pas forcément de rapport avec les auteurs des films à partir desquels il fait ses flip books car ce n'est probablement qu'une partie de son activité. Cela valide aussi notre hypothèse qu'il a été actif dans ce domaine entre 1895, date de l'invention du cinéma et 1900 puisqu'il est mort au début de l'année 1901 et même probablement entre 1896–1897 et 1900 avec notamment l'invention du Petit Bio-graph Parisien, le petit feuilleteur conçu pour ses flip books, en 1898 (voir le brevet pour ce dispositif reproduit à la fin et sur mon site internet).[2]

Comme il est né à Paris on a une chance de retrouver la date de sa naissance même si les actes de naissance ne sont conservés pour Paris qu'à partir de 1860, car l'état civil parisien a été détruit pendant la Commune de Paris (l'insurrection de mars à mai 1871). Pour les périodes antérieures on dispose d'un fichier nominatif partiel (environ un tiers des actes perdus) également numérisé et on y trouve effectivement un Joseph Léon Beau-lieu né à Paris, 6ᵉ arrondissement, le 6 juin 1857 soit effectivement 43 ans avant son décès. Ce qui prouve qu'il s'agit bien du même personnage (sachant qu'il y a au moins deux autres Léon Beaulieu dans l'état civil parisien mais qui ne correspondent pas).

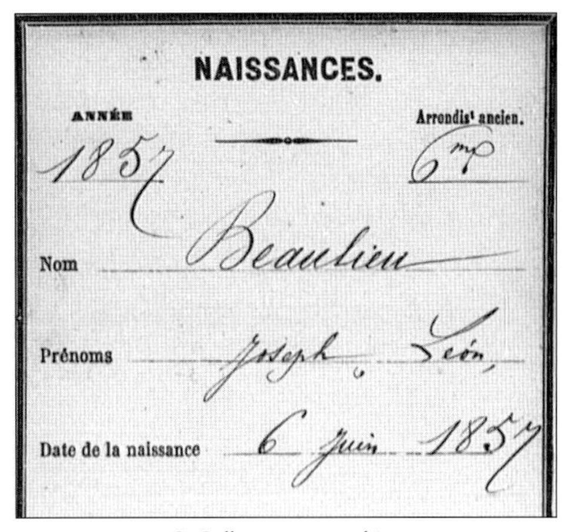

© Collection particulière.

Ses états militaires

Quelques recherches complémentaires aux Archives de Paris ont permis de retrouver son parcours militaire (sous la cote D4R1 186).

Joseph Léon Beaulieu de la classe 1877 (la classe de ses 20 ans) a été enregistré au 1ᵉʳ bureau militaire de Paris cette année-là sous le matricule 2103. Le tirage au sort lui donne le numéro 59 (à cette époque les petits numéros font le service complet de 5 ans).

Au moment de son incorporation, ses parents sont déjà tous les deux décédés et Joseph Léon Beaulieu, qui réside à Aubervilliers (canton de Saint-Denis), déclare la profession de « Fumiste » (un ouvrier qui s'occupe des conduits de cheminée). Il a les cheveux châtains, les yeux gris et mesure 1,56 m. Il sait lire et écrire et a un niveau d'instruction primaire mais n'est pas allé jusqu'au brevet (niveau d'instruction 1, 2 et 3). Il est affecté à la 2ᵉ section d'Infanterie militaire le 12 septembre 1878.

Sa période militaire, qui durera jusqu'à sa mise en congé du service actif le 10 octobre 1884 et son passage dans la réserve, est marquée par plusieurs événements :

> – une condamnation à trois ans de prison par le Conseil de Guerre le 28 avril 1881 pour « outrages par paroles et menaces envers son supérieur en dehors du service » – il obtiendra une remise de peine d'un an et est libéré le 9 avril 1883 ;
>
> – une campagne en Algérie du 6 novembre 1883 au 18 mai 1884.

Passé dans la réserve à compter du 1ᵉʳ juillet 1885 (sans certificat de bonne conduite), on continue malgré tout à suivre son parcours judiciaire : il est condamné une première fois à deux mois de prison pour coups et blessures puis à deux ans de prison et 50 francs d'amende pour escroquerie le 18 février 1886 et à nouveau pour coups à deux mois de prison le 1ᵉʳ février 1888.

Il fait deux périodes militaires du 1ᵉʳ au 13 octobre 1888 et du 28 août au 18 septembre 1889. Il est ajourné en 1893 pour maladie et réformé n° 2 le 8 août 1896 pour asthme et obésité. Il sera encore condamné le 29 janvier 1901 à 100 francs d'amende pour outrages aux bonnes mœurs et son décès est inscrit le 22 février.

Ses domiciles mentionnés sont le 64, rue du Moutier à Aubervilliers en 1888, le 25, rue de Montmorency à Paris en 1893 et le 23, rue de Bretagne à Paris en 1895.

Sa succession

Célibataire et de parents décédés, Léon Beaulieu n'a pour héritiers qu'une cousine germaine dans la ligne paternelle et un oncle dans la ligne maternelle selon une déclaration de succession également retrouvée aux Archives de Paris (sous la cote DQ7 27667). Finalisée le 22 août 1901, elle récapitule les avoirs du défunt et donc le montant de sa succession. Un point intéressant est qu'elle fait apparaître qu'il est appelé « Léon Joseph ou Joseph Léon », ce qui montre bien qu'il utilisait plutôt Léon comme prénom pour son activité commerciale.

Il en ressort qu'un inventaire a été dressé en mai 1901 à la requête d'un administrateur provisoire désigné en vertu d'une ordonnance de référé du tribunal civil de la Seine. Sa succession comporte :

> – du mobilier et une garde-robe qui ont été vendus aux enchères pour la somme de 188,50 francs ;
>
> – un fonds de commerce de bimbeloterie vendu sur adjudication pour 220 francs ;
>
> – du matériel et des marchandises vendus pour la somme de 513 francs ;
>
> – des loyers perçus d'avance et qui ont été remboursés pour une somme de 600 francs ;
>
> – un livret de la Caisse nationale d'Épargne contenant 1 414,84 francs ;
>
> – 100 francs en espèces ;
>
> – un compte courant s'élevant à 7 599,05 francs ;
>
> – 5 obligations de la Ville de Paris réalisées pour 1 821,25 francs ;
>
> – 17 obligations de la Banque Foncière de la Noblesse Russe réalisées pour 6 205 francs.

Soit un total d'actif de 18 661,64 francs.[3]

Malheureusement en l'état actuel des recherches on ne peut savoir à qui ont été vendues les marchandises car les archives du notaire chargé des ventes ne sont pas disponibles ou ont disparu (alors que les minutes notariales sont censées être conservées).

Son activité commerciale

On ne connaît quasiment rien de son activité commerciale si ce n'est les cinq adresses de sa carrière de fabricant de flip books qui sont inscrites sur les flip books eux-mêmes :

– 37, rue du Vert-Bois, Paris (il l'écrit comme ça sur les flip books mais c'est écrit Vertbois sur le brevet du 22 juin 1898 ; il semble qu'au 19e siècle on l'écrivait couramment en deux mots) ;

– 46, rue Volta, Paris ;

– 1, rue de la Courneuve, Aubervilliers ;

– 144, rue Oberkampf, Paris ;

– 257, rue Saint-Denis, Paris.

Par ailleurs, Léon Beaulieu à une époque qui semble être celle de son apogée en matière commerciale rédige une demande de brevet français le 27 février 1898, enregistré le 9 mars et délivré par arrêté le 22 juin sous le n° 275.851 pour un « Effeuilloir mécanique pour cinématographes de poche » (rappelons que l'adresse déclarée est le 37, rue du Vertbois, Paris) [ill. 27–28]. Pour donner suite aux recherches de Pascal Fouché, nous noterons que ce qui est révélateur dans la terminologie que Beaulieu utilisa, c'est la dénomination spécifique des livrets en « cinématographes de poche ». L'appellation rapproche bien sa production de bandes cinématographiques dont ses flip books sont très certainement issus. Cet effeuilloir mécanique est une espèce de petit jouet en métal émaillé, dénommé « Petit Biograph Parisien » (on y trouve aussi inscrit la mention « scènes animées » et ses initiales LB) qui permet de visionner

Le Petit Biograph Parisien[4] © Pascal Fouché.

manuellement ses flip books d'un mouvement allant de l'arrière vers l'avant (la dernière page feuilletée est celle de la partie supérieure du flip book).

En outre, Léon Beaulieu figure dans l'*Annuaire-almanach du commerce, de l'industrie, de la magistrature et de l'administration, Didot-Bottin* 1898 sous la rubrique « cinématographe ». L'adresse figurant dans l'annuaire est le 46, rue Volta, Paris. Il est identifié dans le *Paris-Hachette 1898* sous la rubrique « cinématographe » également et à la même adresse.[5] Compte tenu des délais demandés aux professionnels pour figurer dans les annuaires commerciaux paraissant en toute fin d'année civile au titre de l'année suivante, on peut en déduire que Léon Beaulieu était résidant vers septembre-octobre 1897 rue Volta. Ses adresses commerciales pourraient être dans l'ordre chronologique :

    – 144, rue Oberkampf, Paris ;

    – 46, rue Volta, Paris (septembre 1897) ;

    – 37, rue du Vert-Bois, Paris (27 février 1898) ;

    – 1, rue de la Courneuve, Aubervilliers ;

    – 257, rue Saint-Denis, Paris (22 février 1901, décès).

On le retrouve donc à plusieurs étapes de sa vie personnelle et professionnelle à Aubervilliers et à Paris, mais il est étonnant qu'il ait eu autant d'adresses pour son activité en si peu de temps. Est-ce une conséquence de sa vie brève mais assez agitée ?

L'inventaire des adresses mentionnées sur les livrets (tous ne comportent pas d'adresse car la première page est assez régulièrement déchirée) donne le résultat suivant :

    – rue Oberkampf : 4 flip books ;

    – rue Volta : 3 flip books ;

    – rue du Vert-Bois : 9 flip books ;

    – rue de la Courneuve à Aubervilliers : 20 flip books ;

    – rue Saint-Denis : 13 flip books.

On notera l'hétérogénéité typographique : prénom, adresse, ville et l'oubli du « p » à Oberkampf

© Onno Petersen – Collection Pascal Fouché.

Si on considère que le nombre de flip books diffusés-retrouvés est proportionnel à la durée d'installation professionnelle de Beaulieu à ses différentes adresses alors nous pourrions envisager à plus ou moins 2 mois près :

  – 6 mois d'activités rue Oberkampf : d'octobre 1896[6] à mars 1897 ;

  – 6 mois d'activités rue Volta : d'avril 1897 à septembre 1897 ;

  – 8 mois d'activités rue du Vert-Bois : d'octobre 1897 à mai 1898 ;

  – 20 mois d'activités rue de la Courneuve à Aubervilliers : de juin 1898 à janvier 1900 ;

  – 13 mois d'activités rue Saint-Denis : de février 1900 au 22 février 1901.

Bien entendu, ces données statistiques sont à prendre avec recul car on peut envisager une plus grande rareté et survivance des flip books les plus anciens.

Il est bien difficile de donner avec précision le prix de vente du flip book, ne disposant pas d'information éditée dans la presse ou sur un prospectus. Cependant un exemplaire sur les 107 étudiés porte un tarif inscrit en seconde de couverture : 25 centimes. Ce tarif parait cohérent au regard de différents indicateurs financiers de l'époque même s'il nous est impossible de dater cette annotation.[7]

© Thierry Lecointe.

Notes

1. Pour ce chapitre, la recherche et la rédaction reviennent à Pascal Fouché.

2. http://www.flipbook.info/blog.php ; pour le brevet : http://www.flipbook.info/brevets/brevet_baulieu.htm

3. Selon des données statistiques, 500 francs en février 1901 équivaudraient à un peu moins de 2 000 € en décembre 2018. Compte tenu de son état de locataire, du mobilier, garde-robe et espèces détenus, Beaulieu semble être un citoyen aux faibles revenus. La valeur du fonds de commerce et matériels associés attestent une entreprise modeste. En revanche, ses loyers payés d'avance et son épargne estimée à 67 500 € actuels montrent une forme de prudence financière de Beaulieu, ce qui peut dénoter avec ses déménagements professionnels successifs matérialisant une forme d'instabilité.

4. Léon Beaulieu fait fabriquer son « effeuilloir mécanique » par l'usine de ferblanterie de MM. Picard et Launay, découpeurs de métaux, installée 6–10 rue Florian à Pantin dès 1894. L'usine fabrique des boîtes et récipients métalliques en fer blanc ensuite peints. « Elle comprend un atelier de construction mécanique avec l'emploi d'un marteau mouton, un atelier de vernissage des métaux et une fabrique de fer blanc », voir Cécile Katz, *Territoires d'usines. L'architecture industrielle en Seine-Saint-Denis*, Grâne, CréaphisEditions, 2003.

5. Sources Jean-Claude Seguin.

6. Méliès aurait tourné ses premiers films en mai-juin 1896 et débute la vente début-août 1896 : « **Photographies animées**. Fabrication spéciale d'appareils et de vues de toutes sortes prêtes à livrer. Les acheteurs peuvent voir défiler nos films, tous les jours de 2 à 6 heures au théâtre Robert-Houdin ou le soir à la représentation. MÉLIÈS et REULOS, 8, boulevard des Italiens. Tous les jours nous créons des sujets nouveaux », dans *L'Industriel Forain*, 2/8 août 1896. L'activité « flip book » de Beaulieu ne peut donc démarrer qu'au début du dernier trimestre 1896, si Beaulieu est effectivement lié à la production de Méliès.

7. Par comparaison, le prix d'un pain de 1 kg était de 35 centimes, la douzaine d'œufs valait 50 centimes, les journaux en moyenne 5 centimes.

Le corpus Léon Beaulieu : état des lieux, inventaire et analyse préliminaire

Pascal Fouché possède une collection de plus de 10 000 flip books dont ceux de Beaulieu. Il dispose de vingt-quatre (24) ouvrages différents qu'il a attribués originellement à ce fabricant (dont certains en plusieurs exemplaires).

Les 24 flip books originellement attribués à Beaulieu (Collection Pascal Fouché)
© Pascal Fouché.

En outre, à ce stade de nos investigations, trois autres flip books de sa collection présentaient des caractéristiques techniques similaires à celles observées sur les Beaulieu. Le corpus s'établissait donc potentiellement à 27 exemplaires différents (auquel s'ajoute un vingt-huitième aux images identiques à l'un d'eux mais dont le format est sensiblement différent). Nos recherches (sur internet, auprès d'autres collectionneurs ou archives institutionnelles) depuis 2013 n'ont pas permis de mettre en évidence l'existence d'autres titres complémentaires appartenant à Léon Beaulieu. En l'état actuel, la collection de Pascal Fouché est réputée complète et exhaustive. Si nous avons isolé 27 flip books différents, en revanche notre étude s'est basée sur un ensemble composé de quatre collections, celles de Pascal Fouché, François Binétruy, Thierry Lecointe et Carlo Montanaro. Nous possédons ainsi une base de données de 107 flip books. Lorsque nous éparpillons sur une table ces 107 flip books fermés, force est de constater qu'il est bien difficile au premier coup d'œil de trouver une quelconque différence entre ces exemplaires même si nous relevons quelques formats distincts en matière de longueur, largeur et épaisseur. Cependant, en y regardant de plus près et toujours sans les ouvrir, nous remarquons que des exemplaires se présentent avec des reliures différentes. Nous en avons distingué trois types. Les flip books ont été regroupés selon ces trois types de reliure. Nous sommes donc en présence d'un premier groupe dont les reliures sont en tissu uniquement (les pages sont collées à leurs extrémités sous la reliure) ; un second groupe dont les reliures sont en tissu également mais qui laissent apparaître une agrafe sous le tissu ; un troisième groupe possédant des reliures en papier doublées d'une agrafe. Ainsi, en examinant chaque flip books, il en ressort que :

– les exemplaires avec une reliure en tissu uniquement sont tous identifiés comme étant des Beaulieu (par la présence de l'identité ou d'une adresse de Beaulieu) ;
– les exemplaires avec une reliure en tissu ou en papier sous laquelle on trouve une agrafe portent pour certains l'identité et l'adresse de l'imprimeur Prissette tandis que les autres sont anonymes en raison de la déchirure de la page (ou des pages) où identité et adresse devaient être inscrites. Dans ces deux groupes, aucun flip book ne porte de marque typographique associable à Beaulieu.

La Danse du cancan et *Loïe Fuller* : reliure tissu et agrafe ; *Déguisement* : reliure papier et agrafe
© Onno Petersen – Collection Pascal Fouché.

À la lecture de ces lignes précédentes, vous remarquerez que nous faisons référence de manière explicite à deux fabricants différents : « Léon Beaulieu » et « Prissette, imprimeur ». Dans la photographie reproduite ci-dessus présentant les vingt-quatre flip books originellement attribués à Beaulieu, nos analyses successives nous ont amené à envisager que quatre d'entre eux ne seraient peut-être pas des exemplaires de Beaulieu mais plus probablement de Prissette (« Train en marche », *La danse du cancan*, *Prestidigitation* et *Loïe Fuller*). Il faut bien avouer qu'une simple approche visuelle de ces vingt-quatre exemplaires ne permettait pas de les distinguer les uns des autres en ce qui concerne leurs origines. Ces différents flip books présentent sans conteste de grandes similitudes qui tiennent dans : un format quasi-identique ; des matériaux identiques (papier, cartons de couverture) ; un sens de défilement des pages identiques ; un tissu de reliure commun pour bons nombres d'exemplaires. A ces éléments physiques, il convient d'ajouter une singularité à ce corpus : plus de 60% des flip books ont des pages déchirées, celles où figuraient l'identité et l'adresse du fabricant afin de les anonymiser. Si dans certains cas une inscription subsiste, dans d'autres les flip books sont complètement vierge de tout indice typographique concernant leurs fabrications. Par conséquent, quelques exemplaires anonymes avaient été classés antérieurement chez Beaulieu parce qu'ils provenaient, lors de leurs acquisitions, d'un lot contenant des Beaulieu. Pour ces exemplaires entièrement anonymes nous ne saurons jamais avec certitude s'il faut les classer chez Beaulieu ou Prissette. Il est assez surprenant que cette anonymisation tardive soit susceptible de toucher deux fabricants différents. Par ailleurs, ces deux fabricants sont parisiens (dans un secteur géographique homogène), contemporains (si Beaulieu décède en 1901, Prissette semble vendre son entreprise en 1899)[1] et ces éléments ne favorisent pas la distinction entre l'un et l'autre. S'il y a bien quelques différences entre ces deux fabricants, les similitudes sont telles que nous envisageons des liens évidents entre eux (Prissette imprimeur pour Beaulieu ?), ce qui nous conduit à étudier ce corpus d'une manière globale, soit les vingt-sept exemplaires.

Les flip books du corpus Beaulieu, tout comme ceux de Prissette ne comportent ni titre officiel, ni numéro d'inventaire. Sur dix-huit (18) exemplaires de la collection de Pascal Fouché figure un titre manuscrit en couverture auxquels s'ajoutent sept autres titres à partir des exemplaires de la collection de François Binétruy. On dénombre quatre écritures différentes. Nous avons choisi de conserver ces titres manuscrits (en italique) pour nommer les flip books et à défaut d'utiliser ceux donnés par Pascal Fouché (entre guillemets). Compte tenu des versions multiples dont nous disposons et au regard des adresses figurant sur ces livrets nous constatons une récurrence de ces titres dans le temps. Nous avons, en particulier, inventorié quatre flip books, *L'Arrivée du train* et *La Danse* vendus rue Oberkampf, *Le Voyeur* vendu rue Volta et *Boxe* vendu rue du Vert-Bois dont nous retrouvons des versions comportant la dernière adresse de Beaulieu rue Saint-Denis. Cette permanence des quelques titres à son catalogue (si tant est que l'on puisse parler de catalogue) de 1896–1897 à 1901 tend à démontrer que le corpus Beaulieu est limité et semble circonscrit à ces vingt-sept ouvrages.

Nous avons choisi, avec Robert Byrne et Pascal Fouché, de numériser et animer l'intégralité des 27 flip books attribuables à Beaulieu quel que soit leur origine cinématographique supposée (Méliès, Gaumont, etc.).

Concernant la notion de classification, il convenait d'inventer un système permettant de valider l'appartenance des images des flip books à l'une des nombreuses filmographies connues en 1896–1900. J'ai proposé d'établir des critères qui nous permettraient de classifier les flip books selon cinq catégories (par rapport aux filmographies) :

– « filmographie inconnue » ;
– « probable filmographie _ / confiance faible » ;
– « probable filmographie _ / confiance moyenne » ;
– « probable filmographie _ / confiance élevée » ;
– « certifié filmographie _ ».

C'est donc le nombre et la nature des critères qui permettent à un flip book de passer d'un niveau de classification à un autre.[2] Il faut préciser que lorsqu'un flip book est annoncé « probable x – confiance… », c'est parce que tous les critères se rapportent à la filmographie « x », aucun à une filmographie « y » ou « z ».

Préalablement à ce travail de numérisation, nous avons procédé à une étude physique de chaque flip book afin de définir des axes de recherche et déterminer si chacun d'eux présentait des points communs ou différences significatives. En fait, trouver autant de critères techniques permettant de constituer des familles de flip books au sein du corpus Beaulieu. Notre étude statistique repose sur l'analyse de 28 flip books, l'un d'eux présentant deux formats différents. L'étude technique est circonscrite à l'exemplaire le plus ancien de chaque flip book lorsqu'il en existe plusieurs pour un modèle déterminé. Nous avons également pris en compte la totalité des flip books dont l'adresse commerciale est encore visible, soit 49 exemplaires. Nous avons ainsi collecté les informations suivantes pour chaque flip book (sur la base de 27, 28 ou 49 exemplaires)[3] :

– longueur totale ;
– largeur totale ;
– épaisseur totale ;
– nombre total de pages ;
– étude qualitative du papier utilisé ;
– hauteur du photogramme ;
– largeur du photogramme ;
– sens de défilement ;
– vitesse de défilement constaté ;
– présence d'un titre manuscrit sur la première page de couverture et comparaison graphologique ;
– présence d'une numérotation de page infra-photographique et typographie utilisée ;
– présence d'une numérotation de page intra-photographique et typographie utilisée ;
– présence d'une numérotation de page intra-photographique manuscrite et comparaison graphologique ;
– mention de l'adresse du fabricant.

À l'issu de la numérisation/animation des flip books, la recherche s'orienta vers la collecte de données permettant l'identification de détails visibles dans les images et éventuellement associables à des films connus comme :

– les décors ;
– les accessoires (lits, tabourets, ustensiles, baignoire, etc.) ;
– les costumes de scènes (robes, gilets, gaines, complets, canotier, bonnet de nuit, postiches, etc.) ;
– l'identification de personnages ;

– l'identification du lieu de tournage et éléments contextuels ;
– l'analyse de la mise en scène, du cadrage, des mouvements, etc.

Nous avons pu établir, tel que consigné dans des tableaux en annexe :

(1) Regroupement par nombre de pages (sur la base de 27 flip books).

(2) Regroupement par taille, longueur x largeur, (sur la base de 28 flip books).

(3) Regroupement par épaisseur du papier (sur la base de 28 flip books).

(4) Regroupement par taille de photogrammes (sur la base de 28 flip books).

(5) Regroupement par vitesse de défilement (sur la base de 27 flip books).

(6) Regroupement par vitesse de défilement du film originel (sur la base de 27 flip books).

(7) Longueur totale exploitée de la bande cinématographique (sur la base de copie 35 mm).

(8) Durée du flip book à vitesse de défilement optimale (sur la base de 27 flip books).

(9) Regroupement par sens de défilement (sur la base de 28 flip books).

(10) Regroupement par adresse de commercialisation (sur la base de 49 flip books).[4]

Enfin, sans rentrer dans plus de détails concernant l'analyse de notre mini base de données, nous avons procédé à des « regroupements de regroupements » afin de définir des points de cohérence entre tout ou partie des flip books.

Dans ce corpus marqué par une extrême hétérogénéité en matière de formats (nombre de pages, taille, épaisseur et qualité du papier, format des photogrammes), nous pouvons malgré tout définir quatre grandes familles homogènes au sein desquelles on détermine des sous-groupes aux liens beaucoup plus proches.

Famille 1 :

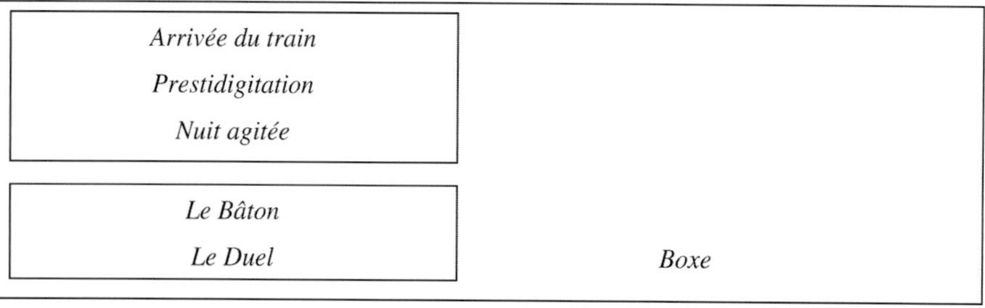

Famille 2 :

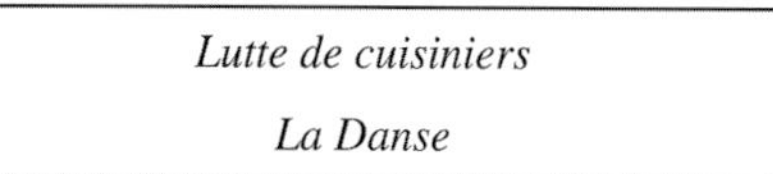

Famille 3 :

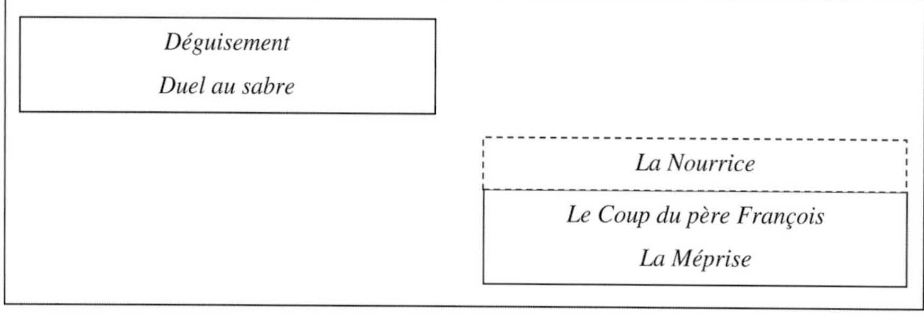

Famille 4 :

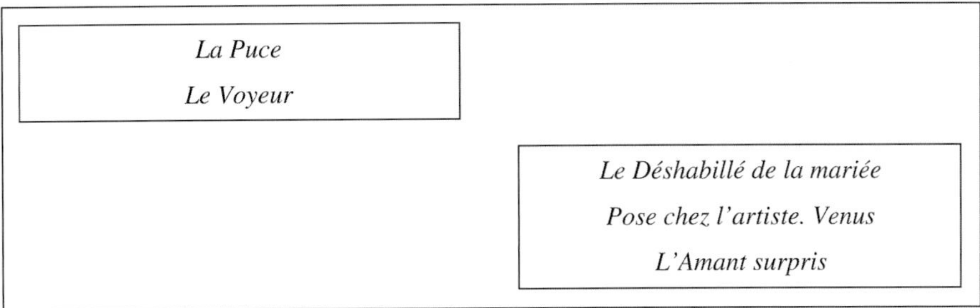

Outre trois flip books qui comportent un copyright Gaumont identique, six autres sont pour ainsi dire orphelins : *Les Deux baisers*, *Le Bain*, *Loïe Fuller*, *Lutte*, « Partie de cartes à trois » et « Train en marche ». Ces familles sont établies sur des critères techniques liés aux livrets eux-mêmes. En conséquence, les liens bâtis reposent sur des modes opératoires qui pourraient regrouper en quelque sorte des dates (ou des lots) de fabrication des flip books.

Enfin, il était capital de relire la bibliographie sur Méliès depuis les écrits de Georges Méliès lui-même, Maurice Bessy et Lo Duca, Richard Deslandes et Jacques Richard, Georges Sadoul, Madeleine Malthête-Méliès pour les plus anciens, jusqu'aux ouvrages les plus récents, richement documentés et d'un contenu analytique remarquable établi notamment par Jacques Malthête et Laurent Mannoni. Et bien sûr, un visionnage complet de la filmographie Méliès rendu possible avec le coffret édité par Lobster films évoqué plus haut. Cependant, la recherche ne pouvait pas se concentrer exclusivement sur la filmographie Méliès, les images récupérées par Beaulieu pouvant provenir d'autres sources. Je me suis également intéressé aux sociétés Georges Mendel et Clément & Gilmer, distributrices de bandes cinématographiques et qui commercialisèrent toutes deux, au sein de leurs catalogues respectifs, à la fois des films Méliès et d'autres fabricants (Pathé, De Bedts, Pirou, Joly).

Notes

1. Selon Pascal Fouché, il s'agirait d'Étienne Charles Prissette, imprimeur typographe à Paris, né en 1853 et mort en 1910.

2. Un principe utilisé par les armées dans l'évaluation technique d'un contact (d'inconnu à ami ou ennemi).

3. 27 flip books aux sujets différents ; 1 sujet est représenté par 2 flip books de formats différents (d'où le 28ème exemplaire) ; 49 flip books comportent encore leurs adresses postales.

4. Cf. annexe 3.

Quels liens possibles entre Beaulieu et Méliès : les sources historiographiques

Les recherches originelles, entamées dès juillet 2013, allaient m'amener avec Jean-Pierre Sirois-Trahan à relire les nombreux ouvrages consacrés à Méliès. Force est de constater que dans les écrits de Méliès lui-même on ne trouve aucun mot ou allusion à l'utilisation de ces bandes cinématographiques pour la fabrication de flip books. Dès lors, on pourrait imaginer différents scénarii :

– Méliès n'aurait effectivement jamais participé de près ou de loin à la confection de flip books ;

– des bandes de Méliès aurait été utilisées pour l'élaboration de flip books sans son implication directe ;

– Méliès a contribué de près ou de loin à l'élaboration de flip books mais n'en a jamais parlé car elle ne figurait pas dans son champ d'activité direct (sous-traitance par un partenaire) ;

– Méliès a contribué de près ou de loin à l'élaboration de flip books mais n'a pas jugé l'activité digne d'intérêt.

Il fallait donc chercher ailleurs des points possibles d'encrage entre Méliès et Beaulieu. La première mention, nous la trouvons chez Georges Sadoul, de manière assez furtive, relevée au début de nos recherches par Jean-Pierre Sirois-Trahan. En repartant de la première édition (1946) de *L'Histoire générale du cinéma – L'Invention du cinéma 1832–1897*, on trouve la mention suivante en légende d'une illustration : « Fig. 142. – *La place de la Concorde* en 1896, par Méliès. Vue prise sur pellicule grand format, pour la confection de livrets sur bristol, animés par feuilletage. (Reproduction grandeur nature.) », l'illustration mesurant 66 mm x 50 mm.[1] L'information est reprise à l'identique dans la réédition augmentée de 1948, l'illustration portant dorénavant le numéro 238. La dimension de l'image reproduite étant la même.[2] Enfin, lors de la dernière édition de 1973, l'information est maintenue. L'illustration, numérotée 177, est dorénavant composée de trois photogrammes successifs matérialisant un mouvement, la première image ayant été celle utilisée lors des deux premières éditions. Les photogrammes mesurent 68 mm x 52 mm, l'inter-image 7 mm.[3] Les images proviendraient, selon l'édition de 1973, de la Cinémathèque Française. Malheureusement, ce document n'a pas été retrouvé par Laurent Mannoni et Jacques Malthête dans le fonds Méliès.

Georges Sadoul se fait même plus précis dans son ouvrage *Georges Méliès* paru en 1961. Il écrit :

> En 1897, les deux hommes [Méliès et Reulos] avaient mis dans le commerce leur *Kinetograph*, et, à la même époque, des séries photographiques, petits albums animés par feuilletage. Pour ces images photographiques de 50 x 65 mm de large, Méliès employa des films larges, de 70 mm vraisemblablement.[4]

Les affirmations de Sadoul laissent perplexe. Cependant différentes constantes s'en dégagent. Tout d'abord, l'existence de flip books en rapport direct avec des films tournés par Méliès. Sans que Sadoul n'étaye véritablement cette affirmation, l'information semble, selon lui, irréfutable car répétée. La seconde constante est la taille des photogrammes 65 x 50 mm. Il n'est pas douteux que Sadoul ait eu sous les yeux ces épreuves puisqu'il les a reproduites, et qu'il les ait mesurées. Néanmoins, rien ne permet de définir la nature de ces épreuves. S'agissait-il de planches contact, d'un négatif, d'un morceau de celluloïd ? L'adverbe « vraisemblablement » qu'il utilise, à propos de ce qui semble n'être qu'une hypothèse quant à l'utilisation de films 70 mm, prouve que ce n'était nullement un fragment de celluloïd. Dès lors, quelle que soit la nature du support, rien ne prouve que le format 65 x 50 mm n'était pas un agrandissement d'une épreuve originelle. Par ailleurs, si la trace de flip books élaborés à partir de films Méliès semble se profiler et confirmer les assertions de Sadoul, il n'existe aucune piste de l'utilisation de pellicules en grand format par Méliès.[5] Enfin, l'ultime constante est la datation : les photogrammes de *La place de la Concorde* sont attribués à 1896 (film n° 54), tandis que la note de 1961 mentionne l'élaboration de flip books en 1897. Dans chaque cas, nous sommes dans les tout débuts de la production cinématographique.

Un autre indice nous amène à nouveau sur la piste de flip books ayant pour origine Méliès. Jacques Malthête et Laurent Mannoni ont révélé dans *L'Œuvre de Georges Méliès*,[6] une planche photographique positive, tirage sur papier argentique, composée de 121 photogrammes représentant une séquence chronophotographique. Cette planche, du fonds Méliès du CNC, conservée par la Cinémathèque française, est organisée par un rangement de 11 x 11 photogrammes dont la lecture chronologique se parcourt comme un texte, de haut en bas, de gauche à droite. Si, selon notre hypothèse, les images sont issues d'une bande cinématographique, malheureusement, la découpe de chaque photogramme a supprimé toutes traces des perforations latérales. Par ailleurs, le format de cette planche, 13,5 x 18,4 cm, montre qu'il s'agit certainement d'une photographie en réduction de l'objet originel. Cette planche, unique dans le fonds Méliès, a longtemps interrogé les historiens. C'est avec la découverte de la collection de Pascal Fouché, que cette planche allait trouver tout son sens. En effet, Pascal Fouché dispose d'un flip books Beaulieu constitué des 121 photogrammes de la planche [ill. 29]. Les titres manuscrits inscrits sur deux flip books sont *Nuit agitée* et *La Nuit terrible* (rien n'indique une datation précise pour ces mentions même si les termes employés paraissent être datés, c'est-à-dire contemporain des livrets). L'animation du flip book d'un côté et celle des photogrammes de la planche photographique de l'autre, réalisées par Pascal Duclaud-Lacoste, montre une parfaite gémellité des deux films. Cela confirme que les photogrammes du flip book sont bien ceux de la planche. L'hypothèse de l'existence de flip books, produits dérivés émanant de films Méliès, commençait à s'étoffer. La planche du fonds Méliès de la Cinémathèque

Française est donc l'image d'une série de photogrammes choisis pour élaborer un flip book. Nous analyserons plus en détail ce livret qui apportera quelques nouveaux indices complémentaires renforçant la thèse d'un film Méliès.

Ce flip book, pourrait donc correspondre au film n° 26 *Une Nuit terrible* de Méliès même si nous ne connaissions jusqu'à présent qu'une autre version de ce film [qui semble postérieure en raison d'un décor plus abouti, nous y reviendrons].[7] Au regard de la forte probabilité de la découverte d'images des films n° 26 et 35 de Méliès, par le biais de deux flip books, cela confirmerait l'utilisation de films primitifs de Méliès, tournés en 1896, pour confectionner des flip books, ce qui accréditerait la thèse et la datation de Sadoul.

Revenons encore un peu plus à Sadoul. Dans son opus *Histoire générale du cinéma – Les pionniers du cinéma 1897-1909*, on découvre la reproduction de deux photographies.[8] Toutes deux sont notées comme issues du fonds de la Cinémathèque Française. Elles sont relatives, selon Sadoul, à deux films de Méliès : *Après le bal (le tub)* et *Le Coucher de la mariée*. On ignore, dans l'ouvrage de Sadoul, si les images reproduites sont extraites de photogrammes ou de photographies de plateau. La relecture de *L'Œuvre de Georges Méliès* de Malthête et Mannoni nous confirme que celle du *Coucher de la mariée* est une photographie de plateau, tirage sur papier argentique 13,5 x 18,4 cm (elle est également reproduite dans cet ouvrage).[9] Il s'agit bien de la même photographie. Pour ce qui est de l'image de *Après le bal (le tub)*, ce document iconographique a disparu du fonds Méliès de la Cinémathèque Française. Nous constatons cependant que cette photographie n'est pas conforme à la version que nous connaissons de ce film. La relative netteté du cliché reproduit dans le livre de Sadoul, en comparaison avec celui du *Coucher de la mariée*, tend à démontrer qu'il s'agirait d'une photographie de plateau ou, à défaut, du tirage d'un photogramme de bonne qualité. Ainsi, tout comme *Une Nuit terrible*, les versions cinématographiques actuellement connues de certains films ne pourraient être que des remakes de versions originelles dont il ne subsiste que des documents photographiques. Mais l'élément majeur de notre attardement sur cette image vient de la découverte d'un flip book de Léon Beaulieu qui représente exactement cette scène dans une séquence de 80 photogrammes. La photographie reproduite dans Sadoul semble correspondre à la fin de la séquence, nous-y reviendrons [ill. 30-31]. Le flip book porte le titre manuscrit *Le Bain*, titre se rapprochant du second donné par Sadoul : *Le Bain de la Parisienne*.

Les sources historiographiques mettent donc en exergue deux documents iconographiques attribués à l'œuvre cinématographique de Méliès utilisés dans deux flip books Beaulieu (dont les historiens considèrent reconnaître d'ailleurs Georges Méliès sur l'un – *Nuit terrible* [*Nuit agitée* pour le titre du flip book] - et Jehanne d'Alcy sur l'autre – *Après le bal (le tub)* [*Le Bain* pour le titre du flip book] – ce que nous ne contestons pas). Les liens entre certains flip books et films de Méliès se renforcent donc encore un peu plus.

Au-delà de ces sources historiographiques, pouvait-on trouver un lien tangible entre Georges Méliès et Léon Beaulieu ? Nous nous sommes alors intéressés aux différentes adresses déclarées par Beaulieu, figurant entre autres sur quelques-uns de ses flip books. Aucune d'entre elles ne nous rapprochait ni du studio de Montreuil, ni du théâtre de Méliès installé 8, boulevard des Italiens. Bien sûr, Beaulieu a peut-être fréquenté ce théâtre mais nous n'en avons aucune preuve. Cependant, une adresse peut établir un lien : le 144, rue Oberkampf. En effet, sur le trottoir d'en face, au 141 et 143, Méliès apportait des films celluloïd à Alban Lapipe pour qu'ils soient perforés, condition indispensable pour leur utilisation dans l'appareil de prise de vue. En effet, à ses débuts, Méliès ne disposait que de bandes non perforées qu'il s'était procuré en Angleterre :

> Les pellicules rapportées de Londres n'étaient pas perforées ! [...]. Ce fut un nommé Lapipe, 141, rue Oberkampf, qui se chargea de confectionner un instrument pour perforer les films, suivant le pas des tambours d'entraînement, mais quel instrument ! Un vrai marteau-pilon, se manœuvrant à la main, d'une dureté énorme à faire fonctionner et, pour comble, ne perçant que deux trous à la fois. On se rend compte de la longueur du travail dans ces conditions et de la fatigue énorme qui en résultait. En se servant des deux mains alternativement, on n'en avait pas moins les bras brisés et l'épaule démolie au bout d'un quart d'heure de cet exercice. C'est cependant avec cet outil invraisemblable que Méliès perfora ses premiers films et qu'il put enregistrer sa première vue.[10]

Méliès avait déjà évoqué ce Lapipe en 1926 :« Debrie commençait à nous donner ses premières perforeuses, infiniment plus soignées et plus précises que celles d'un mécanicien nommé Lapipe qui, au début, était seul à en construire ».[11] Lapipe, installé 141 et 143 rue Oberkampf depuis 1868 se spécialisa dans la fabrication d'outils à découpe et déposa le brevet français n° 255 095, le 26 mars 1896, pour une « Machine à perforer les matières flexibles avec amenage automatique », en d'autres termes, une perforatrice de films. Les va et vient de Méliès ont peut-être développé la curiosité de Léon Beaulieu qui n'ignorait sans doute pas les activités de son voisin d'en face. C'est ainsi que l'adresse de la rue Oberkampf serait probablement la première de l'activité de Léon Beaulieu en ce qui concerne la fabrication des flip books.

Enfin, la référence historiographique la plus probante, que nous devons à une relecture attentive des sources par Jacques Malthête, est sans aucun doute celle de la Commission de recherches historiques de la Cinémathèque française, séance du 17 juin 1944, à laquelle assistait, entre autres participants, la veuve de Méliès :

> [...]
>
> M. Langlois. – Il a fait toutes les choses de Lumière, d'après le catalogue, et il a commencé à faire toutes les scènes jouées très vite.
>
> Mme Méliès. – Un jour, ils ont mis le feu au jardin. Avec la boîte à poudre. Celui qui tenait la boîte a eu la figure toute roussie.
>
> M. Pierre Henry. – Il a tourné très peu de temps en plein air, il a presque tout de suite construit un studio.
>
> Mme Méliès. – Il a fait *Le Bain de la Parisienne* et le petit livre qu'on feuilletait très vite. J'ai fait *Le Tub* aussi.
>
> [...].[12]

Méliès a donc bien contribué de près à l'élaboration de flip books même s'il n'en a jamais parlé !

Notes

1. Georges Sadoul, *Histoire générale du cinéma – I L'invention du cinéma 1832–1897*, Paris, Éditions Denoël, 1946, p. 325.

2. Georges Sadoul, *Histoire générale du cinéma – I L'invention du cinéma 1832–1897*, Paris, Éditions Denoël, 1948, p. 381.

3. Georges Sadoul, *Histoire générale du cinéma – I L'invention du cinéma 1832–1897*, Paris, Éditions Denoël, 1973, p. 393.

4. Georges Sadoul, *Georges Méliès*, collection « cinéma d'aujourd'hui » 1, Paris, Éditions Seghers, 1961, p. 178. Intégralement repris dans Georges Sadoul, *Lumière et Méliès*, Paris, Lherminier, 1985, p. 255.

5. En ce qui concerne les grands formats qu'aurait utilisé Méliès, une information a été véhiculée par Will Day dans une revue britannique : *London Illustration News* (J.-P. Sirois-Trahan posséderait la revue qui était disponible sur Ebay le 25 août 2015, lien url transmis à cette date). L'illustration associée à cette information était en fait un film Gaumont 60 mm *Le chemin de fer de ceinture, station de Ménilmontant*. Tout porte à croire qu'il y a eu de la part de Will Day confusion ou amalgame entre films Méliès et Gaumont/Demenÿ 60 mm. Un second article reprenant le fonds Will Day montre *Bord de mer* de Méliès [mais s'agit-il d'un photogramme Méliès ?] sur film 62 mm, 6 perforations (ce qui ne correspond pas au format Gaumont 60 mm), dans Luke McKernan, « Royal Remembrances. La collection des films Will Day » *Cinémathèque* n° 8, Cinémathèque Française / Yellow Now, Paris, automne 1995, p. 117. Un autre élément plus fiable vient confirmer l'utilisation par Méliès d'un format atypique. Un photogramme est reproduit dans Maurice Bessy et Lo Duca, *Georges Méliès, mage*, Prisma, Paris, 1945, p. 15. Ce photogramme, représentant Méliès jeune, montre une impression sur cinq perforations en hauteur et sur la largeur totale du celluloïd. Une péréquation à partir de la taille des perforations atteste qu'il s'agit d'une pellicule 35 mm. On peut s'interroger sur la hauteur du photogramme qui fait vaguement penser au format de la caméra Joly-Normandin.

6. Jacques Malthête et Laurent Mannoni, *L'Œuvre de Georges Méliès*, Paris, La Cinémathèque Française/Éditions de la Martinière, 2008, p. 89. Elle est partiellement reproduite dans *Méliès, magie et cinéma*, Jacques Malthête et Laurent Mannoni (sous la dir.), Paris, Paris-Musées, 2002, p. 127.

7. Comme nous l'a rappelé Jacques Malthête, il subsiste deux variantes film d'*Une Nuit terrible* : une version complète trouvée au Marché aux Puces de Paris et une version expurgée (conservée au BFI) dans laquelle les images du vase de nuit ont été coupées. Voir *Georges Méliès, à la conquête du cinématographe*, Paris, StudioCanal, 2011, p. 125 et DVD3.

8. Georges Sadoul, *Histoire générale du cinéma – II, Les pionniers du cinéma 1897–1909*, Paris, Éditions Denoël, 1947, p. 129. Les photographies sont reproduites dans l'édition de 1973 mais d'une dimension et qualité moindres, p. 114.

9. Jacques Malthête et Laurent Mannoni, *L'Œuvre de Georges Méliès*, op. cit., p. 94.

10. Dans « Mes mémoires par Georges Méliès » cité dans Maurice Bessy et Lo Duca, *Georges Méliès, mage, op. cit.*, p. 171.

11. « En marge de l'histoire du Cinématographe » par Georges Méliès, *Ciné-Journal*, n° 887, 27 août 1926, p. 22.

12. Source aimablement rapportée par Jacques Malthête. C'est nous qui soulignons.

De la bande cinématographique au livret cartonné : quel *modus operandi* ?

Les formats des flip books soulèvent une question quant à leur transformation de l'état de bandes cinématographiques (positives ou négatives) à celui de livrets en papier sortis d'une imprimerie. Puisque les flip books utilisent les images consécutives d'une bande celluloïd ou une image sur deux, celles-ci étaient nécessairement découpées, image par image. La bande cinématographique n'existe plus en tant que telle à ce stade. Le passage du fabricant de films à l'imprimeur suppose un rangement des photogrammes choisis selon un format simple et utilisable par l'imprimeur en vue d'un découpage ultérieur régulier au massicot. Dès lors, on entrevoit facilement un agencement des photogrammes sous un format de planches rectangulaires (des pages) avec un sens de lecture pouvant être de gauche à droite et de bas en haut (nous avons cependant des flip books qui comportent une numérotation intra-photographique manuscrite ou typographique, ce qui constitue un artifice de simplification de la lecture et qui pourrait se substituer à la composition sous forme de planche). On connait d'ailleurs l'existence de ce type de planches grâce à celle retrouvée dans les archives Méliès concernant *Nuit terrible.* Mais néanmoins, chez l'imprimeur, pour la partie reproduction-duplication des images en nombre, il y aura nécessairement un alignement des photogrammes sous un format rectangulaire qui ne peut exactement correspondre à l'organisation de cette planche Méliès. En effet, dans tous les cas, les photogrammes sont sans doute alignés, juxtaposés sous formes de bandes horizontales régulières mais espacées entre elles afin de pouvoir, à l'issu du travail d'impression, découper au massicot le papier en créant un talon où viendra se positionner la reliure. Il faut sous chaque image une zone de papier suffisamment longue pour créer une élasticité en vue du feuilletage. Or, la planche Méliès ne présente pas cette caractéristique puisque les 121 photogrammes sont juxtaposés sans aucun espacement les uns par rapport aux autres entre chaque ligne.

Je possède un flip book de l'arrivée du train. Ma version est incomplète et a sans doute été déstructurée car les pages ne sont plus soigneusement alignées, la reliure en tissu n'est plus présente laissant apparaître une agrafe[1] et la dernière page porte le numéro 110 (page du dessus puisque le feuilletage s'effectue de l'arrière vers l'avant). Vu son état, j'ai décidé de le démonter page par page pour en extraire d'éventuelles informations. Le résultat est intéressant car il confirme que le flip book est constitué chez l'imprimeur de bandes de onze photogrammes juxtaposés, parfaitement alignés de gauche à droite. Un marqueur est présent sous chaque photogramme de fin de bande, c'est-à-dire sous les numéros 11, 22, 33, 44, etc.

Cet exemplaire présente des anomalies de numérotation. Si les bandes 1–11, 12–22, 23–33, 34–44 et 45–55 sont correctement numérotées en suivant l'ordre chronolo-

Troisième bande du flip book © Thierry Lecointe.

gique parfait, la bande suivante, 56–66, est numérotée 67–77. La bande qui devrait être la 67–77 est inexistante mais devait présenter à l'origine les numéros 78–88. La bande 78–88 est numérotée 56–66. La numérotation redevient cohérente pour les bandes 89–99 et 100–110. Bien sûr, sur cette version la bande 111–121 est inexistante [ill. 32]. Ces erreurs de numérotation expliquent sans doute le démontage originel de ce flip book pour une remise en ordre chronologique. Notre démontage a donc permis de confirmer le *modus operandi* sous forme de séries de 11 lignes de 11 photogrammes chacune pour les flip books de 121 images. Enfin, si le feuillet 110 a perdu sa photographie (la page a été déchirée), l'élément résiduel au niveau du talon, masqué par l'agrafe, comporte, outre le numéro 110, la mention « marque déposée ». Cette page 110 était donc bien originellement la dernière de ce flip book, celle où figurait nom et adresse de Beaulieu. Il y avait donc chez Beaulieu une version de l'arrivée du train constituée de seulement 110 photogrammes, probablement des fins de séries.

J'émets par conséquent l'hypothèse selon laquelle c'est le producteur cinématographique qui détermine le nombre de photogrammes choisis. Ce qui conduit Beaulieu et Prissette à utiliser neuf formats originels différents. Si ces deux fabricants de flip books avaient été maîtres d'œuvre, ils auraient sans doute opté pour un format unique comme c'est le cas chez d'autres fabricants.[2]

Livrons-nous à une décomposition du nombre de photogrammes en ppcm (plus petit commun multiple) :

- 121 = 11 x 11 ;
- 98 = 2 x 7 x 7 ;
- 96 = 2 x 2 x 2 x 2 x 2 x 3 ;
- 90 = 2 x 3 x 3 x 5 ;
- 88 = 2 x 2 x 2 x 11 ;
- 84 = 2 x 2 x 3 x 7 ;
- 80 = 2 x 2 x 2 x 2 x 5 ;
- 75 = 3 x 5 x 5 ;
- 64 = 2 x 2 x 2 x 2 x 2 x 2.

Ainsi la décomposition en ppcm nous permet d'appréhender le format rectangulaire requis (le plus adapté) et sans doute proposé à l'imprimeur. Pour chaque famille de flip books, les planches devaient être les suivantes :

- 121 = 11 x 11 ;[3]
- 98 = 7 x 14 ;
- 96 = 8 x 12 (48 = 4 x 12 ou 8 x 6) ;
- 90 = 9 x 10 ;
- 88 = 8 x 11 ;
- 84 = 7 x 12 ;
- 80 = 8 x 10 ;
- 75 = 5 x 15 ;
- 64 = 8 x 8 (32 = 4 x 8).[4]

Une analyse similaire, à celle de mon flip book de l'arrivée du train, des images scannées montre que le flip book à 88 photogrammes a été construit à partir de 8 lignes de 11 images chacune, ceux à 84 photogrammes à partir de 7 lignes de 12 images chacune. Ce sont les imperfections du découpage des images qui permettent de visualiser *in fine* les photogrammes du début et fin de bande (un découpage trop parfait n'aurait pas permis cette approche et d'arriver à ces conclusions). Les flip books à 80 et 90 images sont constitués de bandes de 10 photogrammes chacune. Le flip book de 64 images est conçu à partir de 8 bandes de 8 images, celui à 96 photogrammes est également constitué de bandes de 8 photogrammes. Ainsi, l'observation physique des livrets confirme notre modèle arithmétique présupposé. Quant au flip book de 98 photogrammes, son analyse allait nous réserver une petite surprise, nous y reviendrons. La dimension spécifique des images et la découpe au massicot du flip book à 75 photogrammes ne nous permet pas de visualiser à ce stade cette règle pour cet exemplaire.[5] Dans ce cas, la longueur des bandes ne relève que d'une simple déduction qui établit à 5 ou 15 le nombre de photogrammes par ligne.

La comparaison des différents formats montre que la planche à 84 images n'a aucun point commun avec les planches à 121, 98, 90, 80 et 75 images, ni même avec celles à 64 et 96 images.

Selon la même approche méthodologique, nous relevons que la planche composée de 96 images n'a pas de point commun avec les planches de 121, 98, 90, 80 et 75 images. Elle ne peut être rapprochée que du format à 64 images. La planche à 80 images possède des points communs avec les planches à 90 images mais aucun avec celles à 121, 98, 96, 84, 75 et 64 images. La planche à 88 images est associable uniquement avec celles à 121 images. La planche à 64 images peut être rapprochée de celle à 96 images.

Nous privilégions dans nos recherches une méthode d'identification dite positive qui consiste à trouver des indices appartenant à une filmographie dûment identifiée. Quand l'exercice semble impossible, nous envisageons une méthode contraire (une sorte de raisonnement par l'absurde) qui consiste à déterminer que des indices n'appartiennent pas à des filmographies identifiées. C'est par cette méthode que nous allons exploiter la piste reposant sur l'analyse des formats des planches.

Nous pouvons ainsi établir que les formats à :

– 121 et 88 photogrammes sont associés ;
– 90 et 80 photogrammes sont associés ;
– 96 et 64 photogrammes pourraient être associés ;
– 98, 84 et 75 photogrammes sont uniques.

L'analyse visuelle des feuillets montre aussi un mode opératoire différent d'un groupe de formats à l'autre. Sur les formats à 121, 90, 88 et 80 images, les bandes de onze et dix images successives présentent une juxtaposition sans inter-image latéral. En revanche, sur les formats à 96, 84 et 64 images, les photogrammes juxtaposés en bandes de douze et huit images présentent un inter-image assez marqué. Enfin, sur le format à 75 images, l'inter-image est tel que la découpe au massicot ne révèle aucune imperfection.

La présence ou non d'un inter-image suscite une interrogation. Si l'imprimeur avait eu la maîtrise du maquettage des bandes, pourquoi opérer de manière si disparate ? Pourquoi, par exemple, s'affranchir d'un inter-image latéral qui risque d'engendrer de mauvaises découpes au massicot ? Ce mode opératoire n'est pas cohérent s'il émane de l'imprimeur. Ces différences visuelles constatées m'incitent à penser que les bandes de 12, 11, 10, 8, etc. photogrammes sont fournies par les producteurs cinématographiques. Ainsi, lorsqu'il y a inversion des images, cela affecterait toutes les images d'une même bande. De la même manière, l'oubli ou la perte d'une bande lors de l'impression affecterait tous les photogrammes d'une même bande, ce que nous avons constaté sur le flip book à 110 images de l'arrivée du train en gare. En conséquence, il parait assez probable que les bandes sans inter-image proviennent d'un seul producteur, celles possédant un inter-image, d'autres. Les bandes seraient donc préalablement montées et organisées par les producteurs cinématographiques eux-mêmes et fournies telles quelles à l'imprimeur.

L'imprimeur à son niveau les organise en planche rectangulaire, laissant un espacement longitudinale suffisant entre chaque bande pour inscrire le numéro de page, créer le talon des feuillets pour le positionnement de la reliure ainsi que de générer le jeu fonctionnel pour le feuilletage.

L'analyse visuelle des feuillets, du flip book à 110 images, montre que la planche rectangulaire est d'abord découpée en bandes verticales. Dans notre cas, en onze bandes verticales, la première regroupant les photogrammes 1, 12, 23, 34, 45, 56, 67, 78, 89 et 100. Les onze bandes ainsi découpées sont superposées les unes au-dessus des autres. Le massicot vient alors couper en paquets réguliers les bandes superposées. Il est créé un premier paquet composé des images 1 à 11, un second des images 12 à 22, etc. Ce procédé explique, dans notre cas, la forme particulière et régulière de la découpe en léger biseau du groupe de feuillets 56 à 66 et celle du groupe 100 à 110.

Dixième et dernière bande du flip book © Thierry Lecointe.

Enfin, en ce qui concerne le procédé technique de reprographie, Robert Byrne établit qu'il consiste en une technique de photogravure en demi-teintes par tramage (similaire à l'impression de photographies de journaux). Chaque photogramme possède une résolution moyenne de 200 points en hauteur et 290 points en largeur.

Notes

1. Il semblerait que cette agrafe ne soit pas contemporaine du flip book. La plupart des exemplaires entiers se présentent avec une reliure en tissu uniquement maintenant l'ensemble des pages, sur d'autres, une agrafe sous le tissu est visible.

2. Nous retrouvons cette logique chez des constructeurs plus structurés. Le grand magasin « Le Bon Marché » fait produire des flip books publicitaires appelés « Cinématographe de poche ». L'impression fut confiée à Camille Sohet, Imprimerie d'Art à Paris, 60, boulevard de Clichy. Au nombre de vingt dans la collection de Pascal Fouché, ils comportent tous 24 photogrammes. Les images proviennent du répertoire chronophotographique Demenÿ et de films Gaumont. La même norme se retrouve dans une série de flip books barcelonais réalisés par l'éditeur Benjamin Miralles dont on dénombre au moins seize numéros (n° 1 : *Baile fantástico* – n° 2 : *Danza serpentina* – n° 3 : *Asalto de armas* – n° 4 : *Baile francés* – n° 5 : *Duelo de damas* – n° 6 : *El Gimnasta* – n° 7 : *Los Pilluelos* – n° 8 : *El Barbero* – n° 9 : *La Jota Aragonesa* – n° 10 : *Marte y las Bravías* – n° 11 : *Paso a dos* – n° 12 : *Baile andaluz* – Otros títulos : *La Menegilda, ¡Olé! ¡Viva España!, La Pulga, El Beso)*. L'auteur des images est identifié sur les flip books à partir du numéro 6 : il s'agit du photographe réputé Pablo Audouard. Ces flip books, « cinematógrafo en la mano », ont été réalisés à partir de films Gaumont pour les cinq premiers [un doute subsiste pour le numéro 2] et comportent tous 80 photogrammes. À partir du n° 6 et jusqu'au 14, il semblerait qu'il s'agisse de vues locales espagnoles ; les deux derniers titres pouvant être associés à deux titres connus chez Beaulieu : *La Puce* et *Les Deux baisers*. Nous ne connaissons aucun exemplaire à partir du numéro 13, ce qui nous incite à penser que les vues « otros títulos » n'ont peut-être jamais été imprimées. Les recherches de Jean-Claude Seguin, à qui l'on doit ces informations, révèlent que ces flip books ont fait l'objet du dépôt d'un brevet le 26 avril 1897. La vente des premiers numéros est attestée dans la presse dès le 2 juillet 1897. Le tarif de chaque flip book était de 2 reales (une unité monétaire espagnole peu usitée à cette époque) soient 50 centimes de pesetas.

3. Ce qui est avéré avec la planche Méliès d'*Une Nuit terrible* et les photographies du train reproduite en cahier central.

4. Nous verrons plus loin les cas particuliers des formats à 96 et 64 photogrammes.

5. Les flip books espagnols Miralles évoqués plus loin sont fabriqués à partir de huit bandes de dix photogrammes.

Visionnage, arrêt sur image et analyse : ce que révèlent les photogrammes

Une vue Edison : *Les Deux baisers* [collection P. Fouché] ou *Le Baiser* [collection F. Binétruy], (75 photogrammes)

© Pascal Fouché et Onno Petersen – Collection Pascal Fouché.

vant de revenir sur les deux précédents flip books évoqués plus haut, nous continuons notre étude par l'un d'entre eux présentant des caractéristiques singulières. Il porte les titres manuscrits *Les Deux baisers* et *Le Baiser* sur un second exemplaire. Ce flip book est le seul à comporter 75 photogrammes.[1] Il se feuillette de l'avant vers l'arrière, à l'inverse de 25 flip books Beaulieu et Prissette sur les 27 de la collection, au regard de la numérotation de pages infra-photographique. Ce flip book qui défile de l'avant vers l'arrière porte l'adresse de la rue Volta, il mesure 52 x 42 mm. Pascal Fouché, Carlo Montanaro et moi-même possédons d'autres exemplaires dont le défilement s'effectue de l'arrière vers l'avant. Ils portent les adresses plus tardives de la rue du Vert-Bois et de la Courneuve à Aubervilliers. Si ces versions plus tardives, au regard des adresses, se mettent en phase avec le principe de feuilletage avec le Petit Biograph Parisien, il ne s'agit que d'un artifice de numérotation : l'organisation des images est la même, c'est la numérotation infra-photographique des pages qui est inversée. Ce sont les seuls exemplaires dont la largeur est 46 mm (62 mm de longueur).[2] Ces versions pourraient avoir été réalisées en marge des précédentes éditées rue Volta par un autre imprimeur.[3] Toutes les versions possèdent une numérotation typographique intra-photographique identique ; le photogramme n° 1 étant situé au-dessus, le n° 75 en-dessous. Il y a donc sur les exemplaires de la rue du

Vert-bois et de la Courneuve une ambivalence entre les numérotations intra et infra-photographiques.

Les images proviennent du film Edison *May Irwin Kiss*, tourné en avril 1896 et portant le n° 155 dans le catalogue Edison reconstitué.[4] La comparaison du flip book avec le tronçon résiduel du film Edison originel montre qu'il y a deux séquences distinctes correspondant à deux baisers, d'où l'un des titres manuscrits qui lui a été donné sans doute à l'époque. Pour un défilement de l'arrière vers l'avant, la première séquence s'étend du photogramme n° 75 (selon la numérotation typographique dans l'image) au n° 36. Cette séquence défile dans le bon sens par rapport au film. Le second baiser s'étend du photogramme n° 35 (selon la même numérotation typographique dans l'image) au n° 1. Là, en revanche, cette séquence défile dans le mauvais sens par rapport au film originel. Bien sûr, si l'on fait défiler le flip book dans le sens croissant de la numérotation intra-photographique, la première séquence de 35 images se déroule dans le bon sens tandis que la seconde de 40 images défile dans le mauvais sens.

La césure au photogramme n° 35 entre les deux séquences montrerait que le format global serait constitué de 15 lignes de 5 photogrammes. En effet, les 35 premiers photogrammes seraient agencés en 7 lignes de 5 images. Le deuxième tronçon composé de 40 photogrammes (des images n° 36 à 75) de 8 lignes de 5 images chacune. Un alignement par bande de 15 images positionnerait la césure, entre les deux séquences, au premier tiers de la troisième bande, ce qui parait peu plausible au regard de l'inversion du sens de défilement des images. La chronologie des images au regard du film originel est donc du numéro intra-photographique 1 au numéro 35 puis, après une césure importante, du numéro 75 à 36. Au regard de cet agencement des images, il semblerait que l'imprimeur ait eu un doute quant au sens de défilement des photogrammes 36 à 75. Le choix qu'il fit l'a amené à numéroter chaque photogramme des 8 bandes de la droite vers la gauche avant le découpage, à l'inverse des sept autres bandes numérotées de la gauche vers la droite. Il pourrait avoir eu recours à deux planches différentes lors de l'impression.

La comparaison du flip book Beaulieu avec celui édité en 2007 par Optical Toys (135 photogrammes) montre que celui de Beaulieu n'utilise globalement qu'un photo-gramme sur deux. À de rares moments, nous observons des enchaînements de une image sur une, une image sur quatre ainsi qu'une inversion de deux images. Le flip book Beaulieu défile correctement à la vitesse de 12 images/seconde, ce qui signifie que le film fut enregistré à 24 images/seconde. Les hiatus constatés sur le flip book Beaulieu tendrait à démontrer que l'imprimeur n'utilise pas à son niveau des tronçons de bandes cinématographiques mais plus probablement des images positives déjà préalablement sélectionnées, rangées et organisées en bandes de cinq photogrammes inamovibles. Nous pouvons déduire de la vitesse de défilement qu'il s'agit bien d'un film Edison tourné pour le Vitascope et non pour alimenter les kinétoscopes.[5] Une bande cinématographique d'une longueur totale de 3 mètres a été nécessaire pour l'élaboration de ce livret.

Ce flip book Edison n'a donc pas été conçu par Beaulieu pour être utilisés dans son « effeuilloir mécanique » ou aurait été conçu avant l'élaboration de son dispositif breveté en mars 1898. Le défilement des images de l'avant vers l'arrière est, en effet, le principe physique naturel pour un feuilletage au pouce. Or, tous les flip books dont le défilement s'effectue de l'arrière vers l'avant sont répartis sur toutes les adresses commerciales connues. Il semble donc que la conception du « Petit Biograph Parisien » ait germé dès l'origine de la conception des flip books chez Beaulieu. Ce livret au défilement atypique constitue donc une anomalie dans le corpus Beaulieu. Nous pourrions même envisager que sa conception originelle n'était pas à l'initiative de Beaulieu. Il s'agissait peut-être d'une réappropriation opportuniste de matrices pré-existantes. Quoi qu'il en ait été, le principe d'utilisation dans son « effeuilloir » a rapidement trouvé une solution par un subterfuge de numérotation de page.

Le flip book *Nuit agitée* [collection P. Fouché] ou *La Nuit terrible* [collection F. Binétruy], (121 photogrammes)

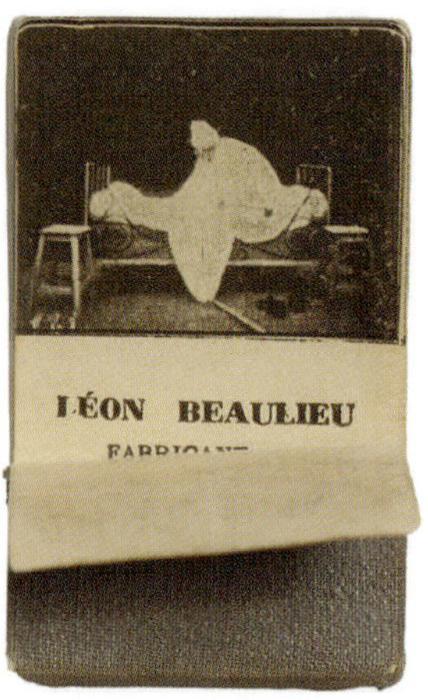

© Onno Petersen – Collection Pascal Fouché.

Si la bande cinématographique du flip book Edison existe encore, aucun des 26 autres flip books ne peut être rattaché à des images cinématographiques existantes, y compris les flip books Gaumont.

Revenons à *Nuit agitée* ou *La Nuit terrible*. Nous savons que ces images proviennent de photogrammes issus du fonds Méliès. Les images montrent un décor minimaliste se composant simplement d'un fond noir. Ce type de fond est assez typique des décors des tout premiers films cinématographiques chez divers producteurs. L'usage du fond noir est utile pour faire ressortir les personnages avec des pellicules à l'époque monochromatique donc très peu sensible.[6] Nous verrons plus loin que ce type de fond n'a pas été étranger, non plus, à Méliès même si nous ne connaissons actuellement que ceux utilisés pour introduire des surimpressions, c'est-à-dire des vues à partir de 1898.[7] En ce qui concerne la physionomie du personnage, nous, comme Jacques Malthête, considérons qu'il s'agit de Georges Méliès avec une probabilité moyenne à élevée. Par ailleurs, son costume, la liquette et le bonnet de nuit sont similaires à ceux visibles dans la version cinématographique connue sous le titre n° 26 *Une Nuit terrible*. Le postiche de la barbe blanche est aussi très comparable à celui porté dans cette vue. D'ailleurs Méliès se mettait très souvent en scène comme il le rappelle en 1926 : « mes journées se passaient à mon premier studio de Montreuil (le premier en date de tous). J'y peignais mes décors, faisais ma mise en scène et jouais les principaux rôles ».[8] Les accessoires sont aussi remarquables. Les deux tabourets d'abord : on retrouve ce couple de tabourets dans pas moins de 37 films compris entre les vues numéros 95 (1897) [ill. 33–34] et 874/876 (1906) (nous nous sommes limités à cette année). La singularité de ces accessoires, c'est qu'ils ne sont qu'au nombre de deux dans chacun de ces films, jamais plus. Le second accessoire est le lit en métal. C'est un modèle assez courant de la fin du XIXe siècle. Un ami en possède un exemplaire de famille quasi identique datant de cette époque. Il mesure 1,80 x 0,80 m, dimension que j'avais estimée initialement. Ce lit suffisamment spécifique allait devenir une sorte de fil rouge de notre recherche. Il est identifié dans sept films depuis le numéro 26 *Une Nuit terrible* (dans la version filmique connue) [ill. 35] jusqu'au numéro 325/326 (1900) [ill. 36–37], ensuite il disparait. Il est quasiment toujours positionné par Méliès pour rendre les volutes en S apparentes (à l'exception de la vue 209 de l'affaire Dreyfus où il est positionné dans l'autre sens pour donner l'illusion d'un lit de prisonnier).

Jacques Malthête a effectué plusieurs études sur l'évolution du studio de Méliès.[9] On perçoit plusieurs aménagements successifs dont l'un d'eux était son allongement progressif. Méliès au fur et à mesure des années était désireux d'éloigner sa caméra de la scène. Il écrivit en 1926 : « successivement, l'atelier [de Montreuil-sous-Bois] s'allongeait pour reculer l'appareil et prendre un champ de plus en plus vaste ».[10] Ainsi, Jacques Malthête établit que la distance de la caméra par rapport à la scène est passée de 8 à 14 mètres entre 1897 et 1902–1903 en se basant sur l'architecture du studio. C'est ce point particulier qui va nous intéresser plus spécifiquement, posant comme hypothèse que les tournages les plus anciens allaient être matérialisés par une distance plus courte entre la scène et la caméra par rapport aux tournages plus récents.[11] La position de la caméra et la focale de l'objectif utilisée allaient donc montrer les objets disposés sur la scène sous une perspective particulière. Ainsi, en connaissant les dimensions du lit et dès lors qu'il est parfaitement visible dans son intégralité, j'ai effectué un exercice de triangulation géométrique. Cette triangulation effectuée à partir de ce fameux lit allait donner la position de la caméra par rapport au lit. Enfin, compte tenu de la dimension du lit, une extrapolation pour déterminer la distance couverte par le champ de l'objectif allait me permettre de calculer la focale. Bien entendu, ces calculs sont entachés d'une légère incertitude compte tenu de l'imprécision relative des mesures. Néanmoins la marge d'erreur reste assez faible et c'est davantage la comparaison des valeurs trouvées deux à deux qu'il conviendra de considérer. J'ai donc travaillé sur quatre films où le lit se situe entièrement dans le champ de la caméra :

    – n° 26 *Nuit terrible*, 1896 (version du flip book) [ill. 38] ;

    – n° 26 *Une Nuit terrible*, 1896 (version film) [ill. 39] ;

    – n° 122/123 *L'Auberge ensorcelée*, 1897 [ill. 40] ;

    – n° 209 *Suicide du colonel Henry*, 1899 [ill. 41].

Les conclusions sont les suivantes :

– n° 26, (version du flip book), distance caméra/bord du lit : 2,75 m, focale : 25 mm ;

– n° 26, (version film), distance caméra/bord du lit : 5,38 m, focale : 45 mm ;

– n° 122/123, distance caméra/bord du lit : 7,06 m, focale : 54 mm ;

– n° 209, distance caméra/bord du lit : 10,06 m, focale : 63 mm.

Pour chacun de ces films le champ couvert par l'objectif au niveau du lit (côté du lit le plus proche) vaut 2,82 m – 2,94 m – 3,29 m – 4,00 m.

L'ouverture angulaire de l'objectif à focale 25 mm est de 54° environ et nous pouvons établir que c'est une focale similaire qui a été employée pour le tournage d'*Arrivée du train*.

L'analyse montre clairement un recul de la caméra au fur et à mesure du temps et, bien sûr, un changement de focale pour s'adapter à ces nouvelles conditions de tournages. La conclusion que nous en tirons pour le flip book, c'est qu'il est antérieur à la version filmique n° 26 conservée sur nitrate et transcrit en DVD, ce que nous avions envisagé au regard de l'évolution du décor entre ces deux vues. Cette version (remake ou réédition de la bande préservée sous la forme du flip book) elle-même antérieure au film 122/123 de 1897, lui-même antérieur au film 209.

Les dix secondes d'images du flip book, comparées à la séquence équivalente du film connu, sont révélatrices d'un scénario tout à fait comparable à celui de ce film et conforme au résumé paru dans le catalogue américain de 1905.[12]

La vitesse optimale de défilement des photogrammes est de 12 images/seconde. Elle correspond à la première vitesse énoncée par Méliès, et probablement utilisée par lui à ses débuts, selon ses souvenirs publiés en 1907. Notons au passage que la version filmique défile à 16 images/seconde, autre paramètre technique le rendant chronologiquement postérieur à la version du flip book (sans doute de plusieurs mois). De toute évidence, les 121 images sont extraites d'une bande de 2,42 mètres ne présentant aucune discontinuité à partir d'une bande originelle de 20 mètres. Cette vitesse de défilement confirme une datation de ce film le positionnant parmi les tous premiers de Méliès.

Ce flip book peut donc être classifié comme « certifié Méliès », sans doute une première version du film n° 26 *Une Nuit terrible*.[13]

Le flip book *Le Bain* [collection P. Fouché], (80 photogrammes)

© Onno Petersen – Collection Pascal Fouché.

En continuant l'analyse des photogrammes des flip books, nous nous sommes arrêtés sur celui intitulé *Le Bain*.

Revenons à la photographie reproduite par Sadoul de cette saynète. Nous l'avons comparée avec le photogramme 80 du flip book, le seul qui puisse correspondre à cette photographie. La comparaison deux à deux est sans appel : la photographie de Sadoul n'est pas la reproduction d'un photogramme du flip book. Le cadre sur la photographie est légèrement plus large (à gauche comme à droite), plus haut mais moins bas que le flip book. Si les positions des deux personnages semblent similaires, nous notons quelques différences significatives : l'ombre de la servante – Jeanne Brady selon Sadoul – portée sur la porte est différente ; l'inclinaison de sa tête par rapport à la tenture présente une différence angulaire de 5° ; la position de la main droite de Jehanne d'Alcy – identifiée comme telle par Sadoul dans son ouvrage de 1947[14] – est différente et génère une ombre dissemblable sur la baignoire. Enfin, le grain photographique du flip book n'aurait pas permis une reproduction dans l'ouvrage de Sadoul de la qualité proposée. Le document de Sadoul est sans doute la reproduction d'une photographie issue d'un photogramme extrait d'une bande cinématographique. Il est juste postérieur au photogramme 80 du flip book (nous pourrions lui attribuer le numéro 81 ou 82 tant les différences sont minimes).

À gauche photographie © Cinémathèque Française / À droite Image 80 du flip book
© Onno Petersen – Collection Pascal Fouché.

Nous avons passé des heures de visionnage sur les 10 secondes du flip book afin de mémoriser les quelques détails visibles dans le décor de fond. Un jour, l'évidence m'a sauté aux yeux : on retrouvait ce décor dans quatre films Méliès. Parfois, le décor avait subi des transformations substantielles suffisantes pour m'écarter de cette piste. Ces films sont les numéros 102 *L'École des gendres*, 122/123 *L'Auberge ensorcelée* et 128 *Après le bal (le tub)*, (tous de 1897) ainsi qu'une vue publicitaire de 1900, *Le Tortoise Comb*[15] [ill. 44 à 47]. Outre l'identification probable de Jehanne d'Alcy dans le flip book, celle-ci évoluait dans un décor Méliès. Par ailleurs, Mme d'Alcy semble arborer une gaine identique à celle qu'elle porte dans la version celluloïd *Après le bal (le tub)* [ill. 42-43]. Ce flip book peut donc être classifié comme « certifié Méliès », possible première version du film n° 128 *Après le bal (le tub)* ou *Le Bain de la parisienne* (selon la dénomination de Sadoul). Jacques Malthête a retrouvé la source utilisée sans doute par Sadoul et qui lève définitivement le voile sur l'identité de nos deux protagonistes. Jehanne d'Alcy déclara à la Commission de recherches historiques de la Cinémathèque française (juin 1944) :

> Mme Méliès. – Au commencement, les acteurs ne voulaient pas venir, et après ils y couraient. Il y a eu Jeanne Brady. Elle vit encore. Elle habite La Varenne. Elle faisait ma femme de chambre dans *Le Bain de la Parisienne*. J'ai fait *Les Lutteuses* aussi. Il y a eu une certaine Bara, elle était avec Bara du Français. Elle était aussi du café-concert.

Au regard des souvenirs de Méliès, il nous est possible de dater avec plus ou moins de certitude les vues utilisant des décors peints : « c'est à cette époque [écrit Méliès en citant le tournage de la vue *Escamotage d'une dame chez Robert Houdin*] que je peignis, en plein air, mes premiers décors afin de corser l'intérêt de conceptions de plus en plus fantastique, [...], surtout lorsqu'il s'agissait de lieux purement imaginaires ».[16] Or, ce film numéro 70 du catalogue est considéré être l'un des derniers de l'année 1896. Nous avons donc tout lieu de penser que ce flip book est contemporain de cette période. En outre, l'adresse inscrite sur le flip book, rue du Vert-Bois, nous indique que le film dont il est issu ne peut-être postérieur à mai 1898. La cadence optimale de ce livret est de 8 images/seconde. Le fabricant utilise très probablement une image sur deux de la bande cinématographique, enregistrée à une cadence de 16 images/seconde. Il a donc été utilisé un tronçon de film comportant originellement 160 photogrammes, soit une longueur de 3,20 mètres de celluloïd. Nous noterons dans la composition du flip book trois inversions de photogrammes entre les numéros 23 et 24, 44 et 45, enfin 54 et 55.

Un second flip book à 80 photogrammes *Le Voyeur* [collection P. Fouché]

© Onno Petersen –
Collection Pascal Fouché.

Ce flip book à 80 photogrammes se présente dans un décor qui semble avoir été repeint car il présente dans sa partie inférieure ce qui peut être identifié comme des récipients. Il parait être positionné dans un jardin car l'arrière-plan semble montrer des feuillages de buissons. Le titre manuscrit, en lettres capitales inscrites au crayon graphite, est à rapprocher du point de vue graphologique des flip books *L'Amant surpris* et *Le Déshabillé de la mariée* analysés ci-après. Le décor est identifié à trois reprises au sein de la filmographie Méliès dans les n° 180, *Luttes extravagantes* (1899),[17] n° 183, *L'Illusionniste fin de siècle* (1899) et n° 309/310, *Nouvelles luttes extravagantes* (1900) [ill. 48 à 51].

Le décor sans équivoque nous permet de classifier ce flip book comme « certifié Méliès ». En outre, l'analyse du personnage principal au regard de sa morphologie et sa gestuelle nous permettrait d'envisager qu'il s'agirait de Georges Méliès lui-même mais, bien qu'il apparaisse de face, son identification formelle nous parait excessive, le doute subsiste.[18] Il pourrait aussi s'agir d'un de ses premiers acteurs choisis dans son entourage. En effet, si Méliès joua souvent les rôles principaux, il s'entoura à ses débuts d'acteurs amateurs : « puis vinrent les petits sujets comiques, joués, non par des acteurs (ces messieurs nous méprisaient profondément alors) mais par des amis ou connaissances ou par les employés de la maison ».[19] Nous remarquons par ailleurs des accessoires de costume que nous retrouverons dans d'autres flip books : le canotier et une canne. En revanche, ni le pantalon, ni la veste ne réapparaitront dans d'autres images de flip books.

La vitesse de défilement optimale est de 8 images/seconde pour un film tourné originellement à 16 images/seconde. Une image sur deux a donc été utilisée d'une bande mesurant initialement 3,20 mètres.

L'adresse inscrite sur le flip book est la rue Volta, la seconde du point du vue chronologique. A ce titre, le film dont les images sont issues pourrait ne pas être postérieur à septembre 1897.

Les flip books *Le Coucher de la mariée*, *Le Déshabillé de la mariée* ou *La Toilette de la mariée* et *L'Amant surpris* [collection P. Fouché], (90 photogrammes)

Le Coucher de la mariée © Onno Petersen – Collection Pascal Fouché.

L'Amant surpris © Onno Petersen – Collection Pascal Fouché.

En partant du décor vu dans *Le Bain*, nous avons trouvé deux autres flip books Beaulieu qui l'utilisent à nouveau. Il s'agit de films dans la même veine que *Après le bal (le tub)* (ou *Le Bain de la parisienne*), un peu grivois ou licencieux. L'un des nouveaux flip books tourné dans ce décor comporte 90 photogrammes et porte le titre manuscrit *La Toilette de la mariée* (deux autres exemplaires portent les titres *Le Coucher de la mariée* et *Le Déshabillé de la mariée*. Le titre *Le Coucher de la mariée* se retrouve dans un exemplaire Binétruy). Là encore, au regard de la photographie de plateau du *Coucher de la mariée* éditée chez Sadoul puis Malthête et Mannoni, les 11 secondes du flip book ne correspondent pas à cette image. Dès lors, nous envisageons encore très sérieusement la possibilité de deux versions de ce film, la plus ancienne étant celle du flip book. La mariée nous fait penser à Jehanne d'Alcy avec un niveau de confiance moyenne à élevée (Jacques Malthête est plus formel et l'identifie clairement dans ce flip book). Cette fois, l'accessoire marquant du flip book est un lit en bois. Ce lit, nous le retrouvons dans le film n° 102 (1897) [ill. 52] et dans la photographie de plateau de ce qui semble être le remake du flip book, le film n° 177/178 (1899), *Le Coucher de la mariée* [ill. 53].[20] La concordance des titres entre le flip book et le film de Méliès conforte l'hypothèse d'une double version de ce titre. Nous noterons que le titre *Le Déshabillé de la mariée* est d'une calligraphie en majuscule, réalisée au crayon graphite, qui ne nous parait pas contemporaine du livret.

L'adresse inscrite sur le flip book, rue du Vert-Bois, nous indique que le film dont il est issu, comme c'est le cas pour *Le Bain*, ne peut-être postérieur à mai 1898.

Le second flip book tourné dans ce même décor porte le titre manuscrit *L'Amant surpris* (il présente les mêmes caractéristiques calligraphiques que le titre *Le Déshabillé de la mariée*). Il comporte également 90 photogrammes. Nous commençons alors à échafauder l'hypothèse selon laquelle les flip books Beaulieu qui comportent à la fois 121, 90 et 80 photogrammes proviendraient de films Méliès. La courtisée dans le flip book, vu sa corpulence, pourrait être encore Jehanne d'Alcy (niveau de confiance moyenne à élevée) ; Jacques Malthête infirme cette possibilité d'identification. Bien entendu, dans ce genre de saynètes tout se passe autour d'un lit. Et cette fois, c'est le retour du lit en fer à volute, le même que décrit précédemment. S'il parait indéniable qu'il s'agisse d'un film Méliès, en revanche il ne correspond à aucun titre connu dans sa filmographie. Ce qui laisse supposer l'existence de vues « hors catalogue » pour une production dite « grivoise »[21] dont Méliès lui-même fit rapidement l'allusion. Dans son opus de 1907, il énumère dans le thème cinématographique, « les sujets composés », des vues comme « les sujets scabreux, les poses plastiques ».[22] Bien que ce texte rédigé par Méliès se veuille généraliste, il est très largement émaillé de ses propres souvenirs et d'exemples émanant de son parcours cinématographique.

L'animation de ces deux flip books montre que la vitesse de défilement adéquate se situe pour chacun à 8 images/seconde. Dans ces cas, qui semblent relever d'une série, le fabricant utilise une image sur deux des bandes cinématographiques. Il a donc été utilisé un morceau de film comportant 180 photogrammes, soit une longueur de 3,60 mètres de celluloïd d'un film tourné à 16 images/seconde. Ces deux flip books peuvent être classifiés comme « certifié Méliès ».

Les flip books Beaulieu recèlent donc à ce stade cinq films certifiés Méliès (compte tenu du cumul de critères classifiant) et un sixième « probable Méliès – confiance élevée », auxquels s'ajoutent un Edison.

L'Amant surpris – *Le Coucher de la mariée* – *Le Bain* – © Onno Petersen – Collection Pascal Fouché.

film No. 102, *L'École des gendres* (1897) – © Cinémathèque Française.
On constate l'utilisation du même décor entre les trois flip books et le film n° 102.

Les autres flip books composés de 121 photogrammes

Nous avons déterminé que *L'Arrivée du train* en gare de Joinville était très probablement un film Méliès. *Nuit terrible* est confirmé Méliès. Tous deux étant composés de 121 photogrammes, nous allons continuer l'analyse des flip books de ce format. Il en existe sept autres. Nous rappellerons que tous sont réalisés par l'imprimeur de la même manière, la juxtaposition des images par ligne présente les mêmes caractéristiques. L'un d'eux porte le titre manuscrit *La Danse*, on y voit une danseuse effectuer différents pas dans une chorégraphie qui parait mal définie. Un autre, *Prestidigitation*, représente un magicien sortant d'un chapeau haut de forme un lapin. Le suivant est *Lutte de cuisiniers*. Puis quatre autres constituent une série, leurs sujets étant similaires. Ils représentent des combats, des duels plus exactement : à l'épée, au sabre, au bâton et des boxeurs. Ces disciplines de combats et les tenues vestimentaires des duellistes font immédiatement penser aux soldats de l'école militaire de Joinville-le-Pont.

– *Prestidigitation* [collections P. Fouché et F. Binétruy]

© Onno Petersen / François Binétruy – Collections Pascal Fouché et François Binétruy.

Les images du flip book *Prestidigitation* montrent de manière certaine que le personnage est David Devant. Cette identification nous connecte avec le film de Méliès n° 101 *David Devant* [film tourné mi-1897 au plus tard compte tenu de sa numérotation]. Voici le résumé du film paru dans le catalogue français de fin 1898-début 1899 : « Prestidigitateur tirant d'un chapeau haut de forme des cartes, des lapins vivants, une carafe pleine de vin, des verres, un pot de fleurs qu'il transforme en une cage contenant une colombe qu'il fait disparaître ».[23] Les 10 secondes du flip book, fragment supposé des 60 secondes du film originel, ne montrent que l'épisode du lapin. Nous pouvons donc prétendre qu'il s'agit d'un film classifié « probable Méliès – confiance élevée ». Nous noterons un décor minimaliste limité à un fond uni clair, spécifique des films les plus primitifs. Le fond clair est choisi par opposition au costume sombre. Le flip book *Prestidigitation* porte l'adresse de la rue Oberkampf. Compte tenu de l'implantation de Beaulieu jusqu'à mars-avril 1897 (avec certes une marge d'erreur), nous en déduisons que ce film pourrait dater de la fin du premier trimestre 1897. Les images du flip book défilent à cadence normale à 12 images/seconde. La vitesse d'enregistrement du film originel par le kinétographe Méliès déduite est donc de 12 images/seconde. Une bande de 2,42 mètres a été nécessaire pour l'élaboration de ce flip book.

– *La Danse* [collection P. Fouché], *Danseuse* ou *La Danseuse* [collections F. Binétruy et T. Lecointe]

© Onno Petersen / Thierry Lecointe – Collections Pascal Fouché et Thierry Lecointe.

Comme pour le flip book *Prestidigitation*, on note l'absence totale de décor. La classification ne peut donc reposer que sur l'identification du personnage et la nature de ce qu'il exécute devant la caméra. Une multitude de fabricants de vues cinémato-graphiques ont mis en images des personnalités féminines qui tenaient l'affiche dans les grands cabarets parisiens. Nous avons opéré un recensement exhaustif des titres mettant en scène ces danseuses ou artistes. Les images du flip book révèlent une corpulence, des mouvements d'une fille résolument jeune, au sortir de l'adolescence. Nous avons donc cherché les âges de Caroline Otéro, Liane de Pougy, Emilienne d'Alençon, les trois grâces régulièrement filmées, d'Yvette Guilbert, sans oublier Louise Willy, Carlotta Zambelli et Régina Badet. Elles avaient toutes en 1896 entre 27 et 28 ans[24] sauf Willy, 23 ans, Zambelli, 21 ans et Badet qui n'en avait que 20. Il ne pouvait raisonnablement s'agir d'une des quatre premières protagonistes, pas plus que Zambelli et Badet, danseuses étoiles, dont les répertoires et les physiques ne semblent pas compatibles avec les images du flip book, ni même Louise Willy dont la danse ne figurait pas dans son répertoire. J'allais donc m'intéresser au film disparu n° 45 *Miss de Vère, (gigue anglaise)* de Méliès. Tout d'abord, nous constatons un point de convergence entre les images du flip book et le titre du film de Méliès. Les images ne montrent qu'un personnage, la danseuse, exécutant un type de danse. Le titre du film ne décrit rien d'autre : il nomme le personnage – Miss de Vère – (potentiellement identifiable compte tenu d'un cadrage adéquate et à l'inverse d'autres titres chez Méliès où les danseuses sont anonymes comme *Danse serpentine* n° 44 – 1896, *Danseuses au Jardin de Paris* n° 92 – 1897, *Danse au sérail* n° 132 – 1897, *Danse du feu* n° 188 – 1899) et le type de danse : une gigue anglaise. Les recherches allaient donc s'orienter vers ce personnage. Élise de Vère est née en 1879 (on ne connait pas précisément la date). Les registres de l'immigration aux États-Unis, lors de ses quatre arrivées à New-York (les 4 septembre 1901, 28 juillet 1903, 13 octobre 1911 et 13 mai 1917) mentionnent un âge de la jeune Constance Élise de Vère qui fait varier son année de naissance entre 1879, 1880, 1882 et 1883 ! Quoi qu'il en soit, en 1896, Élise de Vère a tout au plus 17 ans. Et cet indice est tout à fait compatible avec les images du flip book. Les mêmes registres américains signalent qu'Élise de Vère mesure 5 pieds 3 pouces ou 5 pieds 4 pouces (1,60 ou 1,63 mètres), elle était brune et avait les yeux bruns. Élise de Vère était la fille de Charles de Vère, un prestidigitateur installé à Paris en 1892 où il tenait une boutique de magie. Méliès le connaissait fort bien, ils étaient amis. La jeune Élise de Vère a démarré sa carrière en France en janvier 1897 au Théâtre-Concert-Parisiana :

> Le directeur du Théâtre-concert-Parisiana vient de ramener de Londres une artiste dont l'apparition sur la scène parisienne ajoutera un nouvel élément aux attractions si nombreuses qu'offre déjà cet établissement.
>
> Il s'agit de Mlle Élise de Vère, une toute jeune femme réputée dans toute l'Angleterre pour sa beauté.[25]

Le 25 janvier 1897, *L'Intransigeant* souligne l'exécution de « danses à transformations » de la jeune artiste en rappelant qu'elle obtint un « prix de beauté en Angleterre ». La jeune Élise continue ses armes en France où on la retrouve en mai 1897 au Concert de l'Horloge.[26] Elle est de nouveau au Parisiana début octobre 1897.[27] Début juillet 1898, elle se produit à l'Alcazar-d'été[28] puis, à partir du 15 octobre, à la Scala.[29] Le 17 juillet 1899, lors de la fête du *Gil Blas*, elle remporte un prix de beauté. Le *Gil Blas* signalait en juin 1900 un « public épris de ses troublantes chansons et de ses danses lascives ».[30] Valérien Tranel, administrateur et chroniqueur de l'hebdomadaire *L'Art lyrique et le music-hall* ne semble guère apprécier la jeune anglaise. Sa critique est acerbe mais au-delà des mots, elle nous renseigne sur le répertoire et les qualités artistiques de la jeune actrice. Voilà ce qu'il en disait en 1897 :

> […]. Exécute une espèce de gigue en poussant des petits cris sauvages comme un chat auquel on aurait pris la queue dans une porte. [au Concert Casalta-Dupays].
>
> […] Danse un mélange de gigue anglaise, de pas de flèche[31] et de chahut français à la mode des irlandaises. [au Parisiana].
>
> […] Mlle Élise de Vère est une gentille Emission anglaise et un mignon bonbon anglais, mais pourquoi à propos de… rien éprouve-t-elle le besoin de se déhancher et d'esquisser des pas de gigue ? [au Parisiana].
>
> […] Mme Élise de Vère ne mérite guère sa place au programme : c'est une chanteuse anglaise comme il en pullule dans les boîtes de Mme Jacob au Havre, elle danse comme les irlandaises dans les faubourgs londoniens et je ne m'explique pas sa vedette.

Les qualités chorégraphiques critiquées par Tranel confirment quelque peu les mouvements visibles sur le flip book. En effet, si les 10 secondes restituées par le flip book attestent que les mouvements n'ont globalement strictement rien du ballet classique, nous n'y voyons qu'une esquisse de gigue anglaise à défaut d'une autre danse bien spécifique. Laurent Guido, professeur d'université, spécialiste entre autres des films représentant des danses dans le cinéma des premiers temps nous écrivait à propos de cette séquence :

> Sur la gigue, oui, on pourrait imaginer que quelques esquisses des mouvements effectués au niveau des chevilles, après le premier tourner sur soi de la danseuse (au tout début du flip book), ressemblent vaguement à l'un des mouvements caractéristiques de cette danse. Mais c'est un peu tout ce qui s'y apparente : les mouvements des bras sont incroyablement amples et tout en arrondis et arcs (comme dans le ballet), et la danseuse abuse des sauts, des battements très hauts d'une jambe, et des grandes pirouettes (certes il y en a aussi dans la gigue, mais elles sont exécutées

plus prestement en principe, pour revenir à l'attitude de base, où l'on maintient le plus possible une position verticale, face au spectateur).

Surtout, il n'y a pas les éléments-clés qui permettraient d'identifier immédiatement une gigue anglaise : le bâton évidemment, et aussi le jeté-battu sur place (le petit saut avec les chevilles qui se croisent vite avant de retomber au sol).[32] Bref, la fille tourne trop sur elle-même et dans tous les sens. Et je ne parle pas du costume, un peu trop tutu les amis.

Par rapport à la gigue, c'est comme si on retenait les possibles à-côtés et on ne se concentrait pas sur l'essentiel.

Mais évidemment, on peut imaginer, en projetant les informations qu'on a sur Miss de Vère, qu'il s'agit là d'une jeune fille qui a mis son tutu et qui fait quelques gestes chorégraphiques vaguement liés à la gigue dans son esprit et celui de ses spectateurs – les quasi-pertes d'équilibre qu'on voit sur les fins de mouvements témoignent soit d'une certaine insouciance, soit d'une absence de professionnalisme.

De toute façon, même si il y avait là l'exécution d'une gigue parfaitement identifiable, on ne pourra jamais être sûr qu'il s'agit bien du film de Méliès sans avoir une autre source visuelle. On peut seulement émettre cette hypothèse.[33]

Je lui précisais en retour que les images ne reflétaient ni des pas de danse classique, ni du french-cancan, ni une danse folklorique quelconque et encore moins une espèce de danse serpentine ou autre, à la mode à l'époque. En quelque sorte, on voyait bien des pas du genre gigue anglaise même si d'autres pas, plus ou moins bien assurés, venaient compléter la scène limitée à 10 secondes pour un film qui devait originellement durer 50 à 60 secondes. Méliès, comme le souligne Laurent Guido, ne pouvait dénommer cette danse que gigue anglaise puisqu'elle semblait être la spécialité (plus ou moins aboutie) d'Élise de Vère au regard des comptes rendus d'époque :

Si Méliès a appelé son film *Miss de Vère – Gigue anglaise*, ce n'est pas parce qu'il y voit « any dance », c'est évidemment en référence à un numéro connu (il fait de même quand il évoque les gymnastes de Joinville, les danseuses au Jardin de Paris, et aussi les artistes de music-hall qu'il enregistre sur le mode Edison en 1896). Le fait qu'Élise de Vère interprète explicitement sur scène une gigue (sa danse signature en quelque sorte…) comme un numéro dans des revues, numéro qu'on remarque d'ailleurs comme gracieux et enlevé, et qui, du coup, ne semble pas trop correspondre à ces quelques sauts désinvoltes. [ce qui est contesté par Valérian Tranel].

Mais je n'y vois pas de contradiction impossible à résoudre : si elle était actrice de music-hall, elle pouvait très bien y aller plus franchement, de manière joyeuse et directe, et agrémenter cette gigue de moments supposément plus spectaculaires (tels que ceux que l'on voit). Peut-être, aussi, n'a-t-on là pas l'entier de la bande et a-t-on retenu que le passage qui faisait le plus ballet.[34]

L'identification de cette danse comme une gigue n'est donc pas exclue même si elle ne peut pas être qualifiée comme telle au regard de ce fragment de film ne représentant que le 1/5ᵉ ou 1/6ᵉ de la bande cinématographique complète. Il nous fallait trouver des documents iconographiques d'Élise de Vère afin de comparer silhouette, taille et éventuellement costume de danse. Car Élise de Vère porte sur le flip book un vêtement se rapprochant plus du tutu comme le remarque Guido. Parmi les actrices citées plus haut, aucune ne s'affichait avec ce genre de vêtement. Les nombreuses représentations photographiques d'Élise de Vère datent des années 1900, lorsqu'elle se trouve à l'apogée de sa carrière. Elle porte ses costumes de scènes plus ou moins habillés. Il fallait trouver une photographie d'elle plus jeune, vers 1897. Un document arriva à point nommé : Élise de Vère, jeune, au visage plus émacié que dans les années 1900 et portant un… tutu [ill. 54 à 56] !

Élise de Vère [ca 1897] au début de sa carrière française. © Thierry Lecointe.

Une animation particulière du film centrée sur le visage allait confirmer nos hypothèses par l'identification des traits généraux de la danseuse.

Carte postale datée d'octobre 1904. © Thierry Lecointe.

D'un point de vue technique, l'animation du flip book a été effectuée à 12 images/seconde, cadence qui correspond parfaitement aux mouvements d'ensemble. Il semble bien que le tronçon de bande cinématographique utilisé pour ce flip book n'ait fait l'objet d'aucun découpage, 12 images/seconde correspondant à l'une des vitesses de défilement usitée par Méliès. La bande cinématographique employée mesurait donc 2,42 mètres.

Nous pouvons donc classifier ce flip book au regard des divers critères « probable Méliès – confiance élevée ».

– *Lutte de cuisiniers* [collections P. Fouché et F. Binétruy]

© Onno Petersen / François Binétruy – Collections Pascal Fouché ét François Binétruy.

Il n'est pas possible de rattacher ce flip book à un titre Méliès ou autres. La séquence filmée en plan large ne permet pas d'identifier l'un des deux personnages. Nous noterons un décor limité à un traditionnel fond noir typique de quelques premiers films de Méliès comme chez quelques autres producteurs (en plus des films à surimpressions, selon ce qui est actuellement sauvegardé). Quant aux accessoires, il est bien difficile d'en extraire des conclusions probantes. Seul le baquet en bois en forme de demi-tonneau pourrait être apparenté à celui visible dans le film n° 95 *L'Hallucination de l'alchimiste* (1897) [ill. 57-58], photographié dans la vue de plateau du film n° 390 *Le Piqueur de fûts*, de celle du n° 399/411 *Voyage dans la Lune*[35] (1902) et dans le n° 585/588 *Sorcellerie culinaire* (1904). Mais il est probable d'en trouver de similaires dans d'autres filmographies. Seuls les critères techniques de ce flip book, comme le nombre de photogrammes, le mode de fabrication, le format, l'apparentent à cette série dont plusieurs flip books sont identifiés Méliès ou probable Méliès avec un niveau de classification élevé. Sa vitesse de défilement est de 12 images/seconde, ce qui le relie aux vues les plus primitives du corpus. Une longueur de 2,42 mètres de celluloïd a été nécessaire pour sa réalisation. Nous attribuons donc à ce flip book la classification « probable Méliès – confiance moyenne ».

– Les quatre flip books de duels : *Le Duel*, *Le Bâton* [collection P. Fouché], *Boxe* et *Escrime* ou *Duel au sabre* [collections P. Fouché et F. Binétruy]

Le Duel © Onno Petersen / Pascal Fouché – Collection Pascal Fouché.

Le Bâton © Onno Petersen / Pascal Fouché – Collection Pascal Fouché.

Boxe © Onno Petersen / Pascal Fouché / François Binétruy – Collections Pascal Fouché et François Binétruy.

Escrime ou *Duel au sabre* © Onno Petersen / Pascal Fouché / François Binétruy – Collections Pascal Fouché et François Binétruy.

Nous allons considérer ces quatre flip books dans leur globalité car ils constituent une série homogène. Les images possèdent le même décor : un fond noir. Elles sont enregistrées sous un même cadrage montrant des duels au sabre, à l'épée, au bâton, à la boxe française. Compte tenu des éléments découvert concernant les flip books à 121 photogrammes, il nous parait cohérent de croire en un fournisseur unique pour ces produits particuliers. Nous sommes quasiment sûr que les flip books de ce format sont sortis des mêmes ateliers cinématographiques.

Quelques historiens voient dans Méliès l'inventeur de génie de genres cinématographiques comme les films à trucages, les grandes féeries, les fantasmagories ou les films fantastiques.[36] Cependant, il faut bien avouer que Méliès, à ses débuts, au regard des titres de sa filmographie, réalisa des films comme ses concurrents avec des mises en scène assez similaires et donc minimalistes. Ainsi, écrivait-il dans ses mémoires : « pendant les neuf premiers mois de 1896, Méliès ne fit, comme les autres [citant plus avant « Pathé, Gaumont et d'autres »], que des scènes de plein air ou des petites vues comiques sans grande importance ».[37] Si ses premiers films des années 1896 et 1897 ont quasiment tous disparus, les titres, les photographies subsistantes ou les quelques copies retrouvées de ces années-là confirment un dispositif scénique en devenir. Méliès ne s'est pas caché d'utiliser à ses débuts des bandes de kinétoscope avec un projecteur acheté à Londres à Robert William Paul : « peu de temps après la séance historique du Grand Café, je projetai d'abord des films de Kinétoscope, puis mes premiers films ».[38] Méliès réitéra cette affirmation en étant plus précis sur la nature de ses premiers films : « Je projetais d'abord des bandes de Kinétoscope, des escrimeurs, des boxeurs, la Loïe Fuller. <u>Mes</u> personnages apparaissaient en blanc sur fond noir ».[39] Non seulement, l'emploi du fond noir est avéré mais trois titres sont mentionnés dont deux qui nous interpellent : escrimeurs et boxeurs. Ces deux sujets se retrouvent dans la filmographie Méliès aux numéros 136 et 148 : *Match de boxe, professeurs de l'école de Joinville* et *Assaut d'escrime, école de Joinville*. Si ces deux vues sont inscrites au catalogue Méliès, nous relèverons un anachronisme les concernant. Compte tenu de la numérotation, la vue n° 136 daterait de la fin d'année 1897 et celle n° 148 de 1898. Comment Méliès peut-il alors annoncer que ces films faisaient partie des toutes premières vues tournées et projetées en 1896 (à partir de juin/juillet 1896, date où il semble tourner ses premiers films) ? En revanche, la Loïe Fuller, c'est-à-dire *Danse serpentine* porte le numéro 44 au catalogue et, à ce titre, date bien des tout débuts cinématographiques de Méliès. De toute évidence, les vues n° 136 et 148 constitueraient certainement, elles aussi, des remakes.[40] Les vues de duels des flip books semblent donc appartenir aux toutes premières vues Méliès, probablement tournées à l'époque du train en gare de Joinville.[41] Compte tenu de l'homogénéité des quatre vues de duels, outre le match de boxe et l'assaut d'escrime décrits par Méliès, *Le Bâton* et *Duel au sabre* seraient deux vues qui pourraient confirmer l'existence d'un « hors catalogue » primitif chez Méliès.[42] Nous noterons que cette notion de « hors catalogue » existe aussi dans la filmographie Lumière et n'est pas contestée (de nombreuses vues ont été tournées sans être intégrées au catalogue officiel).

Bien entendu, il n'existe aucun détail dans les images susceptibles d'augmenter le niveau de classification. L'identification éventuelle des protagonistes n'apporterait rien à ce sujet puisque Méliès ne cite personne en particulier (à l'inverse des films *Miss de Vère*, *David Devant*, la série des *Paulus* et *Auguste et Bibb*). Nous classons donc ces quatre titres, au regard de l'ensemble des critères techniques et historiographiques, comme des vues « probable Méliès – confiance moyenne » (même si nous pourrions envisager d'augmenter la classification pour deux d'entre eux au regard des titres figurant dans la filmographie). D'un point de vue technique, l'animation de ces flip books a été effectuée à 12 images/seconde, cadence qui correspond parfaitement aux mouvements d'ensemble. Il semble bien que le tronçon de bande cinématographique utilisé pour ces flip books n'ait fait l'objet d'aucun découpage, 12 images/seconde correspondant à l'une des vitesses de défilement usitée par Méliès. Nous esquissons de ce fait un ensemble cohérent entre les flip books enregistrés à une vitesse de 10–12 images/seconde et filmés sur fond noir, leurs datations établies comme étant les plus anciennes du corpus.

Les bandes cinématographiques employées pour ces quatre flip book mesuraient donc 2,42 mètres.

Les autres flip books constitués de 90 photogrammes

La collection est constituée de huit flip books comportant 90 photogrammes. Nous avons vu précédemment que deux sont identifiés comme étant des films Méliès. Six autres comportent des titres manuscrits notés sur les premières de couverture. Ce sont :

- *Pose chez l'artiste. Vénus* ;
- *La Puce* ;
- *La Méprise* ;
- *Le Coup du père François* ;
- *La Nourrice* ;
- *Loïe Fuller.*

– *Pose chez l'artiste. Vénus* [collection P. Fouché]

© Onno Petersen – Collection Pascal Fouché.

Six flip books à 90 photogrammes ne peuvent être rapprochés de titres de la filmographie Méliès. Cependant, l'un d'eux analysé précédemment, *L'Amant surpris*, est certifié Méliès. En conséquence, l'absence de rattachement des flip books à des titres du catalogue ne constitue pas un critère d'exclusion par rapport à la filmographie Méliès, d'autant que la thèse de films « hors catalogue » se profile nettement. Ainsi, les titres qui suivent demandent une analyse plus particulière.

La visualisation des photogrammes 10 à 15 de *Pose chez l'artiste. Vénus* est sans appel : nous y reconnaissons Méliès dans le rôle du peintre. Mais plus encore que cette identification formelle du personnage, c'est la comparaison avec une photographie reproduite dans *Georges Méliès mage*[43] qui allait définitivement nous convaincre sur l'origine du flip book. Si la photographie n'est pas directement extraite du flip book (il s'agit d'une photographie de plateau), elle montre une scène dont la composition est strictement analogue : positions du peintre et du modèle, cadrage général et perspective, position du chevalet et éléments de décors [ill. 59 à 61]. En outre, les vêtements de Méliès nous interpellent également : la veste est identique mais surtout le magnifique pantalon à carreaux ! Ce type de pantalon (pas tout à fait identique) qu'arbore aussi Méliès dans le film n° 112 *Entre Calais et Douvres* (1897) et que l'on retrouve encore rapidement dans le film n° 312–313 *Le Déshabillage impossible* (1900) [ill. 62–63]. Nous n'avons cependant pas trouvé de trace du décor peint en arrière-plan, preuve de la multiplicité des décors réalisés par Méliès. En revanche, nous retrouvons la petite table basse sur laquelle trône le modèle dans sept autres films du n° 78/80 *Le Manoir du diable* (1897) [ill. 64], puis au n° 96 *Le Château hanté* (1897) [ill. 65] au n° 371/372 *Le Chapeau à surprises* (1901). Ce flip book est donc « certifié Méliès ». Très récemment Serge Bromberg et Eric Lange m'ont transmis quelques photogrammes d'un fragment de film correspondant à la photographie de plateau. La comparaison de ces photogrammes avec ceux du flip book nous enseigne une fois encore sur le fait que Méliès a réalisé non seulement des films hors catalogue mais aussi des remakes. Nous connaissons trois titres dans la filmographie Méliès auxquelles pourraient se rapporter les images du flip book (n° 130/131 *Le Modèle irascible*, n° 165 *Rêve d'artiste* et n° 166 *Atelier d'artiste (farces de modèles)*). Néanmoins, tout rapprochement avec ces titres ne serait que spéculation. La vitesse de défilement optimale est de 8 images/seconde pour un film tourné originellement à 16 images/seconde. Une image sur deux a donc été utilisée d'une bande mesurant initialement 3,60 mètres.

L'adresse inscrite sur le flip book, rue du Vert-Bois, nous indique que le film dont il est issu ne peut-être postérieur à mai 1898. A ce titre, il pourrait davantage correspondre à la vue n° 130/131 *Le Modèle irascible* (fin 1897) – les vues n° 165 et 166 dateraient de fin 1898 – ou du moins à une première version de cette vue si l'on considère le fragment de celluloïd retrouvé comme version ultérieure de ce titre (en raison d'un décor plus abouti et d'une caméra placé sensiblement plus loin de la scène).

Fragment de la seconde version de la saynète [*Le Modèle irascible*] – © Collection Lobster films.

Photogrammes 1, 10, 15 et 20 du flip book © Onno Petersen – Collection Pascal Fouché.

— *La Puce* [collection P. Fouché] ou *Madame cherche ses puces* [collection F. Binétruy]

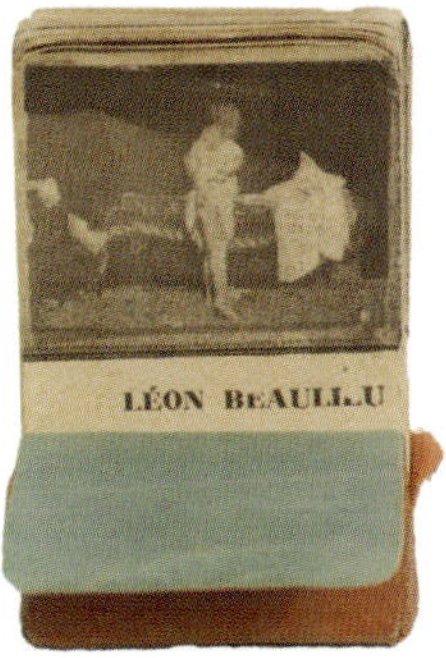

© Onno Petersen – Collection Pascal Fouché.

La scène représente une femme se levant précipitamment de son lit, dérangée par ce qui semble être des puces. Le titre de ce flip book n'est pas sans rappeler celui du film Pathé *La Puce*, n° 783 (1897–1899).[44] Cependant, la silhouette du personnage quasiment debout durant toute la séquence nous évoque celle de Jehanne d'Alcy (même impression pour Jacques Malthête, sans certitude cependant). Le visage visible sur le photogramme 35 nous permet également de soutenir cette hypothèse. Le film se déroule également sur fond noir, sorte de point commun à ces vues primitives du cinéma des premiers temps. L'accessoire principal est le lit mais aucun détail n'est visible et on ne peut donc l'apparenter à l'un des deux modèles connus. L'appartenance de ce flip book à une famille plus large composée du même nombre de pages dont plusieurs sont certifiés Méliès nous conduit à le classifier comme un « probable Méliès – confiance faible ». Il nous restait cette couverture aux motifs très particuliers. Méliès ne déroge pas à une règle qui consistait à utiliser les mêmes accessoires, décors, costumes. La couverture apparaît dans les films n° 82 *Le Cauchemar* (fin 1896) et n° 122/123 *L'Auberge ensorcelée* (1897) [ill. 66 à 68]. Ce flip book obtient finalement la classification « confirmé Méliès ». La cadence optimale de défilement est établie à 10 images/seconde par Robert Byrne. L'enregistrement de ce film s'est sans doute effectué à cette vitesse. Une bande cinématographique de 1,80 mètre fut donc nécessaire pour l'élaboration de ce livret utilisant les photogrammes de manière consécutive.

– *La Méprise* [collection P. Fouché] ou *Méprise* [collection F. Binétruy]

© Onno Petersen –
Collection Pascal Fouché.

En ce qui concerne *La Méprise*, le décor est unique et ne présente donc pas de point commun avec d'autres vues connues. Le personnage qui salue l'ecclésiastique nous interpelle. Sa gestuelle, sa taille, sa corpulence, la calvitie qu'il présente nous font penser à Georges Méliès. Un seul photogramme sème le doute par la longueur de ce qui semble être des rouflaquettes. Mais ce détail n'est pas franc et peut-être s'agit-il d'un défaut d'impression sur ce seul photogramme. Jacques Malthête n'y reconnait pourtant pas Méliès. Ce personnage porte aussi un canotier, élément de costume qui apparaît dans quatre films (entre 1896 et 1901), dans d'autres flip books et sur quelques photos prises dans l'atelier de pause de Montreuil [ill. 69 et 70]. Il tient également une canne, accessoire que l'on retrouve dans le flip book *Le Voyeur*, précédemment décrit. Compte tenu des similitudes observables entre le personnage principal et celui que l'on retrouve dans *Le Voyeur*, des accessoires communs (canotier et canne), des éléments de mise en scène, l'ensemble des critères recueillis pour *La Méprise* nous amène à nous prononcer pour un film « probable Méliès – confiance élevée ». Ainsi, la mise en scène dans des décors peints, la typologie des sujets scabreux, les accessoires de costume (canne et canotier) tendent à montrer que les flip books *La Méprise* et *Le Voyeur* semblent apparentés.

La vitesse de défilement des images du flip book s'effectue à 8 images/seconde. Nous en déduisons qu'une image sur deux a été utilisée pour son élaboration à partir d'un film enregistré originellement à 16 images/seconde. Une bande celluloïd de 3,60 mètres a été nécessaire pour la fabrication du flip book.[45]

– *Le coup du père François* [collection P. Fouché]

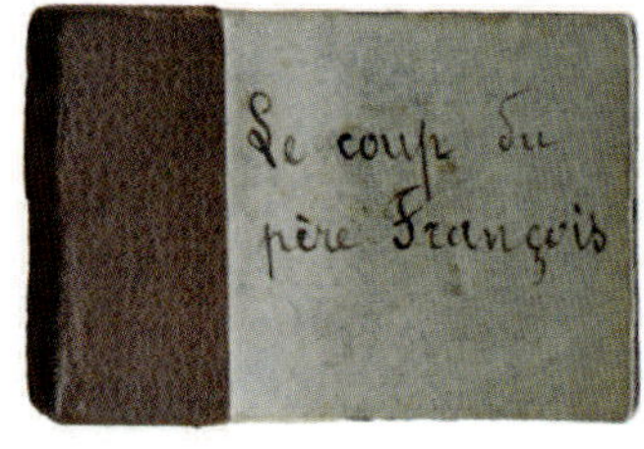

© Onno Petersen – Collection Pascal Fouché.

Ce flip book met en scène trois personnages dont deux vont user d'un stratagème pour détrousser le troisième d'où le titre manuscrit. Cette expression n'est plus vraiment usitée de nos jours d'où notre intuition que ce titre est certainement contemporain du livret.[46] Nous noterons qu'un exemplaire de la collection de François Binétruy porte le même titre. Deux personnages ont attiré notre attention. Le volé d'abord dont la physionomie générale n'est pas sans rappeler le personnage dans *Le Voyeur* et *La Méprise* analysés précédemment. Comme dans ces flip books, il porte également un canotier, élément de costume récurrent chez Méliès. Par ailleurs, si certains photogrammes nous incitent à penser qu'il pourrait s'agir de Méliès, lorsqu'il perd son canotier à la fin de la séquence, les images ne montrent pas la calvitie caractéristique de Georges. Le second personnage est la dame dont la jupe longue dotée d'un liseré dans sa partie inférieure semble très nettement être la même que celle portée par la servante dans *Le Coucher de la mariée* et *Le Bain*, ces deux flip books étant certifiés Méliès puisque tournés dans le décor de la vue *L'École des gendres* entre autres. Ainsi, par transitivité à partir du décor de *L'École des gendres*, de ce même décor et d'une jupe vue dans *Le Bain* et *Le Coucher de la mariée*, de cette même jupe vue dans ce flip book, celui-ci se rapproche encore davantage de Méliès. En conséquence, l'appartenance de ce flip book à une famille plus large composée du même nombre de pages, dont plusieurs sont certifiés Méliès, l'utilisation de costumes et accessoires de manière récurrente dans des images Méliès nous conduit à apporter à ce flip book, selon mon protocole, la classification « probable Méliès – confiance élevée ».

Bien que tourné sur fond noir, sans décor particulier, la cadence optimale de ce flip book est établie à 8 images/seconde. L'enregistrement de ce film s'est sans doute effectué à 16 images/seconde, vitesse associée au flip books les plus récents. L'adresse de notre exemplaire étant la rue Volta, nous estimons que la bande originelle ne peut être postérieure à septembre 1897. Une bande cinématographique de 3,60 mètres fut donc nécessaire pour l'élaboration de ce livret utilisant un photogramme sur deux.

– *La Nourrice* [collection P. Fouché] ou *Le Banc* [collection F. Binétruy]

© Onno Petersen – Collection Pascal Fouché.

Assis sur un banc à côté d'une nourrice, un militaire a engagé la conversation. Comme il devient un peu trop entreprenant, la nourrice lui confie son bambin, prétextant probablement une course urgente, tandis qu'un autre personnage s'assoit en lisant son journal à l'autre extrémité du banc. Malheureusement, il semble bien que le nourrisson se soulage dans les bras du soldat qui se lève brusquement du banc avec la nourrice, ce qui provoque la chute du lecteur. L'effet comique était garanti. Le film a été tourné sur fond noir, le banc étant le seul accessoire. La qualité du tirage, certainement la plus mauvaise du corpus, ne permet pas d'identifier les personnages. On remarque que, comme dans la quasi-totalité des flip books attribués à Méliès, les acteurs sont en costumes comme pour une représentation théâtrale alors que la séquence n'impose pas ces artifices. Est-ce un signe de la touche Méliès scénariste ? Ce flip book allait suggérer un rapprochement troublant. Il subsiste, en effet, un fragment de film de trois photogrammes évoquant fortement la saynète de ce flip book, collés sur le premier catalogue connu de Méliès (le recto d'une simple feuille où figurent les 45 premiers films réalisés à Montreuil entre mai et septembre 1896).[47] Les points communs sont nombreux entre le flip book et le fragment sauvegardé : le banc, la nourrice à gauche, le militaire au centre et le lecteur à droite (l'homme bien en chair, probablement joué par Méliès dans le film). On remarque que le mur devant lequel se passe la scène représentée dans le fragment sauvegardé est également visible dans un film de Méliès récemment retrouvé, *Défense d'afficher* (n° 15, 1896).

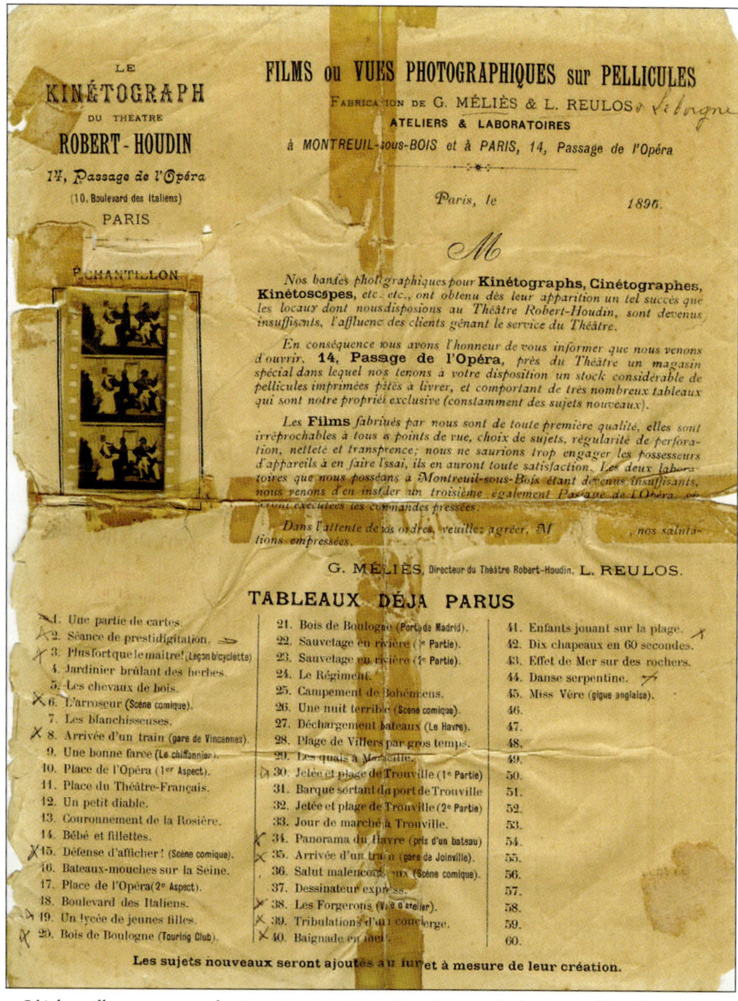

LE **KINÉTOGRAPH** DU THÉÂTRE **ROBERT-HOUDIN** 14, *Passage de l'Opéra* (10, Boulevard des Italiens) PARIS

FILMS ou VUES PHOTOGRAPHIQUES sur PELLICULES

FABRICATION DE G. MÉLIÈS & L. REULOS

ATELIERS & LABORATOIRES

à MONTREUIL-sous-BOIS et à PARIS, 14, Passage de l'Opéra

Paris, le 1896.

ÉCHANTILLON

Nos bandes photographiques pour **Kinétographs, Cinétographes, Kinétoscopes,** *etc. etc., ont obtenu dès leur apparition un tel succès que les locaux dont nous disposons au Théâtre Robert-Houdin, sont devenus insuffisants, l'affluence des clients gênant le service du Théâtre.*

En conséquence nous avons l'honneur de vous informer que nous venons d'ouvrir, **14, Passage de l'Opéra,** *près du Théâtre un magasin spécial dans lequel nous tenons à votre disposition un stock considérable de pellicules imprimées prêtes à livrer, et comportant de très nombreux tableaux qui sont notre propriété exclusive (constamment des sujets nouveaux).*

Les **Films** *fabriqués par nous sont de toute première qualité, elles sont irréprochables à tous les points de vue, choix de sujets, régularité de perforation, netteté et transparence; nous ne saurions trop engager les possesseurs d'appareils à en faire l'essai, ils en auront toute satisfaction. Les deux laboratoires que nous possédons à Montreuil-sous-Bois étant devenus insuffisants, nous venons d'en installer un troisième également Passage de l'Opéra, où seront exécutées les commandes pressées.*

Dans l'attente de vos ordres, veuillez agréer, M , nos salutations empressées.

G. MÉLIÈS, Directeur du Théâtre Robert-Houdin. L. REULOS.

TABLEAUX DÉJA PARUS

1. Une partie de cartes.	21. Bois de Boulogne (Porte de Madrid).	41. Enfants jouant sur la plage.
2. Séance de prestidigitation.	22. Sauvetage en rivière (1re Partie).	42. Dix chapeaux en 60 secondes.
3. Plus fort que le maitre! (Leçon bicyclette).	23. Sauvetage en rivière (2e Partie).	43. Effet de Mer sur des rochers.
4. Jardinier brûlant des herbes.	24. Le Régiment.	44. Danse serpentine.
5. Les chevaux de bois.	25. Campement de Bohémiens.	45. Miss Vère (gigue anglaise).
6. L'arroseur (Scène comique).	26. Une nuit terrible (Scène comique).	46.
7. Les blanchisseuses.	27. Déchargement bateaux (Le Havre).	47.
8. Arrivée d'un train (gare de Vincennes).	28. Plage de Villers par gros temps.	48.
9. Une bonne farce (Le chiffonnier).	29. Les quais à Marseille.	49.
10. Place de l'Opéra (1er Aspect).	30. Jetée et plage de Trouville (1e Partie).	50.
11. Place du Théâtre-Français.	31. Barque sortant du port de Trouville.	51.
12. Un petit diable.	32. Jetée et plage de Trouville (2e Partie).	52.
13. Couronnement de la Rosière.	33. Jour de marché à Trouville.	53.
14. Bébé et fillettes.	34. Panorama du Havre (pris d'un bateau).	54.
15. Défense d'afficher ! (Scène comique).	35. Arrivée d'un train (gare de Joinville).	55.
16. Bateaux-mouches sur la Seine.	36. Salut malencontreux (Scène comique).	56.
17. Place de l'Opéra (2e Aspect).	37. Dessinateur express.	57.
18. Boulevard des Italiens.	38. Les Forgerons (Vue d'atelier).	58.
19. Un lycée de jeunes filles.	39. Tribulations d'un concierge.	59.
20. Bois de Boulogne (Touring Club).	40. Baignade en mer.	60.

Les sujets nouveaux seront ajoutés au fur et à mesure de leur création.

L'échantillon correspond nécessairement à un titre circonscrit dans cette liste du n° 1 au n° 45. © Cinémathèque Française.

Après de multiples visionnages du flip book, Jacques Malthête pense que le fragment pourrait très bien correspondre au n° 36 du catalogue Méliès : *Salut malencontreux*. En effet, dans le catalogue Méliès américain, le titre de ce film est *A Soldier's Unlucky Salutation* et, aussi bien dans le flip book que dans le fragment, il s'agit bien d'un soldat qui salue une nourrice, avec probablement quelque arrière-pensée, et nos trois personnages sont là.

Sur le plan chronologique, nous observons une certaine homogénéité entre ce flip book et d'autres vues analysées. Nous avons déjà effectué des rapprochements entre des flip books et les films de Méliès n°s 26, 35 et 45, auxquels pourrait donc s'ajouter une première version du n° 36. Nous avons ainsi présumé que pour les numéros du catalogue Méliès ultérieurs – n°s 128, 130/131, 136, 148 et 177/178 –, les flip books associés correspondraient à des premières versions de ces titres datant de fin 1896 début 1897. Seul le n° 101 *David Devant* représente en quelque sorte un hiatus chronologique très relatif cependant puisque tourné mi 1897 au plus tard (et sans doute fin du premier trimestre 1897 au regard de l'adresse figurant sur le flip book).

Des critères de classification techniques peuvent en outre rapprocher ce flip book d'autres exemples dont plusieurs sont attribuables à Méliès (nombre de photogrammes, mode opératoire de fabrication, format de pagination).

La cadence optimale du film obtenue par Robert Byrne après différents essais est de 10 images/seconde, ce qui doit correspondre à la vitesse d'enregistrement du film. Cette vitesse, parmi les plus faibles, est à rapprocher du décor noir primitif. Ce film est certainement parmi les plus anciens du corpus. L'exemplaire de Pascal Fouché avec son adresse complète mentionne celle d'Aubervilliers, quatrième du point de vue chronologique. Cependant, les adresses figurant avant le 1er photogramme et sous le 90ème affichent une typographie différente prouvant que ce type de pages sans photogrammes pourraient être des ajouts sans lien chronologique direct avec la fabrication des flip books concernés.

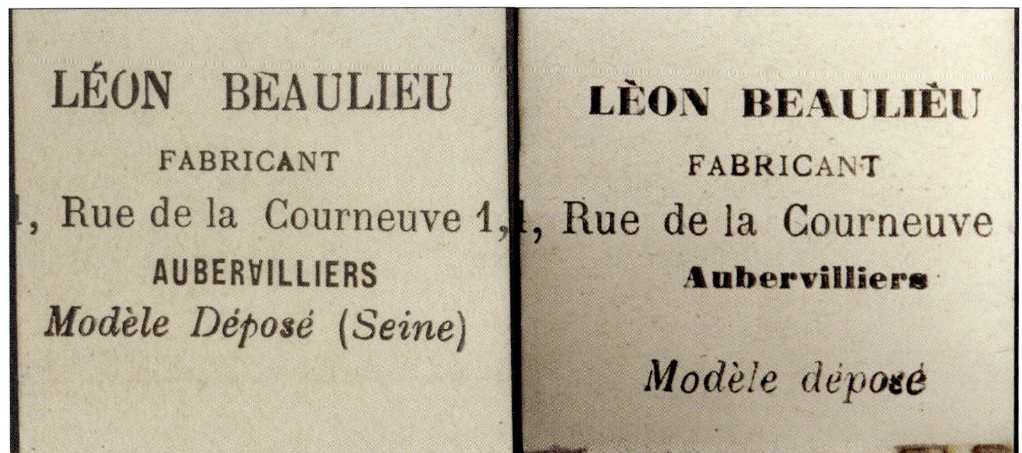

À gauche, page 0, à droite page 90 : les typographies de « Léon Beaulieu », « Aubervilliers » sont différentes. Le V de la ville est un A inversé sur la page 0, « Déposé » prend une majuscule sur cette page. © Onno Petersen – Collection Pascal Fouché.

Une bande celluloïd de 1,80 mètre a été nécessaire pour l'élaboration des 90 feuillets. Nous pouvons donc clairement établir une nouvelle double version correspondant à un titre du catalogue et attribuer à ce flip book une origine « probable Méliès – confiance élevée ».

Trois photogrammes survivants de *Salut malencontreux* – © Cinémathèque Française.

Photogrammes 30, 35 et 40 du flip book *La Nourrice* – © Onno Petersen – Collection Pascal Fouché.

Un autre flip book au format unique : « Partie de cartes à trois » [collection P. Fouché] (96 photogrammes)

© Onno Petersen – Collection Pascal Fouché.

Le flip book composé de 96 photogrammes représente donc une partie de cartes à trois. Robert Byrne, lors du recadrage des images en vue de l'animation, a constaté que les images étaient doublées. Il n'y en a que 48 différentes. Le doublement des images s'est effectué selon le principe suivant : 1–1, 2–2, 3–3,…, 48-48. Le doublement des images, pour la constitution d'un flip book, n'a pas d'autre intérêt que d'augmenter mécaniquement le nombre de feuillets pour rendre le produit homogène avec le reste du corpus. En effet, présenter aux acheteurs un livret de seulement 48 images dans une collection où chaque livret en comporte en moyenne plus de 80 aurait constitué un hiatus.

Le film de Méliès n° 1 *Partie de cartes*, connu, ne correspond pas aux images du flip book. De plus, ce format à 48 images ne semble pas s'inscrire dans ceux relevant des flip books associés à Méliès. Mais si ce flip book était encore une version primitive de *Partie de cartes* et la version filmique connue un remake ? Cela pourrait mettre à mal notre hypothèse. Des recherches ont été menées dans ce sens et c'est ainsi que j'ai relu Madeleine Malthête-Méliès. Elle relate avec précision le tournage de ce premier film :

> En cet après-midi du 10 juin 1896, Georges improvise le scénario de son premier film, un scénario bien simpliste, en vérité. Il a placé Lucien Reulos derrière l'appareil de prise de vues et s'est installé à une table avec son frère Gaston, son ami Leborgne et Roberval, son ancien condisciple du lycée Louis-le-Grand.[48]

Ils sont donc quatre (hommes) autour de la table. Or, sur *La Partie de cartes* que nous connaissons (version filmique), ils ne sont que trois ! Il y a bien une quatrième personne mais c'est une fillette d'abord (Georgette Méliès),[49] laissant sa place à une domestique faisant le service. Dans le livre de Bessy et Duca, on trouve la reproduction de ce qui est énoncé comme un photogramme représentant *Partie de cartes*.[50] Force est de constater que cette photographie n'est pas extraite du film connu. Elle montre cependant bien une partie de cartes mais avec quatre hommes autour de la table, illustration parfaite de la description relatée par Madeleine Malthête-Méliès (l'attribution de cette photographie à Méliès et l'identification des personnages sont incertaines d'après Jacques Malthête). Dans le cas où cette photographie serait effectivement extraite d'un film de Méliès, nous serions donc bien en présence de deux versions possibles de ce film comme pour d'autres vues de Méliès étudiées précédemment. De plus, la version filmique connue défile correctement à 16 images/seconde (confirmé par Serge Bromberg). Or, nous avons constaté que les flip books attribuables à Méliès défilent à 12 images/seconde jusqu'au film numéro 101 daté de mars 1897 au plus tard. Au regard des films retrouvés et numérisés sur DVD, c'est à partir de cette époque, autour de la vue numéro 95, que la cadence de tournage s'établit à 16 images/seconde.[51] Selon mon analyse, la *Partie de cartes* connue ne peut être qu'un remake d'une première version actuellement inconnue, laquelle, selon de forte probabilité, n'aurait été tournée qu'à 12 images/seconde. Quoi qu'il en soit, l'image dans le livre de Bessy et Duca n'est pas comparable à celles du flip book. La possibilité de raccorder ce flip book de 48 images à Méliès s'éloigne donc encore un peu plus puisqu'il ne correspond à aucune des deux versions présumées du film Méliès.

L'analyse physique des scans des photogrammes montre clairement des inter-images latéraux sur une même ligne qui ne sont en aucun cas comparables à ceux, quasi-inexistants, des flip books aux formats à 121, 90 et 80 images, leurs images étant juxtaposées bord à bord. L'inter-image sur ce flip book est très marqué, il détache très bien chaque photogramme. Chaque image est parfaitement délimitée par un cadre noir qui semble avoir été tracé au tire-ligne. Or, ces particularités liées aux photogrammes vont se retrouver dans des flip books, que nous analyserons plus loin, attribués à Gaumont. Nous disposons là d'un nouveau critère physique qui tend à rapprocher ce livret d'une origine Gaumont. Le format à 96 images ne permet d'envisager que des bandes de 8 ou 12 photogrammes, matrice ambivalente avec celles correspondant aux vues Méliès. C'est encore une découpe approximative au massicot qui allait nous permettre de comprendre le mode opératoire quant à la fabrication de ce flip book. Une erreur de découpe montre très clairement une association des photogrammes 87 et 89. D'autres indices infimes mais récurrents confirment l'association de toutes les images impaires. Ces quarante-huit photogrammes impairs sont rangés en six lignes de huit images. Il en est de même pour les quarante-huit photogrammes pairs. L'analyse des découpes montre que ces deux planches sont complètement indépendantes. La planche impaire, constituée des lignes 1 à 15, 17 à 31, 33 à 47, etc. jusqu'à 81 à 95, a été découpée en huit colonnes regroupant les numéros 1, 17, 33, 49, 65 et 81 puis 3, 19, 35, 51, 67 et 83, etc. Il en est de même pour la planche paire. Ce flip book a été réalisé à partir de deux planches de 6 x 8 photogrammes. Sans que nous puissions le vérifier (le démontage du flip book relié ne serait pas anodin), il est probable que les bandes aient été empilées en alternant numéros impairs et pairs (la bande 1, 17, 33, 49, 65, 81 d'abord, suivie de la bande 2, 18, 34, 50, 66, 82, ensuite la bande 3, 19, 35, 51, 67, 83, etc.). Ainsi, seize bandes de six photogrammes auraient été superposées pour une découpe au massicot de six blocs de seize images. Le premier bloc comportant les images 1 à 16, le second les images 17 à 32, jusqu'au dernier avec les images 81 à 96. La superposition des blocs formant par conséquent le flip book de 96 images.

La vitesse de défilement des photogrammes à 12 images/seconde correspond à une cadence optimale. De ce fait, nous en déduisons qu'un tronçon unique de 0,96 mètre a été utilisé pour l'élaboration de ce flip book.

Nous avons donc investigué la *Partie de cartes* Gaumont, film n° 72 du catalogue. La version filmique connue n'est pas celle du flip book. En revanche, nous observons et constatons des similitudes assez singulières. Le film et le flip book comportent trois personnages ; le cadrage, même s'il est plus serré sur le film, est assez similaire à celui du flip book. L'identification des personnages n'a malheureusement rien donné de positif.

C'est en continuant mes recherches sur internet que j'allais trouver un nouvel indice très significatif. Un flip book constitué des mêmes images avait été vendu aux enchères sur un site. Or, ce modèle n'a strictement rien à voir avec le format Beaulieu. Il est présenté comme un exemplaire de l'allemand Max Skladanowsky. Bien qu'il soit anonyme en raison de l'absence de couverture, son format et son feuilletage à l'horizontal sont effectivement exactement identiques aux autres exemplaires connus de ce fabricant germanique. Il est constitué de 48 images uniquement, les mêmes que celles de Beaulieu. Si ce flip book est attribuable à Skladanowsky avec une très forte probabilité, en revanche il est différent de celui connu sous le titre *Eine Parthie Klabrias*. Ce dernier titre extrait de la collection Pascal Fouché a suscité mon intérêt. En y regardant de beaucoup plus près, il s'avère que la composition de la saynète est la même et que deux acteurs sont clairement identiques à ceux de la version reprise par Beaulieu (un doute sur le troisième). La table de jeu est aussi strictement identique ainsi que les chopes de bière.

Nous apportons donc à ce flip book la classification « confirmé Skladanowsky ».

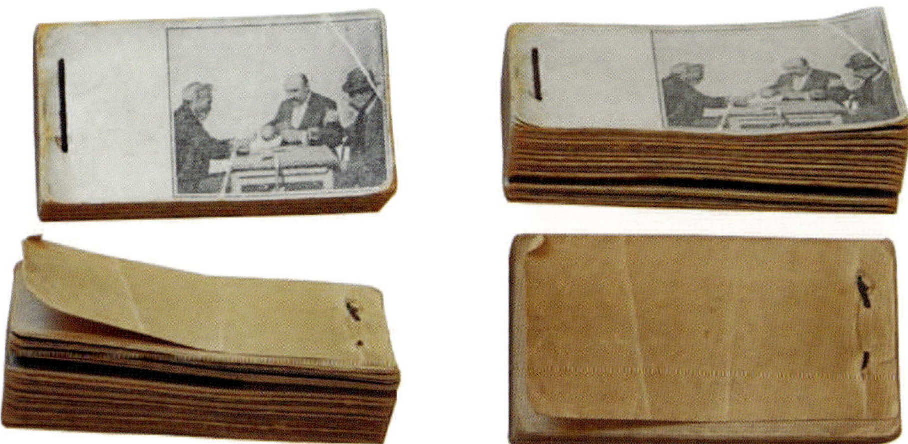

Flip book Skladanowsky, 48 photogrammes, (65 mm x 35 mm) © Collection particulière.

L'existence de deux flip books Beaulieu dont les images proviennent de films Skladanowsky et Edison, ainsi que la nature des autres flip books du corpus, nous éloignent quasi définitivement des distributeurs Mendel et Clément & Gilmer en tant que fournisseurs potentiels de Léon Beaulieu.

Notes

1. Un seul des 7 flip books étudiés dispose de l'image 75 avec l'adresse complète.

2. Je possède une version similaire (62 x 46 mm), feuilletage de l'arrière vers l'avant, éditée rue Saint-Denis (les pages des adresses sont déchirées).

3. Est-ce que l'imprimeur habituel de Beaulieu craignait de faire ce travail pour des problèmes de droit ?

4. Voir Charles Musser, *Edison Motion Pictures, 1890–1900 – An Annotated Filmography*, La Gionate del Cinema Muto / Smithsonian Institution Press, Gemona, 1997, p. 197.

5. Les vitesses de défilement des bandes pour kinétoscopes étaient de 30 à 40 images/seconde.

6. Cette prédominance de l'utilisation du noir et blanc pour renforcer le contraste est toujours présente en 1907 pour les décors et maquillage : « ils [les acteurs] n'échappent pas à la loi qui régit la peinture des décors, dans lesquels le blanc et le noir sont seuls employés. […] Le maquillage se fait exclusivement au blanc et noir », dans Georges Méliès, « Les vues cinématographiques. Causerie par Geo. Méliès », *Annuaire général et international de la photographie*, reproduit dans André Gaudreault, *Cinéma et attraction. Pour une nouvelle histoire du cinématographe*, *op. cit.*, p. 219, texte présenté et annoté par Jacques Malthête.

7. Voir la description de Méliès dans Georges Méliès, « Les vues cinématographiques. Causerie par Geo. Méliès », *ibid.*, p. 215.

8. « En marge de l'histoire du Cinématographe » par Georges Méliès, *Ciné-Journal*, n° 885, 13 août 1926, p. 11.

9. Jacques Malthête, « L'appentis sorcier de Montreuil-sous-Bois », dans *Méliès, carrefour des attractions*, *op. cit.*, pp. 145–155.

10. « En marge de l'histoire du Cinématographe » par Georges Méliès, *Ciné-Journal*, n° 888, 3 septembre 1926, p. 11.

11. Même si Méliès revient épisodiquement à la distance courte tout au long de sa production pour des raisons conjoncturelles liées à la mise en scène, remarque que l'on doit à Jacques Malthête.

12. « A humourous subject, full of action, showing the retiring of a young man who is disturbed by midnight marauders, upon whom he makes an assault, slaughtering four or five in rapid succession. Full of animation ».

13. *Une Nuit terrible* est mentionnée dans *L'Express de Mulhouse*, 19 août 1896 : « "Une Nuit terrible", on croirait assister à une scène de pantomime de cirque », dans Jacques et Chantal Rittaud-Hutinet, *Dictionnaire des cinématographes en France (1896–1897)*, *op. cit.*, p. 317. Jean-Claude Seguin identifie une occurrence antérieure à Lisbonne, dans *A Vanguarda*, 16 août 1896.

14. Jacques Malthête au vu de la morphologie de l'actrice, de son embonpoint et de sa gestuelle, pourrait bien reconnaître Jehanne d'Alcy mais sans certitude aucune. Nous faisons la même analyse.

15. Il est possible que cette vue soit antérieure à cette date.

16. « En marge de l'histoire du Cinématographe » par Georges Méliès, *Ciné-Journal*, n° 888, *op. cit.*, p. 11.

17. Vue reproduite dans le DVD 1 inclus dans Camille Blot-Wellens, *La colección Sagarmínaga (1897–1906) Érase una vez el cinematógrafo en Bilbao*, *op. cit.* Mes remerciements à Jacques Malthête pour cette référence.

18. Jacques Malthête ne reconnait absolument pas Méliès dans cette vue.

19. « En marge de l'histoire du Cinématographe » par Georges Méliès, *Ciné-Journal*, n° 888, *op. cit.*, p. 9.

20. Cette photographie de plateau est associée au titre *Le Vieux galant* [titre hors catalogue] dans l'ouvrage de Maurice Bessy et Lo Duca, *op. cit.*, p. 148.

21. Ce qui pourrait étayer les assertions de Sadoul à propos d'un répertoire de films grivois, dans Georges Sadoul, *Histoire générale du cinéma – II, Les pionniers du cinéma 1897–1909*, Paris, Éditions Denoël, 1973, pp. 107 et 115.

22. Dans Georges Méliès, « Les vues cinématographiques. Causerie par Geo. Méliès », *op. cit.*, reproduit dans André Gaudreault, *Cinéma et attraction. Pour une nouvelle histoire du cinématographe*, *op. cit.*, p. 201.

23. Dans « Liste complète des films cinématographiques de G. Méliès, fabricant, 13, passage de l'Opéra, Paris », citée dans Jacques Malthête, *Méliès, images et illusions*, Exporégie, Paris, 1996, p. 216.

24. La Goulue, personnalité de Montmartre, avait 30 ans. Elle ne semble pas avoir été filmée durant cette période.

25. *La Lanterne*, 16 janvier 1897.

26. *La Lanterne*, 1er mai 1897.

27. *Le Gaulois*, 2 octobre 1897.

28. *L'Aurore* et *Gil Blas*, 8 juillet 1898.

29. *Le Figaro* et *Gil Blas*, 15 octobre 1898.

30.   *Gil Blas*, 21 juin 1900.

31.   Très comparable aux images du flip book.

32.   Ce type de mouvement est perceptible à la seconde 2 sur 10 du flip book animé à 12 images/seconde.

33.   Mail de Laurent Guido du 12 novembre 2013.

34.   Mail de Laurent Guido du 14 novembre 2013.

35.   Voir les deux photographies dans Jacques Malthête et Laurent Mannoni, *L'Œuvre de Georges Méliès, op. cit.*, p. 125.

36.   M. Michel Coissac, écrit Méliès, dans une dédicace qu'il lui a rédigée le 30 septembre 1925 pour la sortie de son livre *Histoire du cinématographe de ses origines à nos jours*, décrivait : « M. Georges Méliès, rois des trucs, prince de la féerie et des transformations », cité dans « En marge de l'histoire du Cinématographe » par Georges Méliès, *Ciné-Journal*, n° 884, 6 août 1926, p. 9.

37.   Dans « Mes mémoires par Georges Méliès » cité dans Maurice Bessy et Lo Duca, *Georges Méliès, mage, op. cit.* p. 169.

38.   « En marge de l'histoire du Cinématographe » par Georges Méliès, *Ciné-Journal*, n° 885, *op. cit.*, p. 11, cité dans Jacques Malthête, *Méliès, images et illusions, op. cit.*, p. 137.

39.   Georges Méliès, *Noir et Blanc*, 10 juillet 1929, cité dans Jacques Deslandes, *Le boulevard du cinéma à l'époque de Georges Méliès*, Éditions du Cerf, Bourges, 1963, p. 27. C'est nous qui soulignons.

40.   Jacques Malthête note qu'il existe d'autres exemples de remakes de films de Méliès réalisés par lui-même comme *L'Illusionniste fin de siècle* [1899], *Le sacre d'Edouard VII* [1902], *Hydrothérapie fantastique* [1909].

41.   Jacques Malthête a toujours eu un niveau de lecture divergent de cet article, renforcé par la parution de ce même article le lendemain avec une ponctuation différente, dans Raymond Thoumazeau et Francis Ray, *Pour vous*, n° 34, 11 juillet 1929, pp. 8-9 : « Je projetai d'abord des bandes de kinetoscope : des escrimeurs, des boxeurs, la Loïe Fuller. Mes personnages apparaissaient en blanc sur fond noir ». Jacques Malthête pense en effet que le terme « <u>Mes</u> personnages » désigne les « escrimeurs », les « boxeurs » et « la Loïe Fuller » d'Edison, que Méliès projetait sur <u>son</u> écran du théâtre Robert-Houdin [c'est lui qui souligne]. Or, si on trouve chez Edison, avant juin 1896, des vues de boxeurs et une danse serpentine parmi une série de danses exécutées par Annabelle Whitford (l'une d'elle a été régulièrement utilisée pour des flip books américains), on ne trouve chez Edison aucun combat d'escrimeurs. Par ailleurs, les images des flip books Beaulieu aux vues de leurs contenus (boxe française et bâton, disciplines spécifiquement enseignées à l'école militaire de Joinville) et de leurs cadences (12 images/seconde) ne peuvent être attribuées à des images du kinétoscope d'Edison.

42.   Pour les films hors catalogue déjà inventoriés voir Jacques Malthête, *Méliès, images et illusions, op. cit.* p. 243.

43.   Dans Maurice Bessy et Lo Duca, *Georges Méliès, mage, op. cit.*, p. 147, *Le Peintre et son modèle*. Le tirage argentique d'époque (11,5 x 16 cm), ayant servi pour la publication, contrecollé sur carton représentant sa femme dans le rôle du modèle [d'après Jacques Malthête, ce n'est pas Jehanne d'Alcy] et lui-même dans le rôle du peintre, intitulé « Le Modèle narcissique, 1896 », a été vendu aux enchères le 17 mars 2018 par la Galerie de Chartres, 7, rue Colin d'Harleville, 28000 Chartres.

44.   Voir Henri Bousquet, *Catalogue Pathé des années 1896 à 1914 – 1896 à 1906*, Editions Henri Bousquet, 1996, p. 854. Résumé du catalogue originel 1900 : « Une jeune et jolie personne en déshabillé cherchant une puce. Jeu de physionomie et poses tout à fait suggestives ». Pour cette vue Pathé, Louise Willy en serait l'actrice selon Bousquet.

45.   Aucun de 4 flip books étudiés ne dispose de l'image 90 en raison des déchirures systématiques de cette page. C'est le seul flip book incomplet de la collection. Le paradoxe de cette mutilation, c'est que la déchirure a supprimé l'image, la reliure préservant l'adresse.

46.   Nous retrouvons cette expression dans le tableau n° 7, *Le Coup du père François*, du film Pathé n° 1309, *Les Apaches de Paris*, sorti en novembre 1905, voir Henri Bousquet, *Catalogue Pathé des années 1896 à 1914 – 1896 à 1906*, *op. cit.*, p. 916.

47.   Cette vénérable feuille, conservée par la Cinémathèque française, a été montrée pour la première fois lors d'une table ronde qui s'est tenue dans le cadre du Conservatoire des techniques de la CF le 15 janvier 2015 : « 1896/2016 : Lumière/Méliès, les débuts du spectacle cinématographique », présentée et animée par Maurice Gianati, Jacques Malthête et Laurent Mannoni.

48.   Madeleine Malthête-Méliès, *Méliès, l'enchanteur*, Hachette, Paris, 1973, pp. 161-162.

49.   Source Jacques Malthête.

50.   Maurice Bessy et Lo Duca, *Georges Méliès, mage, op. cit.*, p. 74.

51. Sur les 15 films préservés du numéro 1 au numéro 128 (1, 15, 26, 70, 78-80, 82, 95, 96, 100, 105, 106, 110, 112, 122-123 et 128), tous transcrit à 16 images par seconde, seuls les numéros 15, 70, 78-80 et 82 montrent une cadence tout ou partiellement accélérée (l'évaluation d'une bonne vitesse de défilement n'est surtout décelable que sur des mouvements rapides). Ainsi, je pause l'hypothèse que les vues n° 1 et 26 retranscrites sur le DVD, défilant correctement à 16 images/seconde, seraient des remakes tournés vers le printemps 1897.

Des flip books initiés par Beaulieu imprimés et vendus par l'imprimeur Prissette ?

Si pour les vingt flip books précédents il ne fait aucun doute qu'il s'agit de produits commandés par Léon Beaulieu pour une fabrication à son seul profit, pour les sept qui suivent le lien est plus mince. Pascal Fouché possède neuf flip books attribuables à un imprimeur parisien, Prissette, dont sept sous forme d'images photographiques dont les formats, matériaux utilisés sont en tous points équivalents aux exemplaires Beaulieu[1] mais qui se distinguent par la présence d'une agrafe reliant les pages. Trois d'entre eux sont constitués de 84 photogrammes et portent tous la mention « Clichés, L. Gaumont et Cie, Paris » sur la page inférieure. La marque Prissette est imprimée sur la seconde de couverture. Pour cinq de ces sept livrets, l'adresse de l'imprimeur figure sur une page. Pour deux d'entre eux, l'anonymisation en raison des déchirures des pages d'adresse est totale et ne permet de les associer formellement ni à Beaulieu, ni à Prissette. Pour d'autres exemplaires qui sont des doubles, les pages déchirées qui les rendent complètement anonymes ne correspondent pas à la pagination observée sur les exemplaires Prissette intègres. Pour ces sept flip books, compte tenu d'un format global similaire, d'un procédé de fabrication identique, de la similitude des matériaux utilisés, de la proximité géographique entre l'adresse de Prissette et celles de Beaulieu, de l'unité temporelle commune pour la fabrication de ces deux corpus, il est bien difficile de ne pas envisager un lien précis entre Beaulieu et Prissette, voire même une certaine perméabilité entre ces deux fabricants. Car n'en doutons pas, si Beaulieu s'affichait comme fabricant, il lui fallait bien un imprimeur, ce qu'il n'était pas.

Si le corpus Beaulieu montre une certaine cohérence en ce qui concerne l'origine des films, les formats qu'il donne à ses flip books, montrant par là un véritable positionnement d'éditeur dans l'élaboration de sa collection, celui de Prissette est beaucoup plus hétéroclite et surtout limité à sept exemplaires.[2] L'ensemble des points de convergence ou même des quelques différences nous incitent à penser que les deux corpus sont liés, Prissette ayant peut-être récupéré à son compte des bandes cinématographiques exclues par Beaulieu. Mais ceci n'est qu'une proposition subjective.

Un flip book à 90 photogrammes : *Loïe Fuller* [collection P. Fouché]

© Onno Petersen – Collections Pascal Fouché et Thierry Lecointe.

Nous nous sommes intéressés à ce livret dont l'un des exemplaires avait été originellement attribué à Beaulieu. En effet, le flip book en question, anonyme, comporte 90 images, se présente avec un format comparable aux autres flip books (largeur 42 mm) et d'un feuilletage qui s'effectue de l'arrière vers l'avant, autant d'éléments qui le connecte aux huit autres flip books de la série Beaulieu comportant le même nombre d'images. Nous possédons cinq flip books représentant cette danse serpentine exécutée, selon le titre manuscrit sur un exemplaire (identifié chez Prissette), par Loïe Fuller (graphologie pourtant identique à quelques exemplaires Beaulieu). Tous sont coloriés (les couleurs utilisées se sont pas synchrones d'une version à l'autre). Pour les cinq versions, les 90 images sont strictement identiques et chacune présente une numérotation typographique intra-photographique.[3] On peut aussi rapprocher ce principe de numérotation à ceux constatés sur des flip books Beaulieu notamment sur *Les Deux baisers* tiré d'un film Edison. Sur un seul exemplaire l'origine du fabricant est mentionnée : « Prissette, Imprimeur Fabricant. Passage Kuszner, 17, Paris » ; sur les quatre autres versions, la première page est déchirée ainsi qu'une dernière sous le photogramme numéro 1. Les cinq versions sont agrafées, seul élément physique qui les distingue des flip books Beaulieu. En revanche, les reliures sont toutes en tissu, matière commune à tous les exemplaires Beaulieu.

Au regard des cinq exemplaires que nous possédons, peut-on imaginer qu'il y ait eu pour cette danse serpentine à la fois des flip books Beaulieu et Prissette ? Les versions dont les pages sont déchirées, rendant anonyme les livrets, pourraient être de ce fait attribuables à Beaulieu ? C'est une hypothèse cohérente au regard du corpus mais certes invérifiable en l'état. Nous noterons que tous les flip books mutilés sont à priori des Beaulieu alors que tous les flip books Prissette paraissent être intègres à l'exception – peut-être – de ces premiers exemplaires de danse serpentine. Si le corpus Beaulieu et Prissette est établi à 27 livrets différents, notre base de données est constituée de 75 flip books formellement attribués à Beaulieu (61 dans la collection Pascal Fouché et 14 chez Thierry Lecointe, hors exemplaires portant l'adresse Prissette) auxquels s'ajoutent 26 exemplaires appartenant à François Binétruy et Carlo Montanaro. Or, nous dénombrons 61 flip books présentant la mutilation de la première page pour les rendre anonyme, soit plus de 60 % ! En outre Pascal Fouché précise que ce chiffre lui parait être un taux à minima et « très loin de la réalité » car « entièrement faussé par

[sa] propre collection », dans la mesure où il s'est évertué pendant des années à chercher et trouver des exemplaires complets. En fait, précise-t-il, « plus de 90 % de ceux que l'on voit passer sur les sites en ligne ou aux enchères ont la première page déchirée », ce qui est le cas pour les exemplaires de Binétruy, Montanaro et Lecointe (97,5 % sont mutilés). Il ajoute que « c'est le seul exemple à [sa] connaissance d'amputation volontaire » sur des flip books, précisant au regard de son expérience : « quand il manque des pages ce sont plus souvent les couvertures qui ont souffert ». Or, pour corroborer son analyse, bon nombre de flip books Beaulieu mutilés présentent un état de vétusté modéré. C'est peut-être à la suite de la vente du stock de Beaulieu après sa mort que ces mutilations ont eu lieu puisque le propriétaire des flip books invendus avait changé (nous en reparlerons). Mais qu'en est-il des éventuels flip books Prissette mutilés ? Pour quelle raison y aurait-il eu un sort similaire pour des livrets Prissette, à une période contemporaine à celle de l'activité de Beaulieu ? Nous n'avons pas de réponse même si les recherches montrent que Prissette semble avoir arrêté son activité en 1899. Le stock Prissette aurait pu subir le même sort que celui de Beaulieu de la part du repreneur de l'imprimerie.

Sur les quatre exemplaires mutilés, une page inférieure est également déchirée derrière le photogramme numéro 1. Sur l'exemplaire Prissette complet, cette page n'existe pas. Il s'agit là d'un premier hiatus constaté entre les flip books Prissette complets et ceux mutilés. Il y a donc des incohérences en matière de pagination sur un corpus qui se veut homogène puisqu'il émanerait de l'imprimeur Prissette lui-même. Or, nous possédons plusieurs flip books Beaulieu comportant cette page inférieure sans photo-gramme sur laquelle est inscrite « Léon Beaulieu fabricant » et son adresse. Nous disposons également de plusieurs flip books Beaulieu qui possèdent deux fois ce type de mention : une fois sur la page supérieure, sous la dernière photo ; une fois sur la page inférieure, avant la page du photogramme 1. Les déchirures des pages d'identité et d'adresse présentent donc deux caractéristiques : lorsque la page ne comporte que les inscriptions d'identité et d'adresse, l'impression est sur la partie haute de la page et la déchirure supprime toutes les mentions ; lorsque l'identité et adresse sont imprimées sous le dernier photogramme, l'impression est circonscrite sur la partie basse de la page et la déchirure laisse encore apparaître des mentions typographiques sous la reliure. Ce qui explique que certains flip books mutilés sont complètement anonymes et d'autres pas. Nous trouvons parfois aussi des exemplaires Beaulieu où identité et adresse sont inscrites sur la page supérieure, située avant le dernier photogramme.

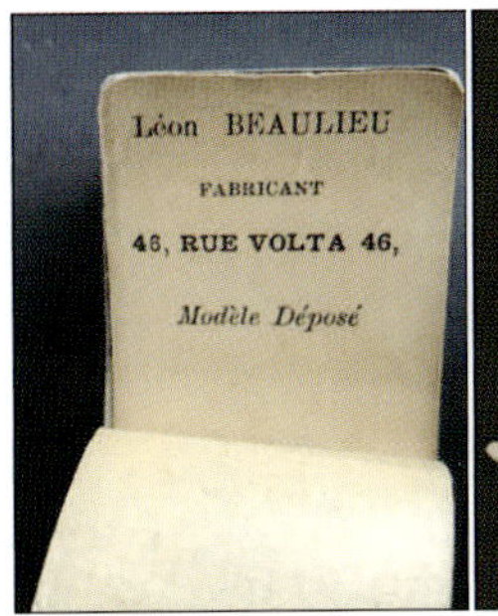

Trois exemples de pagination. Dans le premier cas, la déchirure de la page ferait disparaître toutes les mentions ; dans le second cas, la déchirure de la page laisserait entrevoir sous la reliure les mentions « Paris » et « Modèle déposé » ; dans le dernier cas, le photogramme est déchiré mais toutes les mentions sont présentes. © Robert Byrne / Pascal Fouché – Collection Pascal Fouché.

La pagination des exemplaires mutilés se rapproche donc davantage de celle des flip books Beaulieu. En conséquence, nous pourrions aussi envisager que les quatre flip books *Loïe Fuller* mutilés pourraient être des Beaulieu qui devaient comporter à l'origine deux fois l'adresse. Mais cette hypothèse, certes fondée, relève quand même d'une forme de spéculation.

On peut rapprocher cette danse serpentine sur fond noir à la description qu'en faisait Méliès en 1929 qu'il nomme d'ailleurs comme étant « Loïe Fuller ». Par ailleurs, parmi toutes les danses serpentines sur fond noir identifiées chez les concurrents français et étrangers, les images du flip book se différencient de toutes les versions connues (il existe cependant de nombreuses versions inconnues). A ce titre, on peut légitimement rapprocher ce flip book de la filmographie Méliès dont le film est réputé perdu. La version la mieux définie change de teinte tous les dix photogrammes passant par le bleu, vert, blanc, rouge, sépia, blanc, rouge, bleu et rouge. Parmi les exploitants de kinétographe Méliès, on trouve à Pau la mention de la diffusion d'une danse serpentine coloriée. Cette attestation contribue à valider l'origine Méliès de ces images en couleurs :

> [...] Le Cinématographe de M. Lumière et le Technitographe (appareil Méliès et Rolos [sic][4]) sont, actuellement, les derniers perfectionnements de l'application de la photographie animée. [...] Depuis quelques temps un appareil de ce genre, le Technitographe, fonctionne dans notre ville [Pau], place Royale [...].
>
> [...] Quelques scènes sont particulièrement remarquables : l'arrivée d'un train express en gare de Vincennes, où l'on voit le train stopper, les voyageurs descendre, et se bousculant, réclamer leurs bagages, assaillir le chef de gare, les employés, affolés, se multipliant à droite et à gauche, etc...[5]
>
> Ajoutons que le Technitographe reproduit, en couleurs, les évolutions dansantes de la Loïe Fuller et que ceci est un perfectionnement de plus. [...][6]

Par ailleurs, Jean-Claude Seguin a identifié une « *Danse serpentine* » en « quatre couleurs » parmi d'autres vues Méliès projetées à Lisbonne en août 1896.[7] Or, le nombre de couleurs correspond à celui du flip book.

Si la *Danse Serpentine* inscrite au catalogue Méliès est anonyme (rien n'indique qui danse), les articles de presse se rapportant à cette vue précisent qu'il s'agit de Loïe Fuller, tout comme le stipulait Méliès à postériori. Etait-ce réellement elle sur cette vue ou s'agissait-il d'une accroche publicitaire ? Force est de constater que le personnage Loïe Fuller est quasiment toujours considéré comme une sorte de marque dès lors qu'une danse serpentine est exécutée à l'écran, à l'époque, en France. Même si les traits de la danseuse du flip book peuvent évoquer ceux de Loïe Fuller, la ressemblance ne nous parait pas franche. Il faut bien avouer que nous n'avons pas de cliché photographique de l'artiste à cette période, ce qui rend la comparaison délicate. Selon des spécialistes américains de Loïe Fuller et des danses serpentines interrogés par Pascal Fouché, ils ne reconnaissent pas Loïe Fuller sur les images et envisagent qu'il pourrait plutôt s'agir de la danseuse américaine Crissie Sheridan. Au regard des images du film Edison n° 427 *Crissie Sheridan / Serpentine Dance in National Colors*,[8] nous n'avons pas été davantage convaincu par la ressemblance. Quoiqu'il en soit, nous n'y reconnaissons pas plus Bob Walter ou Lina Esbrard, deux danseuses françaises contemporaines exécutant ce type de danse. Il reste donc envisageable d'y voir Loïe Fuller elle-même sur les images du flip book,[9] à moins qu'il ne s'agisse d'une parfaite anonyme. Nous avons également comparé ces images avec celles de la vue de Méliès n° 188, *La Danse du feu*, (1899) où une danseuse exécute une danse serpentine. Il y a ressemblance entre les deux personnages, essentiellement par la coiffure. Cependant, il serait excessif de prétendre qu'il s'agit de la même actrice compte tenu de la modeste définition des images du flip book. Nous noterons cependant que Méliès confirma à deux reprises l'identité de Loïe Fuller comme actrice de ses films. Merritt Crawford et Paul Gilson, après des entretiens avec Méliès, la cite ainsi également.[10] Enfin, Jehanne d'Alcy réitéra cette affirmation en 1944 : « Méliès avait fait un film sur la Loïe Fuller ».[11]

D'un point de vue technique, ce film défile à cadence normale à 10 images/seconde. La bande est segmentée, elle présente des ruptures après les photogrammes 11, 54 et 58. Elle est donc parfaitement continue de l'image 1 à 11, de la 12 à 54, puis de la 54 à 58 et enfin de la 59 à 90. La vitesse d'enregistrement de cette vue au cinématographe a dû s'effectuer à 10 images/seconde. Une longueur totale cumulée de 1,80 mètre a été utilisée pour l'élaboration de ce flip book. Cette vitesse de défilement particulièrement lente rapproche ce flip book d'*Arrivée du train*, *La Puce*, *Déguisement* et *La Nourrice*, c'est-à-dire des vues parmi les plus anciennes du répertoire de Méliès.

Par ailleurs, l'analyse des images montre l'absence d'un espacement significatif latéral entre chaque photogramme comme constaté sur les flip books constitués d'images Méliès (et à l'inverse de ceux attribués à Edison, Skladanowsky et Gaumont, nous-y reviendrons). Cet autre élément technique permet de rapprocher ce flip book d'une origine Méliès.

Ainsi, Prissette aurait pu avoir accès aux mêmes fournisseurs que Beaulieu, à moins que Beaulieu soit le fournisseur des bandes photographiques imprimées par Prissette. Les cinq flip books Prissette à images photographiques font 42 mm de large, c'est-à-dire la dimension observée sur les flip books Beaulieu. La découpe au massicot semble avoir été effectuée par les mêmes ateliers selon un mode opératoire similaire. Ces points communs nous permettent de renforcer le lien supposé entre ces deux fabricants (Prissette et Beaulieu) sans toutefois pouvoir aller plus loin dans nos hypothèses. L'ensemble de toutes ces données tendrait à démontrer que Beaulieu n'avait qu'un rôle très marginal dans le processus de fabrication des flip books, tout au plus un travail de reliure (en dehors de ses activités de conception et de commercialisation).

L'identification de ce flip book aurait pu en rester là mais c'était sans compter le voisin barcelonais Miralles dont on trouve un titre, *Danza serpentina*, en noir et blanc, n° 2 de sa liste. L'analyse des images de l'imprimeur catalan montrent une continuité chronologique quasi parfaite des 80 photogrammes qui composent son flip book. La comparaison des flip books Miralles et Prissette/Beaulieu révèlent 58 images communes. Les photogrammes 1 à 14 Miralles correspondent à ceux 59 à 72 Prissette, les images 15 à 31 Miralles correspondant à celles 74 à 90 Prissette. Les 39 images comprises entre 42 et 80 Miralles trouvent une correspondance dans 27 images

Prissette se situant au niveau des photogrammes 2 à 29. Nous sommes donc en possession de deux flip books différents issus d'un même film dont nous possédons 112 photogrammes différents (90 chez Prissette/Beaulieu, 80 chez Miralles dont 58 en commun).

La comparaison des deux flip books, telle que consignée dans le tableau ci-dessous, confirme également une segmentation importante de la version Prissette/Beaulieu. Ainsi, le segment 1 à 29 Prissette montre une absence de 12 photogrammes dont 3 consécutifs entre les images 11 et 12. Les photogrammes 28 et 29 sont inversés. La bande présente deux segmentations chronologiques importantes entre les images 54 et 55 puis 58 et 59 en raison de l'inversion chronologique du segment 59 à 90.[12] Si la segmentation fait davantage penser à l'architecture de la bande de *La Danse du Cancan* issue d'un film Gaumont (nous le verrons plus loin), il nous parait difficile d'en tirer une quelconque conclusion (on remarque aussi dans *Le Bain* une inversion de deux photogrammes).

Loïe Fuller					**Prissette / Beaulieu**					59	60	61	62	63	64	65	66	67	68	69	70	71
Danza serpentina					**Miralles**					1	2	3	4	5	6	7	8	9	10	11	12	13
72	73	74	75	76	77	78	79	80	81	82	83	84	85	86	87	88	89	90				
14		15	16	17	18	19	20	21	22	23	24	25	26	27	28	29	30	31	32	33	34	35
						1	2		3	4		5	6	7		8	9	10	11			
36	37	38	39	40	41		42	43	44	45	46	47	48	49	50	51	52	53	54	55	56	57
12		13	14			15	16	17	18	19	20	21		22	23		24	25	26	27		29
58	59	60	61	62	63	64	65	66	67	68	69	70	71	72	73	74	75	76	77	78	79	80
28	30	31	32	33	34	35	36	37	38	39	40	41	42	43	44	45	46	47	48	49	50	51
52	53	54	X	55	56	57	58															

Les cases grisées signifient l'absence d'un photogramme. Les cases grisées avec une croix signifient l'absence de plusieurs photogrammes d'un nombre indéterminé.

Sachant que quatre des cinq premiers flip books Miralles sont tirés d'images Gaumont, dès lors, cette *Danza serpentina* serait-elle un film Gaumont ? Le lien est possible même s'il n'y a aucune référence d'auteur des photographies sur les livrets Miralles jusqu'au flip book n° 6. Cependant, rappelons que chez Prissette nous trouvons trois flip books à 84 photogrammes portant tous la mention « Clichés, L. Gaumont et Cie, Paris », ce qui n'est pas le cas dans la version complète du *Loïe Fuller* Prissette composé, rappelons-le, de 90 images. Enfin, le titre catalan *Danza serpentina* est la traduction parfaite de celui du film Méliès. En conséquence, même si le nombre d'indices favorise le rattachement de ce flip book au film de Méliès, rien ne permet d'écarter définitivement la piste Gaumont.

Les recherches autour de Miralles effectuées par Jean-Claude Seguin montrent que la première mention dans la presse catalane pour la vente des flip books Miralles intervient le 2 juillet 1897.[13] Trois titres y sont relatés dont *Danza serpentina* que nous pouvons, de ce fait, dater.

Nous noterons aussi qu'il est bien difficile d'établir une différenciation entre la vue Méliès et Gaumont tant les comptes-rendus de presse sont similaires. D'autant plus que l'apparition de la danse serpentine de Loïe Fuller, en couleurs également, par Gaumont intervient dès le 27 septembre 1896,[14] soit quasiment en même temps que celle tournée par Méliès. Un détail important est à relever lors des projections de cette vue Gaumont : la récurrence des mentions se rapportant à Loïe Fuller y compris lorsque Gaumont lui-même présente sa vue.[15] Selon de forte probabilité Gaumont aurait réellement filmé Loïe Fuller.

Ainsi, pour *Loïe Fuller*, compte tenu de l'ensemble des critères collectés, nous pouvons établir la classification « probable Méliès – confiance élevée ou Gaumont – confiance faible » correspondant soit au film Méliès n° 44 *Danse serpentine* ou au film Gaumont n° 12 *Danse serpentine : Loïe Fuller*.

Un flip book à 88 photogrammes : *Déguisement* [collection P. Fouché]

© Onno Petersen –
Collection Pascal Fouché.

Ce flip book est entièrement anonyme car la page supérieure déchirée, qui devait comporter l'adresse, ne laisse apparaître aucune inscription. Cet exemplaire faisait partie d'un lot Beaulieu. Il y figure d'ailleurs un titre manuscrit dont la graphologie est commune à des flip books Beaulieu. Il se feuillette de l'arrière vers l'avant. En revanche, les pages sont reliées entre elles par une agrafe recouverte d'une reliure en papier. Or, ce type de reliure ne semble affecter que les exemplaires Prissette.

Le format est unique et tout à fait spécifique mais en analysant chaque image, nous constatons qu'il fut construit à partir de huit lignes de onze photogrammes juxtaposés. Sa construction est donc exécutée selon le même processus que les flip books à 121 images. On ne constate aucun inter-image entre chaque photogramme comme sur les flip books attribués à Méliès. Ces détails techniques l'apparentent par conséquent au groupe des images Méliès à 121 photogrammes. Les images de ce flip book représentent un homme se déguisant en changeant uniquement la forme de son chapeau. Elles peuvent tout à fait correspondre au titre n° 42 *Dix chapeaux en 60 secondes*. Cependant aucun détail ne nous permet de trouver d'autres éléments d'identification. Nous limiterons notre classification à « probable Méliès – confiance moyenne ». Les images défilent correctement à 10 images/seconde, vitesse faible correspondant aux films les plus anciens du répertoire, ce qui est cohérent avec nos éléments d'analyse, notamment le décor uni clair. Une bande de 1,76 mètre a été nécessaire pour la fabrication de flip book.

Nous sommes donc en présence de deux vues attribuables à Méliès dans le répertoire Prissette, ce qui renforce encore un peu plus le lien Beaulieu-Prissette. Si les bandes photographiques proviennent de Beaulieu, pourquoi ne les a-t'il pas utilisées pour son compte ? Nous pouvons avancer deux hypothèses : pour *Loïe Fuller*, des photogrammes trop discontinus ; pour *Déguisement*, un format à 88 images hors norme ?

Une vue Gaumont : *La Danse du Cancan* [collection P. Fouché], (84 photogrammes)

© Onno Petersen – Collection Pascal Fouché.

Ce flip book est l'un d'une série de trois constitués chacun de 84 photogrammes. Une version intègre porte la mention de l'imprimeur « Imp. Prissette, Paris » sur la seconde de couverture ainsi qu'un copyright « Clichés, L. Gaumont et Cⁱᵉ, Paris » sur la page inférieure.

Nous signalerons par ailleurs qu'il existe une version similaire à ce flip book, composé des mêmes images et d'un format strictement identique. Sur cet autre exemplaire, les matériaux utilisés, papier, carton de couverture et reliure en tissu sont équivalents à la fois à l'exemplaire Prissette mais aussi à ceux des autres flip books Beaulieu. En revanche, sur les deux exemplaires les pages sont agrafées, pratique que nous attribuons à Prissette. Ce second livret ne porte aucune mention spécifique le rattachant formellement à Beaulieu ou Prissette. Cependant, il provient lui aussi d'un lot Beaulieu (l'écriture du titre est identique à l'une identifiée sur d'autres Beaulieu) et comporte une première page déchirée, mutilation assez courante et – à priori – spécifiquement observée sur les flip books Beaulieu. Malgré la gémellité apparente de ces deux versions, des différences significatives en matière de pagination nous incitent à prétendre que l'exemplaire mutilé pourrait être un Beaulieu. Sur la version anonyme, il n'y a pas de copyright Gaumont, présent sur la version Prissette, car la page inférieure est inexistante. Pourquoi le copyright aurait-il disparu (puisque cette page n'a pas été prévue) sur l'un des exemplaires s'ils étaient tous deux imprimés et reliés par Prissette ? Carlo Montanaro possède aussi un exemplaire de ce flip book. La première page est également déchirée le rendant anonyme et ne porte aucun copyright. Assez curieusement la page déchirée est nettement plus étroite que celles des photogrammes. Ce découpage atypique de la page d'adresse se retrouve sur un flip book Beaulieu – *Les Deux baisers* – de la collection Montenaro. Se pourrait-il que dans quelques cas la page d'adresse ait été ajoutée par l'imprimeur, à la demande, comme un *addenda* ? Dès lors, ce détail pourrait valider l'existence de versions attribuables à la fois à Prissette et Beaulieu.

Le copyright rattache définitivement cette vue à Gaumont. Ce flip book, portant le titre manuscrit *La Danse du Cancan*, est issu du film Gaumont n° 3 *Moulin Rouge : quadrille*.

C'est le seul flip book attribué à Prissette qui se feuillette de l'avant vers l'arrière. Nous avons cette même anomalie chez Beaulieu avec *Les Deux baisers*. Sa vitesse normale de défilement se situe autour de 16 images/seconde.[16] Il y a des ruptures chronologiques entre quelques photogrammes montrant que ce flip book se compose de groupes d'images segmentées. Les séquences sans rupture chronologique sont constituées pour le premier groupe des photogrammes 1 à 12 ; pour le second des images 13 à 40 (léger hiatus entre 27 et 28) ; le troisième, des photogrammes 41 à 51 ; on trouve ensuite une image 52 totalement isolée qui précède le dernier groupe regroupant les photogrammes 53 à 84. Les images successives utilisées l'ont été d'une bande donc la longueur totale devait être de 1,68 mètre (sur la base d'une copie 35 mm) ou 2,94 mètres si la bande exploitée était au format 60 mm.[17]

Par ailleurs, il existe un flip book issu de ce film Gaumont, réalisé par Benjamin Miralles, éditeur barcelonais.[18] Ce livret, intitulé *Baile francés*, est constitué de 80 photogrammes se présentant sous une chronologie quasi parfaite (un léger hiatus est observable entre les images 33 et 34). Ce flip book se feuillette de l'avant vers l'arrière. Une séquence du flip book Prissette/Beaulieu est commune avec celui de Miralles : 21 images des 28 qui composent la section 13-40 Prissette/Beaulieu sont identiques avec 21 des 23 photogrammes de la section 50–72 Miralles.[19] L'observation de la construction tant technique que chronologique du livret Miralles montre bien que celui de Prissette/Beaulieu semble réalisé avec moins de rigueur et de cohérence, comme si Prissette/Beaulieu avait utilisé trois ou quatre tronçons de bandes cinématographiques. En dehors des images communes, il est donc impossible de déterminer les vraies positions relatives des autres segments de bandes Prissette/Beaulieu. Nous les avons donc consignés dans le tableau ci-dessous en respectant la numérotation des photogrammes Prissette/Beaulieu.[20]

La Danse du Cancan					Prissette / Beaulieu					1	2	3	4	5	6	7	8	9	10	11	12	X
Baile francés					Miralles																	X
1	2	3	4	5	6	7	8	9	10	11	12	13	14	15	16	17	18	19	20	21	22	23
24	25	26	27	28	29	30	31	32	33	34	35	36	37	38	39	40	41	42	43	44	45	46
			13	14	15	16	17	18	19	20	21	22	23	24	25	26	27			28	29	30
47	48	49	50		51		52	53	54	55		56		57	58		59	60	61	62	63	64
31	32	33	34	35	36	37	38	39	40									X	41	42	43	44
65	66	67		68	69	70		71	72	73	74	75	76	77	78	79	80	X				
45	46	47	48	49	50	51	X	52	X	53	54	55	56	57	58	59	60	61	62	63	64	65
66	67	68	69	70	71	72	73	74	75	76	77	78	79	80	81	82	83	84				

Les cases grisées signifiant l'absence d'un photogramme. Les cases grisées avec une croix signifiant l'absence de plusieurs photogrammes d'un nombre indéterminé.

Deux autres vues Gaumont : *Duel de femmes* ou *Le Duel* et *Le Coucher* ou *La Puce* [collections P. Fouché, F. Binétruy et T. Lecointe] (84 photogrammes)

© Onno Petersen/François Binétruy – Collections Pascal Fouché et François Binétruy.

© Onno Petersen/François Binétruy/Thierry Lecointe –
Collections Pascal Fouché, François Binétruy et Thierry Lecointe.

Deux autres flip books de la collection Pascal Fouché sont constitués de 84 photogrammes et portent tout deux la mention « Clichés, L. Gaumont et Cie, Paris » sur la page inférieure. La marque Prissette est imprimée sur la seconde de couverture.[21] À l'inverse de *La Danse du Cancan*, ces deux flip books qui correspondent aux films Gaumont n° 24 *Duel de dames* et n° 142 *Une Nuit agitée*, se feuillettent de l'arrière vers l'avant comme pour la quasi-totalité des flip books Beaulieu ; le feuilletage dans ce sens particulier étant consécutif à l'utilisation de « l'effeulloir mécanique ». Ce détail est assez paradoxal car propre à Beaulieu (dans notre contexte temporel [fin XIXème siècle] et géographique [Paris-Nord]),[22] ce qui nous conduit encore vers un rapprochement implicite entre Prissette (imprimeur-fabricant) et Beaulieu (fabricant). L'exemplaire *Duel de femmes* de Pascal Fouché possède une reliure en tissu, le mien une reliure en papier. Sur mon exemplaire, *Le Duel*, l'adresse figure sur une page supérieure située entre la deuxième de couverture et le photogramme 84, le copyright figurant sur une page avant le photogramme 1 à l'identique de l'exemplaire de Pascal Fouché. Par ailleurs, tout comme pour *La Danse du Cancan*, nous possédons, avec la collection de François Binétruy, une version de ce flip books ne comportant aucune indication (aucun copyright, nom et adresse). La première page est déchirée (celle où devait figurer l'adresse) et il n'y a pas de page déchirée au niveau où figure le copyright sur les autres versions complètes. Après la découverte de l'exemplaire Binétruy, se pourrait-il que ce flip book ait été confectionné en deux versions : l'une avec copyright Gaumont attribuée à Prissette, l'autre mutilée attribuable à Beaulieu ?

Outre la présence du copyright Gaumont sur le flip book, son identification formelle est établie par la comparaison avec trois photogrammes, spécimen d'une planche publicitaire Gaumont. Ces photogrammes montrent effectivement la même scène. Le tirage montre qu'il s'agit d'une vue tournée sur pellicule 60 mm à quatre perforations, format spécifique des premiers films du chronophotographe G. Demé-ny.[23] Nous retrouvons chez Miralles une version de *Duel de femmes*. Ce flip book, portant le n° 5, s'intitule *Duelo de damas* (traduction littérale du titre de la vue Gaumont). Nous avons comparé les photogrammes deux à deux permettant d'établir le résultat suivant.

Duel de femmes					Beaulieu / Prissette													1	2	3	4	5
Duelo de damas					Miralles					1	2	3	4	5	6	7	8	9		10		11
6	7	8	9	10	11	12	13	14	15	16	17	18	19	20	21	22	23	24	25	26	27	28
12			13		14	15		16			17	18		19		20			21	22	23	
29	30	31	32	33	34	35	36	37	38						X	39	40	41	42	43	44	45
24	25	26	27	28	29		30		31	32	33	34	35	36	X			37	38	39	40	41
46	47	48	49	50	51	52	53	54	55	56	57	58	59	60	61	62	63	64	65	66	67	68
42	43	44	45		46		47	48	49		50	51	52			53						
69	70	71	72	73	74	75	76	77	78	79	80	81	82	83	84	X						
																X	54	55	56	57	58	59
60	61	62	63	64	65	66	67	68	69	70	71	72	73	74	75	76	77	78	79	80		

Les cases grisées signifiant l'absence d'un photogramme. Les cases grisées avec une croix signifiant l'absence de plusieurs photogrammes d'un nombre indéterminé.

Si le flip book Beaulieu-Prissette est plus linéaire, ne présentant qu'une césure entre les 38ème et 39ème photogrammes, la version Miralles est plus narrative avec une action qui débute par la distribution des armes pour se terminer à la touche finale de l'une des duellistes.[24]

En ce qui concerne *Le Coucher*, le film est identifié grâce à la reproduction de deux photogrammes consécutifs dans un catalogue Gaumont de janvier 1900[25] qui nous permet sans ambiguïté de l'associer à la vue n° 142 *Nuit agitée*.

Nous avons inventorié trois exemplaires de *Nuit agitée* dont chacun présente les mêmes caractéristiques que *Duel de femmes* : l'un complet (de Pascal Fouché), reliure toilée avec agrafe ; les deux autres anonymes (des collections de François Binétruy et Thierry Lecointe), reliures papier avec agrafe. Ces deux exemplaires sont constitués d'une première page déchirée (celle où devait figurer l'adresse) et d'une absence de page déchirée au niveau où figure le copyright sur la version complète de Pascal Fouché. Nous pourrions de ce fait tirer les mêmes conclusions sur l'existence de versions tant Prissette que Beaulieu.

Deux autres flip books Prissette (exemplaires intègres), constitués d'images photographiques, ne portent aucun copyright et se composent de 98 et 90 photogrammes ;[26] ils ne sont donc à priori pas constitués d'images Gaumont. Nous pouvons déduire de l'analyse de ce corpus que le format des livrets composés de 84 photogrammes est uniquement circonscrit à des films Gaumont. Les flip books figurant des images Gaumont ont tous la même dimension générale : 62 x 42 mm. Cette observation confirme que le choix du nombre de photogrammes parait être à l'initiative du fabricant des bandes cinématographiques. Il parait en effet assez paradoxal que pour un corpus de seulement sept flip books un imprimeur ait eu recours à cinq formats différents s'il avait la maîtrise du choix du nombre d'images (cette remarque vaut également pour le corpus Beaulieu qui comporte cinq formats différents en terme de nombre de pages).

Un flip book à 64 photogrammes : « Train en marche » [collection P. Fouché]

© Onno Petersen –
Collection Pascal Fouché.

Le flip book à 64 images représente un train en marche. Le livret se compose d'une répétition de 32 images afin de constituer un ensemble de 64 feuillets qui le rend plus homogène avec l'ensemble de la collection. Ce principe de construction, qui rappelle celui du livret précédent à 96 images, est sensiblement différent puisqu'il repose sur le rangement suivant : 1-2-3-…-32, 1-2-3-…-32. Il se présente physiquement avec une agrafe, une reliure en toile et une page supérieure déchirée. Il ne peut donc n'être rattaché formellement ni à Beaulieu, ni à Prissette. Nous le rattachons cependant à Prissette en raison de la présence de l'agrafe. Cependant, il se feuillette de l'arrière vers l'avant selon le principe requis par Beaulieu. Chaque photogramme comporte une numérotation manuscrite intra-photographique. Bien sûr, nous avons soigneusement comparé la graphologie de ces chiffres avec ceux visibles sur d'autres flip books. On dénombre au total sept flip books comportant ce type de numérotation : cinq à 121 images, un à 88 images et celui du train à 32 images. La comparaison de chacun des dix chiffres et des nombres montre qu'il s'agit de la même écriture pour l'ensemble à l'exception du flip book à 88 images. L'une des questions est de savoir qui a écrit ces numéros et à quel niveau de fabrication ils ont pu être inscrit. Force est de constater que cette numérotation ne touche que sept flip books sur 24, soit 29% du corpus. Si ce processus avait été à l'initiative de l'imprimeur, il aurait été envisageable de retrouver ce mode opératoire sur un bien plus grand nombre de livrets. Cette raison m'a incité à penser, dans un premier temps, que la numérotation a été réalisée en amont, c'est-à-dire au niveau du fabricant de l'épreuve cinématographique. Ce processus permettait à celui qui avait la maitrise de la chronologie des photogrammes de simplifier le travail pour l'imprimeur (ou pour lui-même) par un repérage simple et lisible du sens de lecture. Nous constatons par ailleurs que cette numérotation manuscrite affecte, en dehors de « train en marche », un livret « certifié Méliès », un autre « probable Méliès – confiance élevée » et quatre « probable Méliès – confiance moyenne ». Il n'y a aucune numérotation manuscrite similaire sur les flip books Gaumont et Edison. Cette numérotation, en l'état, ne semble toucher que les images Méliès du corpus Beaulieu. J'avais donc tout lieu de penser que « train en marche » pouvait relever de la filmographie Méliès, même si cette hypothèse était tangiblement assez faible. Pourquoi tous les flip books attribués à Méliès ne portent pas ce type de numérotation ? Pourquoi deux écritures différentes ? L'hypothèse formulée est que les images n'ont pas été préparées par le même opérateur. Plusieurs personnes auraient contribué à la sélection, découpage et rangement des photogrammes, certaines d'entre elles numérotant les images (on peut être étonné de ce type de travail pour les 32 photogrammes du train dont la chronologie ne prête pas à confusion, ce qui dénote d'une pratique répétitive). Cette numérotation affecte cinq flip books à 121 photogrammes sur neuf, soit 55%. Outre le « train en marche » à 64 images, la numérotation n'affecte qu'un autre livret à 88 images et aucun pour ceux à 90 et 80 photogrammes. Il faut bien constater que cette pratique ne touche en l'état que 7 flip books sur 21 potentiellement attribuables à Méliès, soit seulement 33%. Par ailleurs, en regardant le corpus de l'imprimeur Prissette, nous constatons que deux livrets possèdent une numérotation similaire mais typographique comme c'est le cas chez Beaulieu sur le flip book Edison. Or, de toute évidence ces numérotations chez Prissette se trouvent sur deux flip books dont l'origine cinématographique est complètement dissociable. Ce constat, au regard du voisin Prissette, met donc à mal, *in fine*, notre hypothèse d'une écriture chez le fournisseur cinématographique au profit d'une pratique qui semble, à l'inverse de ma première hypothèse, inhérente à l'imprimeur.[27]

La cadence la plus appropriée pour cette séquence se situe à 8 images/seconde. Un photogramme sur deux a été utilisé, ce que semble confirmer l'analyse de la position du train entre chaque image. Par ailleurs, on note des ruptures de continuité plus importantes entre les photogrammes 13–14, 15–16, 17–18 et surtout 26-27. La bande cinématographique originelle a donc été sectionnée et devait comporter à l'origine au moins 64 photogrammes.

Pourquoi ce flip book a-t-il été réduit à 32 images qui ont été doublées afin de vendre un livret d'un nombre de feuillets comparable aux autres ? Il n'en fallait certes pas davantage pour voir passer le train et son convoi composé de sept wagons dans sa totalité. Beaulieu aurait pu en utiliser directement 64 avec un mouvement plus décomposé. Là encore, s'il ne l'a pas fait c'est sans doute parce qu'il n'en avait pas la possibilité, les images lui étant fournies telles quelles.

L'analyse de chaque photogramme montre très clairement la présence d'un inter-image latéral entre chaque image d'une même ligne, comparable à ceux visibles sur les flip books à 84 et 96 photogrammes. Dès lors, ce critère, conjugué à celui où l'on note que le format à 64 (32) images est multiple de 96 (48), pourrait rapprocher ce flip book d'une production Gaumont (ces deux formats sont réalisés avec des lignes de huit photogrammes). Le format 8 x 8 aurait été associable aussi à celui de 80 photogrammes (8 x 10), mais nous savons que les 80 images sont constituées de 8 lignes de 10 photogrammes et non l'inverse.

Mes recherches étant restées vaines en ce qui concerne l'identification de la locomotive et des voitures sur le réseau français particulièrement, j'ai contacté un spécialiste ferroviaire pour identifier la motrice à vapeur et les voitures afin d'en déduire éventuellement le secteur géographique (le réseau voire la ligne) où ce type de convoi était utilisé. Le secteur géographique devant nécessairement nous rapprocher du terrain de jeu habituel du tourneur. Bruno Carrière de l'association Rails & histoire/A-HICF[28] s'est chargé du dossier. Il fut transmis à Jean-Marc Combe (ancien directeur du musée des chemins de fer français de Mulhouse) et Christian Fonnet (ancien documentaliste à *La Vie du Rail*). Jean-Marc Combe nous livre sans équivoque l'analyse suivante :

Les photos jointes montrent, sans aucun doute possible, l'une des 120 (ou pour être précis une des 1110, les essieux moteurs étant non couplés) compound à 3 cylindres du London and North Western. Elles ont été étudiées par F. W. Webb et produites de 1882 à 1890. Quant aux voitures il s'agit probablement des célèbres voitures du même réseau à 4 essieux semi-rigides.

Christian Fonnet de son côté nous explique :

> A priori, si c'est une 021, elle serait due à John Ramsbotton pour le réseau britannique du London North Western Railway ou ces machines ont été produites entre 1855 et 1872 (et aussi pour d'autres compagnies).
>
> Mais comme elle ressemble aussi aux 120 dues à Webb, successeur de Ramsbotton sur le même réseau, ce pourrait être une compound de la classe TEUTONIC, le gros cylindre BP[29] étant visible sous la porte de boite à fumée à l'avant de la locomotive.

Les deux spécialistes se rejoignent en fin de compte sur le modèle – une 120 (1110) compound à 3 cylindres de la classe Teutonic [ill. 71 et 72] – et surtout sur la localisation du réseau, le London North Western Railway, allant de Londres à Liverpool en passant par Birmingham, Manchester et desservant aussi Crewe et Chester. De plus, une voiture visible sur les images est bien le modèle à quatre essieux, construits pour cette compagnie en 1888 [ill. 73].

L'analyse de la filmographie Méliès ne nous permet absolument pas d'envisager des tournages en Angleterre. Même si Méliès s'est déplacé à Londres, notamment pour y acheter l'un de ses premiers projecteurs, qu'il transforma par la suite en caméra, ainsi que de la pellicule cinématographique, il n'était pas en mesure à ce moment-là d'enregistrer des films. En effet, au moment de son acquisition, son projecteur n'était pas encore transformé en caméra et la pellicule n'était pas perforée.

Il existe chez Robert William Paul une vue hors catalogue intitulée *Royal Train*. Cette vue consultable sur le DVD *RW Paul The collected Films 1895–1908* édité par la BFI montre un convoi similaire mais qui ne correspond pas aux images de notre flip book.

La filmographie Gaumont nous enseigne en revanche l'existence d'une série de 38 films consécutifs dont 33 portent des titres les localisant en Angleterre et à Dublin.[30]

Il semblerait que cette série publiée en novembre 1897, sous la rubrique « série L » avec une numérotation allant de 1 à 64, soit une sorte de reportage outre-Manche. Parmi les 38 titres (il y a, comme de coutume chez Gaumont, de nombreux numéros de vues absents au catalogue, d'où une numérotation de 1 à 64 pour seulement 38 vues inventoriées) figure la vue *Train à corridor, n° 55*. Une voiture à corridor désignant celles à couloir longitudinal faisant son apparition en France au début des années 1890. Bruno Carrière nous rappelle :

> Pour mémoire, la grande majorité des voitures antérieures à cette époque avait la particularité d'avoir des compartiments entièrement isolés les uns des autres, sans possibilité de communication entre eux (chaque compartiment n'était accessible que par deux portes – une par face – ouvrant directement sur l'extérieur, en l'occurrence les quais).

Par ailleurs, nous noterons que les vues britanniques Gaumont inscrites dans la liste de novembre 1897 se situent entre Londres et Dublin. Or, le réseau de la London North Western Railway s'étend de Londres à Liverpool, port qui dessert Dublin. De plus, les voitures à corridor étaient à cette époque réservées sur les grandes lignes. On a donc tout lieu de penser que ce *Train à corridor* est un convoi roulant sur une voie express britannique sans doute située entre Londres et Liverpool, tracté par une Teutonic dont les voitures présentaient la particularité de disposer d'un couloir (un corridor) pour desservir les compartiments.

En outre, il convient de préciser que deux ressortissants britanniques propriétaires dès la fin d'année 1896 de chronophotographe Gaumont 60 mm ont été identifiés et étaient susceptibles d'avoir transmis à la maison mère leurs bandes pour y être développées dès le début 1897.[31] La vue *Train à Corridor* (n° 55) se situant dans la liste entre les vues du jubilé de la reine Victoria du 22 juin 1897 (n° 7 à 23) et la visite du duc et de la duchesse d'York à Dublin du 18 août 1897 (n° 62) et durant 10 jours, tout porte à croire que ce train à corridor roulait sur la London North Western Railway entre ces deux périodes.

Or, les images du flip book montrent bien un train express de type Teutonic sur la ligne de la London North Western Railway. En outre, la référence temporelle de la vue Gaumont est tout à fait compatible avec l'activité connue de Beaulieu.

La vitesse de défilement optimale est estimée à 8 images/seconde pour un film tourné originellement à 16 images/seconde. Une image sur deux a donc été utilisée d'une bande mesurant initialement 1,28 mètre (sur la base d'une copie 35 mm) ou 2,24 mètres si la bande exploitée était au format 60 mm.

Si les flip books, élaborés à partir de vues Gaumont, identifiés chez Prissette et Beaulieu sont réalisés originellement avec des bandes de 12 photogrammes, ultérieurement le format semble se limiter à des bandes de 8 photogrammes (six puis quatre lignes de 8 images). Cette norme est à rapprocher d'un autre fabricant français déjà évoqué (Le Bon Marché), utilisant des vues Gaumont, dont le format est de 24 photogrammes, c'est-à-dire 3 bandes de 8 images.

Ce flip book, pour lequel au début de notre recherche était classifié « inconnu » peut dorénavant atteindre la classification « probable Gaumont – confiance moyenne ».

Un flip book à 98 photogrammes : *Lutte*, [collections P. Fouché et F. Binétruy]

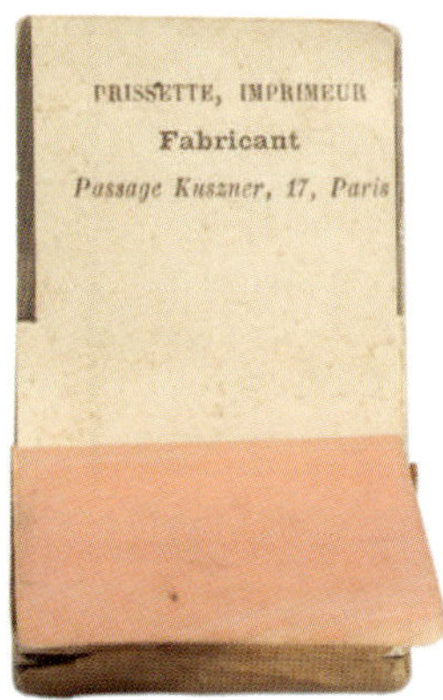

© Onno Petersen – Collections Pascal Fouché et François Binétruy.

Ce flip book, singulier à plus d'un titre, a d'abord été identifié dans la collection de Pascal Fouché où il se présente avec l'adresse de l'imprimeur Prissette sur la page supérieure. Il se feuillette également de l'arrière vers l'avant pour une utilisation dans le dispositif breveté par Beaulieu. C'est avec deux autres exemplaires de la collection de Pascal Fouché et François Binétruy que le rattachement à Beaulieu pouvait être envisagé ou du moins que le doute est entretenu. Ils ne comportent aucune marque d'identification et se présentent avec une page supérieure déchirée comme pour la majorité des flip books Beaulieu. Cependant, les trois exemplaires arborent une reliure en papier qui dissimule une agrafe, éléments qui les associent davantage à Prissette. En revanche, le sens de défilement des images, la mutilation observée sur deux exemplaires nous incitent à croire que ce flip book aurait pu être exploité à la fois par l'imprimeur Prissette et Beaulieu.

Pour ce flip book, nous ne connaissons que deux vues cinématographiques pouvant correspondre à ce titre. L'une issue de la filmographie de George William De Bedts, n° 49, *Lutteurs (à trois)*, l'autre de Pathé *Lutteurs*, toutes deux de 1896. Celle de De Bedts est parfois désignée par la presse régionale de *Lutteurs aux Folies-Bergères*, annoncée à quelques reprises « en couleurs ». La couleur pourrait effectivement se justifier par le nombre de lutteurs (trois) afin de les différencier dans un supposé corps à corps. Sachant qu'ils ne sont que deux sur le flip book nous envisageons une origine Pathé de ces images. Ce film ne porte pas de numéro d'inventaire s'agissant d'un ajout manuscrit de Pathé sur l'une de ses premières listes.[32] Cette origine supposée pourrait expliquer le recours à ce format unique de 98 photogrammes. Il est cependant paradoxal d'être en présence d'un flip book unique de ce producteur français dont la filmographie était non négligeable.

En analysant les images de l'exemplaire numérisé (celui où figure l'adresse Prissette), il apparait plusieurs points singuliers. Les images 89 à 98, complétées par l'adresse, constituent en fait une bande homogène de 11 images (l'adresse étant à la suite du photogramme 98).

La découpe approximative au massicot montre l'extrémité de l'image 98 sur la page de l'adresse qui constitue en somme la 99ème image.
© Onno Petersen – Collection Pascal Fouché.

En continuant l'observation image par image, nous pouvons établir que ce flip book est construit à partir de 9 bandes de 11 photogrammes chacune (à l'exception de la dernière bande dont la 99ème « image » est en fait l'adresse), format qui n'est pas sans rappeler les flip books à 121 et 88 photogrammes. Les 98 images visibles nous avaient amenés sur un format – erroné – qui se voulait être 7 lignes de 14 photogrammes. Par ailleurs l'étude visuelle met en exergue un autre type de hiatus singulier. Certaines bandes présentent des anomalies dans leur continuum : entre les images 5 et 6, 20 et 21, 29 et 30, 30 et 31, 51 et 52, 53 et 54, 64 et 65, affectant cinq bandes au total (Cf. illustrations ci-dessous).

Exemples parmi ceux cités où le numéro d'un photogramme se trouve de part et d'autre de la découpe.
© Onno Petersen – Collection Pascal Fouché.

Pour ces hiatus, nous en déduisons que la planche d'imprimerie ne peut être la même, au moins deux ont été utilisées. Le mélange des bandes s'est effectué lors de l'assemblage du flip book.[33]

Enfin, nous notons une césure chronologique à partir du photogramme 94 s'accompagnant d'un changement de typographie de la numérotation. Des images auraient été ajoutées pour compléter la dernière bande matricielle. En fait les images 95 à 98 sont la répétition des images 1 à 4.

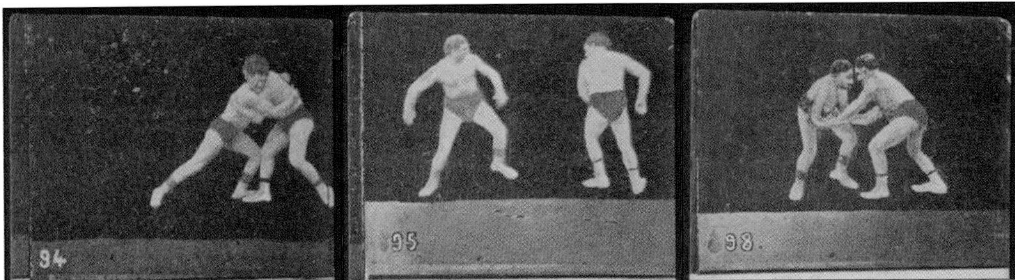

Changement typographique de la numérotation (tapuscrit à manuscrit) et rupture chronologique.
© Onno Petersen – Collection Pascal Fouché.

D'un point de vue photographique, les deux lutteurs semblent être dans les airs. Ils sont devant le fond noir mais ne reposent pas sur le sol marqué d'une teinte plus clair. Nous n'avons aucune explication à ce décalage dans l'image. En tout état de cause, cette anomalie photographique ne correspond pas aux autres flip books ce qui renforce l'idée d'une provenance différente. Bien que le format rappelle ceux attribués à Méliès, ce flip book, sans autre élément technique, est donc classifié « probable Pathé – confiance faible ».

Notes

1. Les deux flip books Prissette dessinés sont radicalement différents de la série composée de photogrammes.

2. Si les longueurs totales des feuillets constituant les flip books sont très variables (entre 52 et 70 mm), la côte en largeur des flip books Prissette, 42 mm (à plus ou moins 2 mm), est commune à tous les livrets Beaulieu (exception faite d'une version du flip book *Les Deux baisers* coupée à 46 mm). La découpe au massicot semble provenir d'un même mode opératoire.

3. La numérotation typographique intra-photographique se retrouve sur un autre flip book Prissette-Beaulieu, *Lutte*, composé de 98 images.

4. Pour Lucien Reulos, l'associé de Méliès.

5. La description faite à Mulhouse le 13 août 1896 est assez similaire : « "L'arrivée d'un train en gare" est saisissante, le convoi lancé à toute vitesse s'arrête brusquement : les employés courent, les portières s'ouvrent, les voyageurs descendent et se dirigent vers la sortie ; on décharge les bagages ; tout cela est si bien représenté qu'il ne manque que le bruit pour être d'un réalisme parfait », dans *L'Express de Mulhouse*, 13 août 1896, cité dans Jacques et Chantal Rittaud-Hutinet, *Dictionnaire des cinématographes en France (1896–1897)*, *op. cit.*, 1999, p. 317.

6. Dans *Le Patriote des Pyrénées*, 8–9 novembre 1896. La vue en couleurs est annoncée dès le 29 octobre, la première mention apparait dans l'étape précédente du technitographe à Agen le 3 septembre 1896, cité dans Jean-Claude Seguin :

   https://www.grimh.org/index.php?option=com_content&view=article&layout=edit&id=7183&lang=fr#le-tech nitographe-octobre-décembre-1896

   Une « *Danse serpentine* » incluse parmi d'autres vues du répertoire Méliès fut annoncée dans *L'Express de Mulhouse*, 19 août 1896, cité dans Jacques et Chantal Rittaud-Hutinet, *ibid.*, p. 317. Nous signalerons que les vues colorisées, notamment les danses serpentines, sont rapidement projetées sur les écrans : « La merveilleuse découverte de la photographie vivante, grandeur naturelle et en couleur, sera visible au théâtre Isola tous les jours », *Le Soleil, petite gazette des théâtres*, 31 mars 1896, et « Il y a notamment une "Loïe Fuller" en couleurs dont on bisse à chaque séance la danse serpentine », *L'Intransigeant*, 6 avril 1896 cités dans Jacques et Chantal Rittaud-Hutinet, *ibid.*, p. 357. Nous notons une appropriation très rapide par des coloristes d'un matériau relativement nouveau : une image de 25 x 20 mm sur du celluloïd se répétant entre 800 et 1000 fois selon la longueur de la bande pelliculaire !

7. Dans *Diaro Illustrado*, 22 août 1896.

8. Film enregistré en septembre-octobre 1897, voir Charles Musser, *Edison Motion Pictures, 1890–1900 – An Annotated Filmography*, *op. cit.*, p. 352.

9. La presse française fait copieusement référence à la star américaine en raison des titres donnés aux vues françaises. Nous noterons ainsi la récurrence des références à Loïe Fuller très largement relayées par la presse à propos des vues se rapportant à la danse serpentine de Gaumont et de Méliès, voir le site de Jean-Claude Seguin : https://www.grimh.org/index.php?option=com_content&view=article&layout=edit&id=1092&lang=fr#3 https://www.grimh.org/index.php?option=com_content&view=article&layout=edit&id=6757&lang=fr#3 Nous relevons chez les fabricants cinématographiques des titres en 1896 qui font directement référence à Loïe Fuller : 1) Gaumont, film n° 12 *Danse serpentine : Loïe Fuller* - 2) Pathé, film n° 19 *Loïe Fuller*, repris dans le catalogue Vitagraphe sous le n° 145 *Danse serpentine* et chez Mazo au n° 17 *La Danse serpentine* – 3) G. W. De Bedts, film n° 17 *Loïe Fuller* – 4) Méliès, film n° 44 *Danse serpentine*, probablement repris au catalogue G. Mendel, film n° 6 *Loïe Fuller* – 5) En revanche, chez Joly-Nomandin nous trouvons *Danse serpentine (de miss Esbrard)* relayée comme telle par la presse d'époque – 6) Nadar, [Danse du papillon ou serpentine] de Bob Walter – 7) Sans oublier le film Lumière n° 765 *Danse serpentine* de décembre 1897 dont nous connaissons deux versions : l'une tournée en Italie exécutée par une danseuse anonyme ; l'autre où il s'agit de Leopoldo Fregoli travesti en danseuse. Voir Michèle Aubert et Jean-Claude Seguin, *La Production cinématographique des frères Lumière*, Bibliothèque du Film / Éditions Mémoires du cinéma, Paris, 1996, pp. 324-325.

10. Dans Aude Bertrand, *Georges Méliès et les professionnels de son temps*, mémoire de recherche de master, Université Lumière Lyon 2 / ENSSIB, juin 2010, pp. 41 et 48.

11. Commission de recherches historiques de la Cinémathèque française, séance du 17 juin 1944, source que l'on doit à Jacques Malthête.

12. Une bande plus complète pourrait être constituée des 112 photogrammes suivants : 59 à 90 Prissette, 32 à 41 Miralles, 1 Prissette, 42 à 80 Miralles, 28 Prissette suivi de 30 à 58 Prissette (11,2 secondes).

13. *La Esquella de la Torratxa*, Barcelona. Source Jean-Claude Seguin.

14. *L'Echo de Saint-Nazaire*, 27 septembre 1896, cité dans Jacques et Chantal Rittaud-Hutinet, *Dictionnaire des cinématographes en France (1896-1897)*, *op. cit.*, p. 430.

15. Voir : https://www.grimh.org/index.php?option=com_content&view=article&layout=edit&id=1092&lang=fr#3, site de Jean-Claude Seguin.

16. L'animation de ce flip book a été réalisée à 12 images/seconde, le logiciel ne permettant que des multiples de 24 (1, 2, 4, 6, 8, 12 ou 24 images/seconde) :
    - pour 24 images/seconde, il faut enchaîner les images n° 1 à 24 de façon consécutive ;
    - pour 12 images/seconde, il faut enchaîner les images n° 1 à 12 en les doublant : 1-1-2-2-3-3-4-4-5-5-6-6-7-7-8-8-9-9-10-10-11-11-12-12 ;
    - pour 8 images/seconde, il faut enchaîner les images n° 1 à 8 en les triplant : 1-1-1-2-2-2-3-3-3-4-4-4-5-5-5-6-6-6-7-7-7-8-8-8 ;
    - pour 6 images/seconde, il faut enchaîner les images n° 1 à 6 en les quadruplant : 1-1-1-1-2-2-2-2-3-3-3-3-4-4-4-4-5-5-5-5-6-6-6-6 ;
    - pour 4 images/seconde, il faut enchaîner les images n° 1 à 4 en les répétant six fois : 1-1-1-1-1-1-2-2-2-2-2-2-3-3-3-3-3-3-4-4-4-4-4-4. Robert Byrne a modélisé des animations à des vitesses intermédiaires (10 et 16 images/secondes). Pour 10 images/seconde, il faut enchaîner les images n° 1 à 10 en triplant quatre images de manière aléatoire, par exemple : 1-1-1-2-2-3-3-3-4-4-5-5-6-6-6-7-7-8-8-8-9-9-10-10. Pour 16 images/seconde, on enchaine les images n° 1 à 16 en doublant les numéros pairs par exemple : 1-2-2-3-4-4-5-6-6-7-8-8-9-10-10-11-12-12-13-14-14-15-16-16.

17. Gaumont a tourné et exploité ses films en 1896 et 1897 sur bandes larges données pour 60 mm (d'après les publicités commerciales d'époque). Laurent Mannoni les mesure précisément à 58 mm. La hauteur des photogrammes se situe autour de 35 mm, là où ceux des bandes 35 mm ne font que 20 mm environ.

18. Nos remerciements à Jean-Claude Seguin pour les scans de ce flip book.

19. Le hiatus observable entre les photogrammes Beaulieu 27 et 28 est identifiable et explicable par comparaison avec le flip book Miralles. Ce livret montre deux images supplémentaires entre les deux photogrammes du livret Beaulieu.

20. Une vue plus complète pourrait être composée des 143 photogrammes suivants : 1 à 12 Beaulieu, 1 à 49 Miralles, 13 à 27 Beaulieu, 60 et 61 Miralles, 28 à 40 Beaulieu, 73 à 80 Miralles et 41 à 84 Beaulieu (8,9 secondes).

21. Je possède en outre une version du flip book *Duel de femmes* où la mention « PRISSETTE, IMPRIMEUR, PARIS » est inscrite sur la page supérieure et la mention « Clichés, L. Gaumont et Cie, Paris », sur la page inférieure.

22. Un fabricant de jeux, Charles Auguste Watilliaux, 110, rue Vieille-du-Temple, à Paris, réalise en 1896 un jouet optique qu'il appelle « folioscope ». Sa description nous est relatée par Gaston Tissandier, « Récréations scientifiques – Le foliosocope », *La Nature*, n° 1190, 21 mars 1896. Pascal Fouché possède deux exemplaires du « Folioscope » de C. Watilliaux décrit dans cet article : ils sont imprimés recto verso et tête bêche contenant donc quatre flip books dessinés. Ces modèles se feuillettent de l'avant vers l'arrière comme le montre également le dessin reproduit dans l'article.
Le 1ᵉʳ mai 1896 Charles Auguste Watilliaux et Siméon Claparède déposent un brevet, obtenu le 10 août 1896 sous le n° 256.039, pour un : « *Appareil donnant l'illusion du mouvement par la succession rapide de photographies ou dessins* ». *Il* en est fait l'écho dans « Le folioscope mécanique », *La Nature*, supplément au n° 1232, 9 janvier 1897 ainsi que dans J. L. Breton, « La Chronophotographie », *Revue scientifique et industrielle de l'année*, Paris, 1897, pp. 209-210. C. Watilliaux après son folioscope d'images dessinées passe un accord avec Georges Demenÿ pour utiliser ses images chronophotographiques et « *au lieu de les monter en cahier, il les monte autour d'un axe placé horizontalement dans une boîte en carton et muni d'une manivelle* », Cf. « Convention avec M. Watilliaux fabricant de jouets 110 rue Vieille-du-Temple pour la fabrication de séries photographiques dans le Folioscope de M. Claparède (Traité du 7 mai 1896) » dans Georges Demenÿ, archives familiales, sources Cinémathèque Française et Pascal Fouché. Ces images se feuillètent dans l'appareil de l'arrière vers l'avant.
Il existe aussi une version intermédiaire entre ces deux dispositifs. Il s'agit de flip books plus traditionnels comme on les connaît à l'époque de Beaulieu en simple recto verso sous le même nom « Folioscope ». Pascal Fouché en possède un exemplaire, François Binétruy un autre. Le premier représente d'un côté un jeune garçon montant et descendant d'une échelle double et de l'autre côté un homme essayant en vain de monter sur un cheval. Le second, présente deux autres séries d'images dont une jeune fille jouant à la corde à sauter. Ils se composent de 110 photographies numérotées qui se feuillettent, cette fois, de l'arrière vers l'avant tel que mentionné sur les livrets eux-mêmes : « Pour voir les sujets s'animer, feuilleter le carnet avec le pouce en partant du premier feuillet de dessous ». Ce sens de défilement préfigure l'utilisation dans l'appareillage rotatif. Nous noterons que ce modèle de « folioscope » semble très légèrement antérieur à ceux de Léon Beaulieu qui aurait pu s'en inspirer. Les images du folioscope de Pascal Fouché sont les mêmes sujets que ceux présentés dans le « folioscope mécanique » conservé à la Cinémathèque Française sous le N° Inventaire : AP-95-1756, voir :
http://www.cinematheque.fr/fr/catalogues/appareils/collection/folioscopeap-95-1756.html

23. Photogrammes reproduits dans Camille Blot-Wellens, *La colección Sagarmínaga (1897–1906) Érase una vez el cinematógrafo en Bilbao*, *op. cit.*, p. 108.

24. La concaténation des flip books Prissette-Beaulieu et Miralles nous permet de constituer un film plus complet de 124 photogrammes, d'une durée 7'' 75/100.

25. Nos remerciements à Jean-Claude Seguin pour la source.

26. Une version *Loïe Fuller* de 90 photogrammes et *Lutte* en 98 photogrammes.

27. Ce constat s'étend également au flip book *La Danse du Cancan*. Issu du même film Gaumont n° 3, le flip book Miralles, n° 4 : *Baile francés*, comporte une numérotation intra-photographique typographique alors qu'aucune ne figure sur les exemplaires Beaulieu et Prissette. La numérotation émane donc bien d'une manipulation locale au niveau de l'imprimeur.

28. AHICF : anciennement association pour l'histoire des chemins de fer.

29. Basse pression. La classe Teutonic, 10 locomotives fabriquées en 1889-1890, était une variante de la classe Dreadnought, 40 produites de 1884 à 1888, elle-même dérivée de la classe Experiment, 30 construites de 1882 à 1884 (l'aspect des locomotives est similaire). Elles ont été mises au rebut entre décembre 1903 et juillet 1907.

30. Voir *La Mise au point, Revue photographique trimestrielle, n° 1, novembre 1897*, citée dans Marie-Sophie Corcy, Jacques Malthête, Laurent Mannoni, Jean-Jacques Meusy, *Les premières années de la société L. Gaumont et Cie – Correspondance commerciale de Léon Gaumont 1895-1899*, Paris, Association française de recherche sur l'histoire du cinéma / Bibliothèque du Film / Gaumont, 1998, pp. 473–474.

31. Dans *ibid*. pp. 192-193.

32. Voir Henri Bousquet, *Catalogue Pathé des années 1896 à 1914 – 1896 à 1906, op. cit*, p. 842.

33. Ce type d'anomalie se retrouve sur l'autre exemplaire de Pascal Fouché mais à des endroits différents, ce qui est fort logique.

Des enseignements de l'analyse de la numérotation, décors, formats et adresses

Nous avons remarqué que le corpus relevant d'images Méliès était constitué des flip books à 121, 90, 88 et 80 photogrammes. Selon une forte probabilité, il semblerait que l'ordre chronologique de fabrication des flip books (et de tournages des films associés) aille du format à 121 images pour les plus anciens à celui de 80 images pour les plus récents. Cette hypothèse repose en partie sur l'analyse des décors. À l'exception du film tourné en décor naturel (l'arrivée du train), sept flip books à 121 photogrammes ont été filmés sur fond noir, ce qui correspond à une pratique de tournage dite primitive (à l'époque dans le seul but de donner du contraste)[1]. Un seul a été enregistré sur fond clair uni, ce qui relève du même principe général que les tournages sur fond noir. Le flip book à 88 photogrammes est tourné sur fond clair. Trois flip books à 90 photogrammes présentent cette caractéristique d'enregistrement sur fond noir, un autre se présente sur un fond clair uni. Le fond clair a été choisi, à chaque fois, parce que les personnages portaient des costumes qui étaient partiellement sombres. Quatre flip books à 90 images ont été filmés dans des décors peints, donc plus élaborés. Les deux flip books à 80 images se déroulent aussi dans des décors peints. Ainsi, nous constatons qu'à l'exception des images enregistrées en décor naturel, 100% des flip books à 121 et 88 images sont tournés sous décors unis (noir ou clair), 50% des flip books à 90 images sont en décors unis et aucun de ceux à 80 images (100% en décors peints).

Si cinq flip books à 121 photogrammes portent une numérotation manuscrite, celui à 88 images qui présente cette même caractéristique est tourné sur fond clair. Ainsi, les flip books possédant une numérotation intra-photographique manuscrite font partie de ceux qui sont très certainement les plus anciens du corpus. Nous remarquons aussi, pour corroborer cette hypothèse, que les trois flip books identifiés rue Ober-kampf, première adresse commerciale selon notre étude, comportent tous 121 pho-togrammes. Dès la seconde adresse, rue Volta, occupée par Beaulieu jusqu'en septembre 1897, nous voyons apparaître un format à 90 photogrammes dans un décor à fond noir et à 80 images dans un décor peint. Ainsi, la numérotation des images sur les flip books d'origine Méliès tendrait à indiquer que les images du « train en marche », qui utilise cet artifice en matière de numérotation, pourraient être parmi les plus anciennes de ce corpus, c'est-à-dire antérieures à septembre 1897 (ce qui est compatible avec la date de tournage de *Train à corridor*). Par extension, les trois flip books à numérotation intra-photographique typographique *Les Deux Baisers, Loïe*

Fuller et *Lutte* pourraient également faire partie des plus anciens du corpus. La numérotation intra-photographique semble être un marqueur de datation. Ainsi, les flip books édités les premiers (compte tenu de cette numérotation dans l'image photographique et d'une édition à la première adresse) seraient : *La Danse, Nuit agitée, Le Duel, Le Bâton, Duel au sabre, Déguisement, Train en marche, Prestidigitation, Arrivée du train, Les Deux baisers, Lutte* et *Loïe Fuller*. De ces douze flip books, seuls *La Danse, Prestidigitation* et *Arrivée du train* comportent l'adresse la plus ancienne, *Les Deux baisers* celle de la rue Volta. Quatre exemplaires que nous possédons de cette liste de douze, édités à Aubervilliers, seraient par conséquent des rééditions. Les quatre autres ne présentent aucune adresse.

Si nous rapprochons cette liste des familles de flip books cités en début d'enquête, nous retrouvons les titres dans les familles 1, 2 et première branche de la 3. Par croisement avec cette première analyse « généalogique », nous pourrions alors ajouter *Boxe* et *Lutte de cuisinier* parmi les premiers flip books édités.

Quant aux vues Méliès les plus anciennes ayant servi de matrices aux flip books, dont nous situerions la borne extrême des tournages à fin 1896, il s'agirait de tous les livrets à 121 et 88 photogrammes, les quatre livrets à 90 photogrammes enregistrés sous décors unis (pour *Loïe Fuller*, l'existence est avérée dès juillet 1897 par la version Miralles) et *Le Voyeur* édité rue Volta. En complément, nous trouverions aussi parmi les vues les plus anciennes : le « train en marche » dont nous présumons la réalisation avant le 18 août 1897, *Lutte* et *Les Deux baisers* (dont la date de réalisation du film est connue en avril 1896). Les films dont sont issus les autres flip books pourraient être postérieurs à septembre 1897 sans toutefois dépasser le milieu d'année 1898[2] (voir la liste « reconstitution chronologique »). Nous ne visualisons, dans les décors peints, aucune marque relative à Méliès (initiale MR, étoile à cinq branches, mention Star Film ou Géo[rges] Méliès), références visibles dans quelques films de 1897 (n° 78/80, 96, 102, 105 et 112 pour les plus anciens). L'absence de marque dans les différents décors peints signifierait que les flip books issus de films enregistrés dans ce type de décors pourraient être des vues datant de fin 1896 ou des tous débuts de 1897 et exploités par Beaulieu fin 1897/début 1898.

Cette observation nous confirme aussi que Méliès a fait assez rapidement évoluer son style pour tourner des saynètes en décors théâtraux dès le début de l'année 1897, ce qui est cohérent avec ce que nous connaissons de sa filmographie. Cela tend aussi à confirmer que Beaulieu a sans doute produit ses flip books de la fin 1896 à mi 1898, probablement pas au-delà. Léon Beaulieu ne semble donc s'inscrire comme un véritable fabricant de flip books cinématographiques, son activité commerciale centrée sur ces produits, que durant cette période assez courte. Elle est d'ailleurs corrélable avec ses inscriptions sur les annuaires commerciaux sous la rubrique spécifique « cinématographe » et par le dépôt de son brevet. Après le milieu de l'année 1898, il semblerait, au regard du corpus et de sa disparition des registres commerciaux que son activité globale se soit recentrée sur la vente de bimbeloterie dont ses flip books ne devait plus constituer que l'un des produits. En fait, son retour à Aubervilliers, rue de la Courneuve, estimé vers juin 1898 marque sans doute une forme de changement, voire de déclin, de son activité commerciale et l'arrêt de sa collaboration avec les producteurs cinématographiques. S'il ne semble plus créer de nouveaux flip books en 1898, il continue cependant à rééditer après cette époque ses matrices les plus anciennes.

Ces différentes analyses confirment en outre une évolution générale, pour la fabrication des flip books à partir de films Méliès, vers le recours à un nombre d'images de plus en plus réduit, signe à priori d'une recherche de réduction du coût de fabrication.

Nous formulons l'hypothèse selon laquelle tous les flip books à 121 photogrammes, ceux à 90 images sous décors unis affectés de l'une des trois dernières adresses commerciales seraient des rééditions, ainsi que ceux à 90 et 80 images sous décors peints affectés des deux dernières adresses.

Les neuf flip books (les livrets eux-mêmes) relevant d'une édition originelle, à partir de bandes cinématographiques Méliès ou autres, seraient *La Danse* (rue Oberkampf), *Prestidigitation* (rue Oberkampf), *Arrivée du train* (rue Oberkampf), *Le Coup du père François* (rue Volta), *Le Voyeur* (rue Volta), *Les Deux baisers* (rue Volta), *Le Coucher de la mariée* (rue du Vert-Bois), *Pose chez l'artiste. Vénus* (rue du Vert-Bois) et *Le Bain* (rue du Vert-Bois), les autres seraient des rééditions.

Note

1. Pratique constatée chez Muybridge, Marey et Edison avec les tournages dans son studio, la Black Maria.

2. Puisque nous trouvons déjà rue Volta (quittée par Beaulieu vers septembre 1897) un flip book dans un décor peint sous le format à 80 photogrammes établi comme le plus récent de ceux proposés par Méliès.

La survivance des flip books Beaulieu après sa mort ?

près le décès de Léon Beaulieu le 22 février 1901, nous avons vu que la succession finalisée le 22 août 1901 allait à une cousine germaine dans la ligne paternelle et un oncle dans la ligne maternelle. Qu'est-il advenu de son activité « flip book » ? De nombreux flip books ont leurs premières et parfois dernières pages déchirées (celles où la mention de son identité et adresse sont inscrites). Est-ce le résultat d'une anonymisation des flip books en raison d'une réappropriation par d'autres afin de les revendre dans un réseau de distribution secondaire ? C'est envisageable car aucune autre raison ne paraît justifier une telle mutilation (il s'agit bien de faire disparaître le nom de Beaulieu car sous la reliure une mention typographique, voire l'adresse, apparaît parfois encore). Ainsi dans notre corpus global, il en ressort que moins de 37 % des flip books ont été vendu du vivant de Léon Beaulieu (et ce taux est probablement à minorer). Pascal Fouché en continuant ses recherches autour de Léon Beaulieu, a remarqué que certains thèmes de ses flip books ont été utilisés par un autre fabricant de jouets au tout début du XXe siècle qui a notamment produit le « Cinématographe-Jouet ». Ce dispositif est bien connu des amateurs de jouets optiques de ces années-là car on le trouve régulièrement dans plusieurs versions différentes. Pascal Fouché en possède deux versions, l'une noire sans nom d'éditeur qui porte seulement la mention « Cinématographe-Jouet » avec une douzaine de bandes différentes, et l'autre plus tardive, de couleur rouge avec seulement 3 bandes, éditée par les Jouets R.J.L. sous le nom « Cinescenic ». Grâce à Éric Lange[1] qui a retrouvé un article dans *La Nature* du 13 décembre 1902, on peut être à peu près sûr que la première version du « Cinématographe-Jouet » date de 1902 et qu'il a été fabriqué par un dénommé M. Mathieu. Si le « Cinématographe-Jouet » reprend en partie des photogrammes provenant des livrets de Beaulieu, en revanche le « Cinescenic » (d'une conception plus tardive) n'est constitué que de dessins sans rapport avec sa production. Parmi la douzaine de bandes du « Cinématographe-Jouet », nous retrouvons cinq sujets de Beaulieu : *Nuit agitée*, *La Danse*, *Le Duel*, *Boxe* et *Lutte de cuisiniers*[2] (l'article de *La Nature* mentionne un « train en marche »). Les bandes Mathieu ne sont constituées que de 48 images. En regardant dans le détail, si la similitude est constatée, on s'aperçoit qu'il n'y a pas gémellité parfaite entre les images Beaulieu et Mathieu. Les images Mathieu ne sont pas des reproductions photographiques, il s'agit d'images principalement dessinées à partir des photogrammes Beaulieu. Ainsi, dans la version *Nuit agitée* de Mathieu, si le personnage semble être issu des photogrammes, le lit a été redessiné (il ne se présente plus sous la même géométrie) et il n'y a plus qu'un seul tabouret (dont la forme est modifiée) sur lequel figure le pot de chambre, le personnage lui-même a été renforcé au tire-ligne. Par ailleurs, ces images sont de moins bonne qualité encore que celles du flip book. Sur les autres bandes nous remarquons également ce principe où les images sont des dessins s'inspirant fortement des photographies originales. La chronologie événementielle de la production Mathieu au regard de l'article paru en décembre 1902 est cohérente avec l'histoire de Beaulieu, ce qui pourrait confirmer une appropriation du travail de Beaulieu par Mathieu. Soulignons également que Mathieu fait fonctionner ses flip books avec un appareillage particulier (primé au concours Lépine selon l'encart publicitaire collé à l'intérieur de la boite de rangement) comme l'avait conçu Beaulieu

Le Cinématographe-Jouet (à gauche)
et le Cinescenic (à droite).
© Pascal Fouché.

marquable; c'est ce qui en fait tout le charme et le rend bon marché. L'appareil se compose d'une bande de papier noire parcheminée mesurant 0m,30 de longueur sur laquelle on a collé les unes à côté des autres, à une distance de 2mm, des photogravures d'une scène quelconque prises au cinématographe et représentant une cinquantaine de positions successives. On a réuni ensuite les deux extrémités de la bande afin d'en former un anneau; dans cette bande on y dépose une simple et grosse bille ordinaire, puis on suspend la bande sur une manivelle qui traverse un petit carré de bois de 2 millimètres d'épaisseur correspondant aux intervalles laissés entre les images, puis on descend la bande dans une grande boîte rectangulaire en introduisant les deux extrémités de la manivelle dans les deux petites fentes réservées à cet effet. Sur la face supérieure de la boîte est fixée une petite patte en métal qui vient heurter chaque image à son passage. Il suffit de tourner la manivelle de gauche à droite pour voir s'animer toutes ces figures qui passent successivement. On y voit un duel, une danseuse, des chiens savants, des clowns, un train en marche, etc., etc. La bille emprisonnée et entraînée par cette petite manivelle donne la tension nécessaire à la bande, suivant le mouvement rotatif. Ce petit cinématographe est un jouet ingénieux, amusant et vraiment curieux. Le cinématographe se trouve chez M. Mathieu, 29, rue de Valois, à Paris.

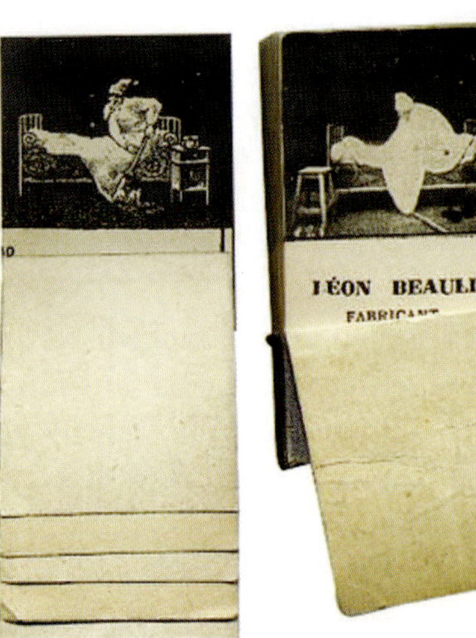

Images comparées entre un dessin du Cinématographe-Jouet Mathieu et un photogramme du flip book Beaulieu. © Pascal Fouché.

Le Nature, 13 December 1902 – © Collection particulière.

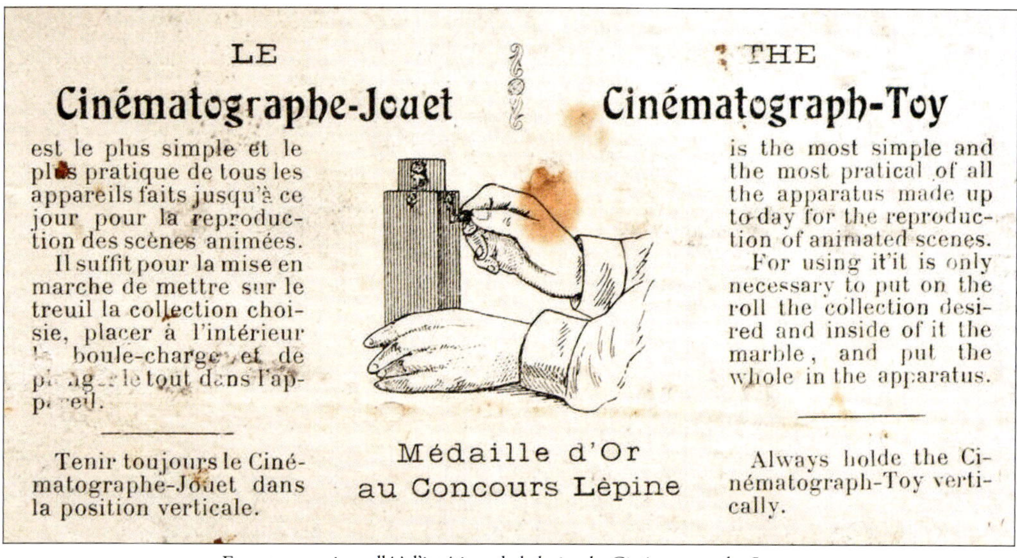

Encart en papier collé à l'intérieur de la boite du Cinématographe-Jouet.
© Pascal Fouché.

en son temps avec son « effeuilloir mécanique ».[3] Ce processus de feuilletage par le biais d'un dispositif mécanique constitue peut-être également une autre relation de cause à effet entre les deux hommes.

Notes

1. On consultera son site internet dédié aux appareils et technologies du cinéma des premiers temps : http://cinema-tographes.free.fr/

2. Le corpus Mathieu se compose en plus de deux bandes réalisées à partir de photographies dont l'origine n'est pas identifiée et de cinq autres composées de dessins.

3. Nous soulignerons à nouveau que les défilements de l'arrière vers l'avant remarqués chez Watilliaux, Beaulieu et Mathieu (flip books d'origine française, contemporains des débuts du cinématographe) sont consécutifs à l'utilisation de dispositifs mécaniques de feuilletage. Lorsque le feuilletage s'effectue au pouce, les pages défilent, dans les pays occidentaux utilisant une écriture de gauche à droite, de l'avant vers l'arrière comme montré sur les images ci-dessous dont une photographie où l'on voit Max Skladanowsky feuilleter un flip book de sa fabrication réalisé à partir de ses vues cinématographiques [ca 1896]. Voir cette photographie sur le blog de Pascal Fouché : http://www.flip-book.info/blog,php?annee=2017&mois=8. Une seule exception cependant pour un folioscope Watilliaux dont le mode d'emploi est explicité sur le livret compte tenu d'un feuilletage atypique voire contre nature. Dès lors, cet aspect confirmerait que les flip books Prissette à feuilletage de l'arrière vers l'avant pourraient être des ersatz de flip books Beaulieu. La production Beaulieu étant cinq fois supérieure à celle de Prissette, j'aurais tendance à croire en une forme de récupération ultérieure par Prissette de matériaux originels fournis ou négociés pour Beaulieu

© Thierry Lecointe.

Conclusion provisoire

« Crowdsourcing », voilà une notion relativement nouvelle, qu'il est bien difficile de traduire en français (recherche participative, collaborative ? Notre langue évoluant moins vite que les techniques), qui a lancé cette enquête. Aurait-on pu imaginer tel cheminement il y a encore quelques années, nous amenant d'Allemagne aux Etats-Unis via la Bolivie et rayonnant ensuite à travers le monde (notamment par le réseau de l'association Domitor) ? Internet, encore, qui met en évidence l'existence, outre le flip book point de départ des recherches, d'un corpus plus global, en France.

Cette collection a donc permis de découvrir quelques fragments de films cinématographiques inconnus et d'autres présumés disparus. Elle nous offre d'abord un nouveau regard sur la filmographie Méliès. Les premiers enseignements sont la récurrence de remakes[1] et l'existence de vues hors catalogue,[2] ce qui amène de nouvelles perspectives (un répertoire grivois) sur une période méconnue. Se pouvait-il que des vues aient pu être spécifiquement tournées pour alimenter un répertoire de produits dérivés comme les flip books ? Notre analyse originelle ne plaidait pas en faveur de cette hypothèse. Les résultats obtenus ne font que la conforter. En effet, sur les vingt flip books certainement ou possiblement attribués à des vues originaires de Méliès, un peu plus de la moitié correspond à un titre du catalogue.[3] C'est bien la preuve d'une récupération d'éléments filmiques. Par ailleurs, aucun spécialiste n'imagine l'utilisation de tronçon de celluloïd de 3 mètres en moyenne à partir de bobines conditionnées en 20 mètres ; aucun spécialiste n'imagine une mise en scène, avec décors et costumes, pour 10 secondes de tournage. Peut-on imaginer un déplacement de Méliès en gare de Joinville dans le seul but d'y filmer 20 secondes pour un flip book ? Outre la découverte du vues inconnues, les animations photogrammes par photogrammes confirment aussi les cadences faibles, à 10 et 12 images/seconde, des premiers tournages puis leur évolution rapide à 16 images/seconde telles que mentionnées par Méliès. Quel est donc le bilan provisoire ? Car peut-être d'autres que nous trouverons des indices complémentaires venant confirmer ou infirmer, pourquoi pas, nos hypothèses. En partant des familles de flip books composées du même nombre de feuillets, nous pouvons afficher les résultats suivants (la première cadence de projection – images/s – est celle du flip book, la seconde est celle estimée du film celluloïd dont est tiré le flip book) :

Flip books Beaulieu :

- 121 : *Nuit agitée*, (12 images/s – 12 images/s), « confirmé Méliès », possible première version de *Une Nuit terrible, n° 26*. Photogrammes existant mais aucune copie de film connue ;

- 121 : *Arrivée du train*, (5 images/s – 10 images/s), « probable Méliès – confiance élevée », *Arrivée d'un train (gare de Joinville), n° 35*. Aucune copie de film connue ;

- 121 : *La Danse*, (12 images/s – 12 images/s), « probable Méliès – confiance élevée », *Miss de Vère (gigue anglaise), n° 45*. Aucune copie de film connue ;

- 121 : *Prestidigitation*, (12 images/s – 12 images/s), « probable Méliès – confiance élevée », *David Devant, n° 101*. Aucune copie de film connue ;

- 121 : *Boxe*, (12 images/s – 12 images/s), « probable Méliès – confiance moyenne », possible première version de *Match de boxe, professeurs de l'école de Joinville, n° 136*. Aucune copie de film connue ;

- 121 : *Le Duel*, (12 images/s – 12 images/s), « probable Méliès – confiance moyenne », possible première version de *Assaut d'escrime, école de Joinville, n° 148*. Aucune copie de film connue ;

- 121 : *Le Bâton*, (12 images/s – 12 images/s), « probable Méliès – confiance moyenne », pas de titre associé. Aucune copie de film connue ;

- 121 : *Duel au sabre*, (12 images/s – 12 images/s), « probable Méliès – confiance moyenne », pas de titre associé. Aucune copie de film connue ;

- 121 : *Lutte de cuisiniers*, (12 images/s – 12 images/s), « probable Méliès – confiance moyenne », pas de titre associé. Aucune copie de film connue ;

- 110 : *Arrivée du train*, (5 images/s – 10 images/s), « probable Méliès – confiance élevée », *Arrivée d'un train (gare de Joinville), n° 35* – variante de la version à 121 photogrammes (sans les images 111 à 121) ;

- 90 : *Le Coucher* (ou *Le Déshabillé* ou *La Toilette*) *de la mariée*, (8 images/s – 16 images/s), « confirmé Méliès », possible première version de *Le Coucher de la mariée, n° 177/178*. Aucune copie de film connue ;

- 90 : *L'Amant surpris*, (8 images/s – 16 images/s), « confirmé Méliès », pas de titre associé. Aucune copie de film connue ;

- 90 : *Pose chez l'artiste. Vénus*, (8 images/s – 16 images/s), « confirmé Méliès », possible première version de *Le Modèle irascible, n° 130/131*. Un fragment de ce film connu mais non restauré ne correspondant pas aux images du flip book ;

- 90 : *La Puce*, (10 images/s – 10 images/s), « confirmé Méliès », pas de titre associé. Aucune copie de film connue ;

- 90 : *La Méprise*, (8 images/s – 16 images/s), « probable Méliès – confiance élevée ». Aucune copie de film connue ;

- 90 : *Le Coup du père François*, (8 images/s – 16 images/s), « probable Méliès – confiance élevée », pas de titre associé. Aucune copie de film connue ;

- 90 : *La Nourrice* [6], (10 images/s – 10 images/s), « probable Méliès – confiance élevée », pourrait correspondre à une première version de *Salut malencontreux, n° 36*. Trois photogrammes subsistant mais ne correspondant pas aux images du flip book ;

- 80 : *Le Bain*, (8 images/s – 16 images/s), « confirmé Méliès », possible première version de *Après le bal (le tub), n° 128*. Aucune copie de film connue ;

- 80 : *Le Voyeur*, (8 images/s – 16 images/s), « confirmé Méliès », pas de titre associé. Aucune copie de film connue ;

- 96 (48 x 2) : « Partie de cartes à trois », (12 images/s – 12 images/s), « confirmé Skladanowsky ». Aucune copie de film connue ;

- 75 : *Les Deux baisers*, (12 images/s – 24 images/s), « confirmé Edison », *May Irwin Kiss, n° 155*.

Flip books Prissette/[Beaulieu] :

- 98 : *Lutte*, (6 images/s – 12 images/s), « probable Pathé – confiance faible », *Lutteurs*, pas de numéro de catalogue. Aucune copie de film connue ;

- 90 : *Loïe Fuller* [24], (10 images/s – 10 images/s), « probable Méliès – confiance élevée ou Gaumont – confiance faible », Méliès, *Danse serpentine*, n° 44 ou Gaumont *Danse serpentine : Loïe Fuller*, n° 12. Aucune copie de film connue.

- 88 : *Déguisement* [22], (12 images/s – 12 images/s), « probable Méliès – confiance moyenne », *Dix chapeaux en 60 secondes*, n° 42. Aucune copie de film connue ;

- 84 : *La Danse du Cancan* [3], (16 images/s – 16 images/s), « confirmé Gaumont », *Moulin rouge : quadrille*, n° 3. Aucune copie de film connue ;

- 84 : *Duel de femmes*, (16 images/s – 16 images/s), « confirmé Gaumont », *Duel de dames*, n° 24. Aucune copie de film connue ;

- 84 : *Le Coucher*, (8 images/s – 16 images/s), « confirmé Gaumont », *Nuit Agitée*, n° 142. Aucune copie de film connue ;

- 64 (32 x 2) : « Train en marche » [1], (8 images/s – 16 images/s), « probable Gaumont – confiance moyenne », *Train à corridor, n° 55, série L.* Aucune copie de film connue.

Voilà donc 25 fragments de films des premiers temps inconnus retrouvés dans un répertoire non-film de 27 flip books. Grace à un corpus atypique précieusement collecté par Pascal Fouché, à la croisée des chemins entre film celluloïd, paper-print et livre, ces flip books préservés par la numérisation de Onno Petersen, magnifiés par l'animation de Robert Byrne révèlent encore un peu plus l'étendue de l'œuvre de Méliès dont bien peu s'imaginaient pouvoir retrouver ses films les plus anciens. Nul doute que le flip book risque d'apporter d'autres découvertes !

Reconstitution chronologique

Il s'agit d'une proposition de classement chronologique des films ayant servi à la fabrication des flip books (ce n'est pas un classement chronologique d'édition des flip books).

Les titres comportent les indications suivantes : le nombre d'images/s correspondant à la vitesse d'enregistrement du film ; le nombre de photogrammes du flip book ; le titre associé au sein de la filmographie ; la date de tournage au regard de la date d'édition du flip book, de la date de première projection connue.

Fragments attribués à Méliès :

- *Boxe* : (12 images/s), 121 photogrammes, possible première version de *Match de boxe, professeurs de l'école de Joinville, n° 136* ;

- *Le Duel* : (12 images/s), 121 photogrammes, possible première version de *Assaut d'escrime, école de Joinville, n° 148* ;

- *Le Bâton* : (12 images/s), 121 photogrammes ;

- *Duel au sabre* : (12 images/s), 121 photogrammes ;

- *Lutte de cuisiniers* : (12 images/s), 121 photogrammes ;

- *Nuit agitée* : (12 images/s), 121 photogrammes, possible première version de *Une Nuit terrible, n° 26*, date de première diffusion connue août 1896 ;

- *Arrivée du train* : (10 images/s), 121 photogrammes, *Arrivée d'un train (gare de Joinville), n° 35*, date de tournage été 1896, date de première diffusion connue août 1896, édition du flip book entre octobre 1896 et mars 1897 ;

- *La Puce* : (10 images/s), 90 photogrammes ;

- *La Nourrice* : (10 images/s), 90 photogrammes, possible première version de *Salut malencontreux, n° 36* ;

- *Déguisement* : (12 images/s), 88 photogrammes, *Dix chapeaux en 60 secondes, n° 42* ;

- *Loïe Fuller* : (10 images/s), 90 photogrammes, *Danse serpentine, n° 44*, date de première diffusion connue août 1896, date de commercialisation des images constituant un flip book juillet 1897;

- *La Danse* : (12 images/s), 121 photogrammes, *Miss de Vère (gigue anglaise), n° 45*, édition du flip book entre octobre 1896 et mars 1897 ;

- *Prestidigitation* : (12 images/s), 121 photogrammes, *David Devant, n° 101*, édition du flip book entre octobre 1896 et mars 1897 ;

- *Le Coup du père François* : (16 images/s), 90 photogrammes, date d'édition du flip book entre avril et septembre 1897 ;

- *Le Voyeur* : (16 images/s), 80 photogrammes, date d'édition du flip book entre avril et septembre 1897 ;

- *La Méprise* : (16 images/s), 90 photogrammes ;

- *Le Bain* : (16 images/s), 80 photogrammes, possible première version de *Après le bal (le tub), n° 128*, date d'édition du flip book entre octobre 1897 et mai 1898 ;

- *Pose chez l'artiste. Vénus* : (16 images/s), 90 photogrammes, possible première version de *Le Modèle irascible, n° 130/131*, date d'édition du flip book entre octobre 1897 et mai 1898 ;

- *Le Coucher de la mariée* : (16 images/s), 90 photogrammes, possible première version de *Le Coucher de la mariée, n° 177/178*, date d'édition du flip book entre octobre 1897 et mai 1898 ;

- *L'Amant surpris* : (16 images/s), 90 photogrammes, date d'édition du flip book entre octobre 1897 et mai 1898.

Fragment attribué à Edison :
- *Les Deux baisers*, (24 images/s), 75 photogrammes, *May Irwin Kiss, n° 155*, date de tournage connue avril 1896.

Fragment attribué à Skladanowsky :
- « Partie de cartes à trois », (12 images/s), 2 x 48 photogrammes.

Fragments attribués à Gaumont :
- *La Danse du Cancan*, (16 images/s), 84 photogrammes, *Moulin rouge : quadrille, n° 3*, date de première diffusion connue décembre 1896 ;

- *Duel de femmes*, (16 images/s), 84 photogrammes, *Duel de dames, n° 24*, date de première diffusion connue juillet 1896 ;

- *Le Coucher*, (16 images/s), 84 photogrammes, *Nuit Agitée, n° 142*, date de catalogage août 1897 ;

- « Train en marche », (16 images/s), 2 x 32 photogrammes, *Train à corridor, n° 55, série L*, date de tournage probable juillet 1897, date de catalogage novembre 1897.

Fragment attribué à Pathé :
- *Lutte*, (12 images/s), 98 photogrammes, *Lutteurs*, pas de numéro de catalogue, date de tournage présumée printemps-été 1896.

Notes
1. 7 flip books sont considérés comme des premières versions de vues du catalogue Méliès (35 % des flip books attribués à Méliès).
2. 8 flip books (40 % des flip books attribués à Méliès).
3. 5 flip books correspondent à des vues cataloguées (25 % des flip books attribués à Méliès), auxquels il convient d'ajouter les premières versions présumées.

George Méliès Flip Book Sets off Crowdsourcing : Crowdsourcing under way to ID George Melies flip book

By Maane Khatchatourian

A South American animation company is spearheading a crowdsourcing effort to ID a flip book that could be a reproduction of one of George Méliès' early films. However, film preservationists, archivists, and even a Méliès' descendant think it's an almost impossible task.

In fact, producer Serge Bromberg – restorer of the color version of Méliès' "Trip to the Moon" – said there's only a one percent chance of accurately identifying the flip book's origin given its poor image quality, as well as the lack of context clues and traditional Méliès trademarks.

But that is not stopping Kobold Charakter Animation co-founder Bernhard Richter, who stumbled upon the flip book at a used bookstore in Germany when browsing for a piece of cinema history to raffle off at an upcoming computer graphics conference in California.

After researching its provenance, Richter said the book depicts Méliès' "lost" 1896 short film "The Arrival of a Train at Vincennes Station," pictured, based on the fact that its publisher Léon Beaulieu's made flip books of movies produced between 1895 and 1898.

Bernhard and Kobold co-founder/his daughter Sara Richter ID'ed the film based on the train depicted in the flip book. "The double-decker was very typical for suburban rail trains around Méliès' birthplace [in Paris]; he could have easily set up his camera there," said Sara Richter. "We haven't found anything 100 percent conclusive tying the book to Méliès, but we have those clues."

However, to others, the train is a giveaway that the film was shot by the first filmmakers in history, Auguste and Louis Lumière, because of its similarity to the locomotive that appeared in their 1896 film "The Arrival of a Train at La Ciotat Station" (http://www.youtube.com/watch?v=v6i3uccnZhQ). According to UCLA Film & Television Archive director Jan-Christopher Horak, the Lumière brothers shot train arrivals at numerous stations in France.

"The camera angle, the camera looking down the platform, the train coming in and riding past the camera – that's identical to the Lumière film," Horak said.

Horak said he wouldn't be able to confidently attribute the movie to either the Lumière brothers or Méliès due to the lack of signage, the indistinguishable train platform, and the hazy background in the flip book images.

Further complicating matters is the fact that this could be a Méliès copycat film of the Lumières' work. Even though Méliès' great- great-granddaughter Pauline said she's skeptical about attributing the film to Méliès because he was such a firm proponent of novelty, Dino Everett, archivist at USC's Hugh M. Hefner Moving Image Archive, said the director could have copied the Lumières' train arrival films to get his foot in the door during the early years of his career. The French helmer was later aggressively against copycat productions.

Regardless of who shot the film, Kobold Charakter Animation is seeking any and all information about the flip book. The company will send a copy of the book to whoever offers the most significant clues to help with the ID process.

Source: https://variety.com/2013/film/global/george-melies-flip-book-sets-off-crowdsourcing-1200564564/

Email infoen@koboldcharakteranimation.com

https://www.youtube.com/watch?v=UTqQeCJLHdE

Kobold Charakteranimation

le 12 juillet 2013

Please, help us identify the origin of this flipbook (from approx. 1893-1898). We suspect it might be the version of the lost movie "Arrive d´un Train" by Georges Méliès. Here are the facts:

- After Méliès saw the presentation of the film "Arrivée d´un Train" by the Lumieres he offered 10.000 Francs to acquire the camera/projector. The offer was rejected.

- Méliès travels to London and buys a similar equipment by Robert W. Paul (an english inventor).

- Méliès starts by copying known scenes of the Lumieres brothers and shows them in his theater.

- Among other movies Méliès shows "Arrivée d´un train gare de Vincennes" in 1896.

- In the time in question between 1895-1898 there are only 2 known famous movies showing a train arrival: one by Lumieres and the other by Méliès. We know it is not the train arrival by the Lumieres.

- No surviving footage of this film by Méliès is known to exist and it is therefore presumed to be lost. Or is it?
http://en.wikipedia.org/wiki/Arrival_of_a_Train_at_Vincennes_Station

- Méliès did not only show his movies in his Théâtre Robert-Houdin but also distributed them to artists working in fairs who then showed his movies among other attractions. Flipbook were typically sold during that time at fairs.
https://en.wikipedia.org/wiki/Georges_Méliès

- Gare de Vincennes lies inside the Île-de-France which is Georges Méliès birthplace.

- Île-de-France is still popularly referred to by French people as the Région Parisienne ("Paris Region") or RP. It consists mostly of the Paris aire urbaine (Paris metropolitan area).

- Double-deck trains -as shown in the flipbook- were used in particular in french suburban railways.

- The french publisher of the flipbook is: "Léon Beaulieu".

9 tableaux regroupant les données techniques d'un échantillon des 28 flip books différents, de premières éditions / Nine technical data tables from a sample of 28 first-edition flip books.

Tableau 1 Board 1	
nb photogramme frame nr	nb flip book nr flip book
121	9
98	1
96 (48x2)	1
90	8
88	1
84	3
80	2
75	1
64 (32x2)	1
	27

Tableau 2 Board 2	
Longueur x largeur (mm) Height x width (mm)	nb flip book nr flip book
68 x 40	2
64 x 40	2
63 x 40	1
62 x 40	2
70 x 42	1
68 x 42	2
65 x 42	6
63 x 42	1
62 x 42	4
60 x 42	3
52 x 42	1
70 x 44	1
62 x 46	1
	28

Tableau 3 Board 3		
épaisseur papier paper thickness (mm)	valeur moyenne average value (mm)	nb flip book nr flip book
entre 0,104 et 0,107	0,107	7
entre 0,119 et 0,124	0,121	5
entre 0,132 et 0,136	0,134	5
entre 0,144 et 0,150	0,146	6
entre 0,155 et 0,163	0,158	3
entre 0,200 et 0,234	0,217	2
		28

Tableau 4 Board 4	
taille photogramme frame size (mm)	nb flip book nr flip book
25 x 34	2
30 x 38	1
30 x 40	5
32 x 40	2
33 x 40	1
26 x 42	1
28 x 42	1
30 x 42	3
32 x 42	8
34 x 42	1
35 x 42	1
36 x 42	1
34 x 44	1
	28

Tableau 5 / Board 5

vitesse défilement flip books flip books scolling speed (images/sec - frames/sec)	vitesse défilement films estimated recording speed (images/sec - frames/sec)	nb flip book nr flip book
5	10	1
6	12	1
8	16	8
10	10	4
12	12	9
12	24	1
16	16	3
		27

Tableau 6 / Board 6

longueur estimée du celluloïd estimated length of celluloid (base 35 mm / mètres - meter)	nb flip book nr flip book
4,84	1
3,60	5
3,20	2
3,00	1
2,42	8
1,96	1
1,80	3
1,76	1
1,68	3
1,28	1
0,96	1
	27

Tableau 7 / Board 7

durée du flip book (sec) flip book duration (sec)	nb flip book nr flip book
4,00	2
5,25	3
6,25	1
8,80	1
9,00	3
10,00	2
10,08	8
11,25	5
16,33	1
24,17	1
	27

Tableau 8 / Board 8

sens de défilement sense of scolling	nb flip book nr flip book
de l'arrière vers l'avant / back to front	25
de l'avant vers l'arrière / front to back	2
hybride / hybrid [2]	1
	28

[2] défilement de l'arrière vers l'avant mais numérotation infra-photographique de l'avant vers l'arrière.

Tableau 9 / Board 9

adresses adress	nb flip book nr flip book	121	96	90	80	75
144, rue Oberkampf, Paris	4	4				
46, rue Volta, Paris	3			1	1	1
37, rue du Vert-Bois, Paris	9	2		3		4
1, rue de la Courneuve, Aubervilliers	20	7	2	9		2
257, rue Saint-Denis, Paris	13	9		2	2	
	49	22	2	15	3	7

Base de données des 107 flip books / Database from 107 flip books.

Tableau 10 / Board 10			
Titres / Titles (coll. P. Fouché + T. Lecointe)	Nombre de / Number of flip books (coll. P. Fouché + T. Lecointe)	Titres / Titles (coll. F. Binétruy)	Nombre de / Number of flip books (coll. Binétruy + Montanaro)
La Danse / La Danseuse	4	*Danseuse*	1
Arrivée du train	4	*Arrivée d'un train en gare*	1 [+ 1 coll. Carlo Montanaro]
[Prestidigitateur]	1	*Prestidigitation*	1
Nuit agitée	4	*La Nuit terrible*	1 [+ 1 coll. Carlo Montanaro]
[Boxeurs]	5	*Boxe*	1
Le Duel	3		1
Le Bâton	2	*Bâton*	1
[Combat au sabre]	2	*Duel au sabre*	1
[Bagarre de mitrons]	3	*Lutte de cuisiniers*	1
La Puce	4	*Madame cherche ses puces*	1
Le Coup du père François	3	*Le Coup du père François*	1
La Nourrice	3	*Le Banc*	1
Le Coucher de la mariée *Le Déshabillé de la mariée* *La Toilette de la mariée*	5	*Le Coucher de la mariée*	1
L'Amant surpris	3		
Pose chez l'artiste. Vénus	4		
La Méprise	3	*Méprise*	1
Le Bain	4		1
Le Voyeur	2		[1 coll. Carlo Montanaro]
Les Deux baisers (46 mm)	4	*Le Baiser*	1 [+ 1 coll. Carlo Montanaro]
Les Deux baisers (42 mm)	1		
[Partie de cartes à trois]	2		
The following flipbooks could be only made by Prissette / Les flip books suivants ne pourraient être que de Prissette			
Déguisement	1		
Loïe Fuller	3 [+ 1 Prissette]		1
[Train en marche]	1		
La Danse du Cancan	1 [+ 1 Prissette]		1
[escrimeuses] / *Duel de femmes*	[2 Prissette]	*Duel de femmes*	1 [+ 1 coll. Carlo Montanaro]
[Le Coucher] / *La Puce*	1 [+1 Prissette]	*Le Coucher*	1
[Lutteurs]	2 [+ 1 Prissette]	*Lutte*	1
	75 [Beaulieu ou anonymes] + 6 Prissette		26 [Beaulieu ou anonymes]

Biographies

Robert Byrne is an award-winning film restorer specializing in early cinema and films of the silent era. Working with film archives and collections worldwide he has led restorations of more than twenty feature films and numerous short subjects. He has lectured at the Library of Congress, University College Cork, Queen's University Belfast, The Reel Thing Symposium, and numerous AMIA and FIAF technical symposiums. Rob publishes regularly on the topics of motion picture restoration and preservation and serves as President of the San Francisco Silent Film Festival, a nonprofit organization dedicated to live cinema performance and educating the public about silent film as an art form and as a culturally valuable historical record.

Pascal Fouché, publisher and historian, publishing specialist, co-founder of IMEC (Institut Mémoires de l'édition contemporaine), collector of flip books. Author of *Bibliographie des écrits de Louis-Ferdinand Céline* with Jean-Pierre Dauphin (BLFC, 1985), *L'Édition française sous l'Occupation 1940-1944* (BLFC, 1987), *Céline. « Ça a débuté comme ça »* (Gallimard, 2001), *Jean Genet matricule 192.102. Chronique des années 1910-1944* with Albert Dichy (Gallimard, 2010) and *Flammarion 1875-2015. 140 ans d'édition et de librairie* with the collaboration of Alban Cerisier (Gallimard-Flammarion, 2015). Editor of the correspondences of Marcel Proust and Louis-Ferdinand Céline with Éditions Gallimard (Gallimard, 1989 and 1991) and *Journal 1939-1945* of Maurice Garçon with Pascale Froment (Les Belles Lettres-Fayard, 2015). Director of the books *L'Édition française depuis 1945* (Éditions du Cercle de la Librairie, 1998), *Gallimard 1911-2011: un siècle d'édition* with Alban Cerisier (BnF-Gallimard, 2011) and *Dictionnaire Encyclopédique du Livre* with Daniel Péchoin and Philippe Schuwer (Éditions du Cercle de la Librairie, 3 volumes, 2002 2011).

Pamela Hutchinson is a freelance writer, critic and film historian who contributes regularly to *Sight & Sound, the Guardian,* Criterion and the BBC, specialising in silent and classic cinema and women in film. She has written essays for several edited collections and is the author of the BFI Film Classic on *Pandora's Box* and the editor of *30-Second Cinema* (Ivy Press). She is a guest lecturer at the National Film and Television School, and a member of both Fipresci and the London Film Critics' Circle. She also writes the silent cinema website Silent London.

Thierry Lecointe, independent researcher, has published numerous articles on the origins of cinema, particularly editions of the Domitor Society for the Study of Early Cinema, published in 2010, 2012 and 2014, and in specialized magazines such as *1895 revue d'histoire du cinéma.* He is also the author of *Le Cinématographe-Lumière dans les arènes (1896-1899),* (UBTF, 2007). He has given several conferences for the

GRAFICS research group in Montreal, the Domitor association, the Jean Vigo Institute in Perpignan and the École Normale Supérieure in Paris.

* * *

Robert Byrne est restaurateur de films spécialisé dans les films à l'ère du muet. Travaillant avec des archives et des collections cinématographiques du monde entier, il a mené des restaurations de plus de vingt longs métrages et de nombreux sujets courts. Il a donné des conférences à la Library of Congress, University College Cork, Queen's University Belfast, The Reel Thing Symposium et dans de nombreux symposiums techniques tels AMIA et FIAF. Rob publie régulièrement au sujet de la restauration et de la préservation de films cinématographiques et est président du San Francisco Silent Film Festival.

Pascal Fouché, éditeur et historien, spécialiste de l'édition, cofondateur de l'IMEC (Institut Mémoires de l'édition contemporaine), collectionneur de flip books. Auteur de la *Bibliographie des écrits de Louis-Ferdinand Céline* avec Jean-Pierre Dauphin (BLFC, 1985), de *L'Édition française sous l'Occupation 1940-1944* (BLFC, 1987), de *Céline. « Ça a débuté comme ça »* (Gallimard, 2001), de *Jean Genet matricule 192.102. Chronique des années 1910-1944* avec Albert Dichy (Gallimard, 2010) et de *Flammarion 1875-2015. 140 ans d'édition et de librairie* avec la collaboration d'Alban Cerisier (Gallimard-Flammarion, 2015). Éditeur des correspondances de Marcel Proust et Louis-Ferdinand Céline avec les Éditions Gallimard (Gallimard, 1989 et 1991) et du *Journal 1939-1945* de Maurice Garçon avec Pascale Froment (Les Belles Lettres-Fayard, 2015). Directeur d'ouvrage de *L'Édition française depuis 1945* (Éditions du Cercle de la Librairie, 1998), de *Gallimard 1911-2011 : un siècle d'édition* avec Alban Cerisier (BnF-Gallimard, 2011) et du *Dictionnaire Encyclopédique du Livre* avec Daniel Péchoin et Philippe Schuwer (Éditions du Cercle de la Librairie, 3 volumes, 2002-2011).

Pamela Hutchinson est une écrivaine indépendante, critique et historienne du cinéma. Elle contribue régulièrement à *Sight & Sound, the Guardian*, Criterion et à la BBC, spécialisée dans le cinéma muet et classique et sur le thème des femmes dans le cinéma. Elle a rédigé des essais pour plusieurs collections éditoriales et est l'auteure pour BFI Film Classic sur *Pandora's Box* et l'éditrice de *30-Second Cinema* (Ivy Press). Elle est conférencière invitée à la National Film and Television School, et membre à la fois du Fipresci et du cercle London Film Critics. Elle écrit également pour le site Web de cinéma muet, Silent London.

Thierry Lecointe, chercheur indépendant, est l'auteur d'articles sur les débuts du cinéma dans des livres (notamment les actes de l'association internationale de recherche sur le cinéma des premiers temps Domitor parus en 2010, 2012 et 2014) et des revues spécialisés (*1895 revue d'histoire du cinéma*). Il a aussi publié *Le Cinématographe-Lumière dans les arènes (1896-1899)*, (UBTF, 2007). Il a donné quelques conférences pour le groupe de recherche GRAFICS de Montréal, l'association Domitor, l'institut Jean Vigo de Perpignan et l'École Normale Supérieure à Paris.

Bibliographie sélective / Selected bibliography

Aude Bertrand, *Georges Méliès et les professionnels de son temps*, mémoire de recherche de master, Université Lumière Lyon 2 / ENSSIB, juin 2010.

Maurice Bessy et Lo Duca, *Georges Méliès, mage*, Prisma, Paris, 1945.

Camille Blot-Wellens, *La colección Sagarmínaga (1897-1906) Érase una vez el cinematógrafo en Bilbao*, Filmoteca Española, 2011.

Henri Bousquet, *Catalogue Pathé des années 1896 à 1914 – 1896 à 1906*, Editions Henri Bousquet, 1996.

Marie-Sophie Corcy, Jacques Malthête, Laurent Mannoni, Jean-Jacques Meusy, *Les premières années de la société L. Gaumont et Cie – Correspondance commerciale de Léon Gaumont 1895-1899*, Paris, Association française de recherche sur l'histoire du cinéma / Bibliothèque du Film / Gaumont, 1998.

Jacques Deslandes, *Le boulevard du cinéma à l'époque de Georges Méliès*, Éditions du Cerf, Bourges, 1963.

Julien Dupuis, *Georges Méliès, à la conquête du cinématographe*, Paris, StudioCanal, 2011.

Wiebke K. Fölsch, *Buch Film Kinetiks – Zur Vor- und Frühgeschichte von Daumenfino, Mutoscop & co.*, Berlin, Freie Universität Berlin, 2011.

André Gaudreault, *Cinéma et attraction. Pour une nouvelle histoire du cinématographe*, Paris, CNRS Éditions, 2008.

Jacques Malthête, *Méliès, images et illusions*, Exporégie, Paris, 1996.

Jacques Malthête et Laurent Mannoni (sous la dir.), *Méliès, magie et cinéma*, Paris, Paris-Musées, 2002.

Jacques Malthête et Laurent Mannoni, *L'Œuvre de Georges Méliès*, Paris, La Cinémathèque Française/Éditions de la Martinière, 2008.

Madeleine Malthête-Méliès, *Méliès, l'enchanteur*, Hachette, Paris, 1973.

Georges Méliès, « Les vues cinématographiques. Causerie par Geo. Méliès », *Annuaire général et international de la photographie*, Paris, Librairie Plon, 1907, pp. 362-392, reproduit dans André Gaudreault, *Cinéma et attraction. Pour une nouvelle histoire du cinématographe*, Paris, CNRS Éditions, 2008, texte présenté et annoté par Jacques Malthête.

Georges Méliès, « En marge de l'histoire du Cinématographe », *Ciné-Journal*, n° 884 du 6 août 1926, n° 885 du 13 août 1926, n° 887 du 27 août 1926 et n° 888 du 3 septembre 1926.

Georges Méliès, *La vie et l'œuvre d'un pionnier du cinéma*, coll. « La petite collection », édition établie et présentée par Jean-Pierre Sirois-Trahan, Paris, Les Éditions du Sonneur, 2012.

Charles Musser, *Edison Motion Pictures, 1890-1900 – An Annotated Filmography*, La Gionate del Cinema Muto / Smithsonian Institution Press, Gemona, 1997.

Jacques et Chantal Rittaud-Hutinet, *Dictionnaire des cinématographes en France (1896-1897)*, Honoré Champion, Paris, 1999.

Georges Sadoul, *Georges Méliès*, collection « cinéma d'aujourd'hui » 1, Paris, Éditions Seghers, 1961.

Georges Sadoul, *Histoire générale du cinéma – I L'invention du cinéma 1832-1897*, Paris, Éditions Denoël, 1946.

Georges Sadoul, *Histoire générale du cinéma – I L'invention du cinéma 1832-1897*, Paris, Éditions Denoël, 1948.

Georges Sadoul, *Histoire générale du cinéma – I L'invention du cinéma 1832-1897*, Paris, Éditions Denoël, 1973.

Georges Sadoul, *Histoire générale du cinéma – II, Les pionniers du cinéma 1897-1909*, Paris, Éditions Denoël, 1947.

Georges Sadoul, *Histoire générale du cinéma – II, Les pionniers du cinéma 1897-1909*, Paris, Éditions Denoël, 1973.

Georges Sadoul, *Lumière et Méliès*, Paris, Lherminier, 1985.

Collectif, Cinémathèque n° 8, Cinémathèque Française / Yellow Now, Paris, automne 1995.

Collectif, *Méliès, carrefour des attractions*, suivi de Correspondance de Georges Méliès (1904-1937), André Gaudreault et Laurent Le Forestier (dir.) et Stéphane Tralongo (coll.), Cerisy-la-Salle/Rennes, Colloque de Cerisy/Presses Universitaires de Rennes, 2014.

View animations of all Léon Beaulieu's
flip books online at:

Les animations de tous les flip books
de Léon Beaulieu visibles sur:

https://silentfilm.org/preservation/flipbooks/